# FOX, FIN, & FEATHER

THE DERRYDALE PRESS
FOXHUNTERS' LIBRARY

# FOX, FIN, & FEATHER

*Tales from the Field*

# HENRY W. HOOKER, MFH

Published in association with
The Masters of Foxhounds Educational Foundation

THE DERRYDALE PRESS
Lanham and New York

THE DERRYDALE PRESS

Published in the United States of America
by The Derrydale Press
4720 Boston Way, Lanham, Maryland 20706

Distributed by NATIONAL BOOK NETWORK, INC.

**Library of Congress Control Number: 2001092603**

ISBN 1-58667-080-8 (cloth : alk. paper)
ISBN 1-56416-203-6 (clamshell : alk. paper)
ISBN 1-56416-202-8 (leather : alk. paper)

♾™ The paper used in this publication meets the minimum requirements of
American National Standard for Information Sciences—Permanence of
Paper for Printed Library Materials, ANSI/NISO Z39.48–1992.
Manufactured in the United States of America.

# CONTENTS

# DEDICATION

Whilst I was courting her in 1955, Alice, my wife to be, took me hunting for the very first time. The sky was a luminous blue, the grass was emerald green, the horses full of run, hounds gay and keen. I viewed a fox that day, which I still see in my fancy. That romance endures. The longer I hunt the more I understand Mason Houghland's advice that he often gave to me: "The time to be happy is now, the place to be happy is here, the way to be happy is to hunt the fox."

The person who started me foxhunting has been my best hunting, shooting, and fishing companion and much more. Game and keen, she keeps a tight seat over the obstacles of life. However, the greatest pleasure of all is seeing her values and character in our children, Bradford Hooker, Lisa Hooker Campbell, and Timothy Hooker, and our grandchildren, Henry Hooker II, Alexander Hooker, Alice Campbell, Eileen Campbell, Palmer Campbell, Charlie Hooker, and Heather Hooker. If my pen is ever to befriend me, I hope it is in this book dedicated to my wife and our family. I am proud of them all.

# EDITOR'S PREFACE

Henry Hooker has, in his Introduction, painted some entirely new images to describe the magic of hunting and what it means, down deep, to the initiated, that are destined to be quoted in the literature of the twenty-first century, much as that famous foreword of his predecessor, Mason Houghland, has been.

*Fox, Fin and Feather* is the sporting memoir of one of the most amusing raconteurs in the outdoor field today. From the hub of his sporting life in Nashville, Tennessee, where he serves as Master of Foxhounds of the Hillsboro Hounds, Henry Hooker takes readers on a raucous jaunt—foxhunting, fishing and shooting—from the dark hills and hollows of the Tennessee night hunters to the exclusive quail shooting plantations of South Georgia. He connects the "Brahmans of the chase" (i.e., English-inspired mounted foxhunters) to their American roots (i.e. southern night hunters and field trialers) and brings his characters to life with hilarious and touching anecdotes. Whether from the podium—he is a highly sought speaker—or from the pages of his memoir, Hooker tells the stories of the celebrated as well as the lesser-known figures of foxhunting and other field sports with humor and reverence.

Norman M. Fine
Millwood, Virginia

# ACKNOWLEDGMENTS

I need to acknowledge those who over the years inspired and encouraged me to write.

Mason Houghland wrote me a letter when I was in law school. It was a reply to my thank-you letter to him for taking me out with his hounds. In it, he was complimentary of the way I had described the hunt. That was my first encouragement to write about hunting. Then, when I began hunting with the Hillsboro Hounds, Vernon Sharp also encouraged me to write. Some of his friends in the Masters of Foxhounds Association of America (MFHA), such as Wilbur Hubbard, did the same. Soon Alexander Mackay-Smith joined the chorus, which was very encouraging to me because I regarded him as the foremost scholar and author of the cultural history of field sports in the United States. Lowry Watkins, the great owner-trainer of the superb steeplechaser Tourist List, also urged me to capture the old times before they were gone. Then John Sloan Sr. asked me to write a piece about him for *The Chronicle of the Horse* when he retired as master of the Hillsboro Hounds. I was very flattered and pleased because I held him in such esteem.

When, as master myself, I began to write letters to the Hillsboro Hounds subscribers inviting them out cubbing, many of them encouraged me by saving the letters and telling me that they would like me to write a book about our experiences.

One of my favorite foxhunters and hunt supporters, Polly Murphy, has always considered writing a book herself to be titled As the Stirrup Twists. We have had many moments of merriment over potential subject matter seen in the field or at the posthunt tea party. When a particularly attractive newcomer comes out hunting, Polly sometimes gives me a look and asks, "Is she going to be in the book?" Polly has a discerning eye. She is certainly uncannily accurate at recognizing potential book material.

Through the years, others have encouraged me. Two literary ladies, Nina Bonnie and Elizabeth Rodgers, read parts of this book and urged me to make it more anecdotal. Certainly the MFHA seminars, at which I started speaking at the request of Ned Bonnie, and *Covertside*, the MFHA journal, in which editor Norman Fine published some of my stories, have given me the opportunity to express the philosophy of this book to many foxhunters, steeplechasers, fishermen, and bird hunters. I acknowledge, with gratitude, their encouraging response.

As you read this book, it will become obvious that my life as a sportsman has been filled with many fun and enriching experiences provided by Joyce and Bill Brown. For example, we were at Fox Camp one night hoisting salutes to the sunset and conjuring up future adventures when someone suggested we plan a trip to Africa. This seemed to interest everybody, and we asked Joyce's mother, Mrs. Drane, to go with us. "Sounds like fun," she said. "Are we going to fly or drive?" We roared with laughter and Mrs. Drane laughed, too. From then on, whenever someone suggested that we go somewhere, the immediate question was not whether we would go, but whether we would "fly or drive."

Alice and I arrived at a compromise solution. We would fly, often with the children, to Alaska or New Mexico or wherever, and meet Bill and Joyce, who had driven there in their camper and had rented a camper for us. Then we would make a caravan through the mountains or the prairies, camping by the streams, until we dropped off the rented camper some place down the line and flew home. Without the Browns, there probably would not have been a book for me to write.

I have a good friend named Charlie Martin who has a delightfully wry sense of humor. He and his wife, Ellen, have a game they play. When the mail is being opened, one of them reads to the other the first few words of one of the letters, and the listener guesses the author. It seems they always get it right when the letter is from me. When they told me about this game, Charlie added, "Henry, you write pretty well. If anything interesting ever happened to you, you could probably make a good story out of it."

Many friends have looked at this book and made suggestions. I appreciate the help of Dave Anderson, Ed Bacon, Rob Banner, Nina and Ned Bonnie, Joyce and Bill Brown, Camille Campbell, Lisa Campbell, Bill Carter, Dorothy Davis, Norman Fine, Dennis Foster, Billy Haggard, Ben Hardaway, Stephen K. Heard, Bradford Hooker, Timmy Hooker, Lin Howard, Kate Ireland, Tommy Lee Jones, Maggie and David Kendall, Mason Lampton, Gigi Lazenby, Richard Mooney, Betsy Burke Parker, Steve Portch, Bill Puryear, Ray Reid, Elizabeth Rodgers, John Seigenthaler, Bill Steinkraus, Jennifer Walker, Ridley Wills, Peter Winants, Daphne and Marty Wood, James L. Young, and, importantly, my wife Alice.

I owe a special thanks to Lynne Thompson for her charming drawings and to Bob Schatz for his help with scanning the photographs and for his spectacular photographs of me bringing in hounds at sunset.

The MFHA Educational Foundation, under the direction of C. Martin Wood III, MFH, has supported the publication of this book. For this encouragement and the work they do to protect our sport, I express my deep gratitude and best wishes for success in their important mission.

Finally, Jane Ann Whitson has done much of the work of producing this book. For her persistence, loyalty, and encouragement I thank her sincerely. If you are writing a book, it is very encouraging to hear someone laughing while she is typing it, and even more so to hear her still laughing while she is reading the later drafts.

# FOREWORD

Henry Hooker's sporting memoir, *Fox, Fin and Feather*, spans seventy-five years chronicling, in his words, "fun in field sports." However, describing his offering as an anecdotal biography would be akin to defining Ernest Hemingway's *Green Hills of Africa* as an African travelogue. Neither does justice to the pristine genius of either author.

With tongue lightly pressed against his psyche's cheek, Mr. Hooker draws his reader into a lively world—the world of larger-than-life characters; a world rife with the warp and woof of sporting adventure. It is a rich tapestry in danger of fading due to the harsh light of modernity.

Hooker tells stories. Oh, how he tells stories! One might be about the chief of the Osage Indians following a "one-legged lady" in the hunting field. Another is the one about his being lured to the Alaskan brine by the fish that hunts—by scent! Henry's passion and pure, unadulterated pleasure in all things feral (whether fin, feather, or feminine) fairly sings with unbridled joie de vivre. In fact, that master of southern hounds, hospitality, and hunting chutzpah, Mason Lampton, master of the Midland Fox Hounds of Georgia, remarked to Henry that "you have sung their song." A paean to the Hook's stories of dogs and hunting people.

This gem is genuine; a unique and precious retrospective of one exceptional man's life with dogs and their human factotums. As a life-long follower of and, lately, breeder of pure, line-bred Virginia-strain American foxhounds, I was enthralled with Hooker's account of the North Cotswold hounds imported from England to Tennessee in World War II. Mason Houghland, in a generous gesture to preserve Cotswold master Bill Scott's boodlines lest they perish due to the exigencies of war, gambled with the Hillsboro American hound-breeding program and entered these English hounds into his pack. The results might startle some houndmen.

True hound aficionados will relish Henry's personal tales of the seminal foxhound breeders of the early twentieth century: Haiden Trigg, Sam Wooldridge, Joseph B. Thomas, E. H. Walker, Wash Maupin, and Burrell Frank Bywaters, among others. I do not know if Henry's yarns about Sam Wooldridge's exploits are true or not, but I really do not care. They alone are worth the price of the book.

Hooker's anecdotes about dogs are not limited to foxhounds alone. Shooting dogs figure notably, and his recollections include quail shoots in the deep South with Parker and Pansy Poe of Pebble Hill Plantation (worthwhile subjects by their own right for a chronicle); shooting driven grouse in Scotland (site of Henry's temptation by the fairer sex); or drawing a bead on the red-legged partridge in Spain. Somewhere in the midst of these shooting adventures is the story of "The Dropper," part setter, part pointer, who was "the meat-providingst dog" ever hunted. He simply required a "beep" before he would "Auk"!

We in the sporting world rarely are treated to lyrical or creative writing. Ours normally is the stuff of didactic or demonstrative essay. But in Hooker's reminiscences we find the serendipitous, the sublime, even the sensuous. Woven into the narrative is genuine conflict, wryly drawn characterization, and age-old themes of faithfulness, constancy, and strength against adversity. Some of the stories really *do* bring a tear to the eye.

There is also creative gambling, unbridled drinking, sexual tension (both canine and human), incisive but gentle humor, and mellifluous poetry.

"Bold fox, you learn eternal truth
For which the histories offer proof.
It's true of all the world's host
Who hunts the best is hunted most."

Well, there you go.

James L. Young, MFH
The Plains, Virginia

# INTRODUCTION

I will make you brooches and toys for your delight
Of bird-song in morning and star-shine at night.
I will make a palace fit for you and me,
Of green days in forests and blue days at sea.
        —Robert Louis Stevenson "Romance"[1]

This is a book about fun in field sports. It celebrates the characters and cultures of foxhunting, steeplechasing, fishing, and shooting. It celebrates life. Some of the practices described may seem to be out-of-date in light of present-day debate. These stories, however, are not intended to be a defense of past practices; they are simply history in which these examples of human nature appeared. Do not be surprised that the same sportsmen show up in different contexts. This is a joyful tour in which reliable old friends reappear, sometimes unexpectedly, to enhance the fun. Many of them are in the chronology of the Hillsboro Hounds, which is included at the end of this book to give a time frame for the stories about hunting and steeplechasing in Middle Tennessee during the last seventy-five years.

The section on our Cornersville, Tennessee, hunt country is intended to provide background to make other segments of the book clearer. It becomes apparent from hunting that temperature, humidity, soil, and scent are intertwined. So, too, there is the realization that the best sport occurs in the company of friends who give it meaning and make the memory of it endure. For me, the hunting, the chasing, the shooting, and the fishing are an interwoven tapestry in which these characters and their exploits are salient threads.

When Mason Lampton read a manuscript of this book, he said, "Henry, I can tell you spent a lot of time hunting with dogs and dog people, and you were listening to what they were telling you. You have their song. Anybody who wants to know what it was like hunting in the South for the last three quarters of the twentieth century should read your book."

Mason made me think about the span of seventy-five years of fox and coyote hunting that this book covers, and the defining changes during that period. Two changes overshadow the rest. They were the stocking and proliferation of the deer population by state wildlife agencies, and the coming of the coyote. Both of these changes brought a need to change the type of hunting hounds used. Ben Hardaway, in his book *Never Outfoxed*,[2] dealt at length with his reaction to the "antlered menace," as he colorfully called the spread of deer. His quest for biddable hounds has had a profound influence on the crossbred hound in America. Moreover, the expansion of the deer population provided a major food source for the migration of the coyote into our hunt country. The coyote was a successful competitor for habitat, virtually displacing the red fox. The advent of the coyote, in truth, not only caused changes in hound breeding, but it also necessitated enlargement and reengineering of most hunt countries because the coyote covers a large country when really pressed. This has caused many hunts to panel their countries extensively and to put in riding gates for more rapid crossing. In some places, radios and whippers-in riding in trucks are employed to turn the quarry back from traffic hazards.

The march of civilization to its manifest destiny (a description used by historians who were employed by the victors) affected the species of wildlife that use the lands on which we live and hunt. Great ferocious beasts and herds, seemingly innumerable, have become extinct or endangered. However, the coyote, branded a rogue and a thief and made the target of frantic hostility and bounties, is so tough, so adaptable, and so resilient that all the trapping, shooting, and poisoning have neither diminished its number nor curtailed its range.

I saw a coyote mousing in a new-mown hay field. I stopped my car and sat very still, watching for a long time. The coyote listened and then pounced, pinning the mouse with a pad. Before it reached down to take the mouse in its mouth, it looked all around, three hundred and sixty degrees. Each and every time, and before every morsel, that coyote looked for danger all around, a full circle. "This," I thought, "is the worthiest game for horse and hound, the wildest and the wariest, the wiliest and most enduring, the foremost survivor of the animal kingdom. When we come again, horn sounding, hounds uncoupled, and horses prancing, our bits and buttons, spurs and stirrups flashing in the sun, the coyote will test us with its cunning, speed, and stamina, and we will confirm for ourselves why throughout history the chase truly has been the sport of kings."

The magic remains. The ancient partnership between the hunter and his hound endures. In the last weeks of summer, signs of the coming autumn appear. Nuts and seed pods, ripening grain, and the tall tasseled corn signal those inexorable changes that beckon hunters to field and forest. Soon the cool lingers longer in the morning, and the nocturnal rambling of the quarry brushes the dew-glistened grass. Beyond the crimson borders of sumac and sassafras, deep in the poplar-brightened woods, still sanctuaries wait for hounds to put game afoot and inaugurate another season of slash and dash. Foxhunters meet at dawn to hear the music and experience the harmony that links hunter, horse, and hound to those stealthy creatures whose magic movement whispers through the woods. Whether they are there for the costume and the finery or the countryside and the camaraderie, these hunters become part of a long procession of the brave. Their presence is affirmed by every note of the huntsman's horn. It remains in the memory, like the afterglow of the night hunter's hilltop fire.

## Notes

1. Robert Louis Stevenson, "Romance." *The Oxford Book of English Verse, 1250–1900.* Chosen and edited by Arthur Quiller-Couch (London: Clarendon Press, 1924), 1023.

2. Benjamin H. Hardaway III, *Never Outfoxed: The Hunting Life of Benjamin H. Hardaway III* (Columbus, Ga.: Benjamin H. Hardaway III, 1997).

L.Thompson

FOX

ONE

# SCARLET COATS AND NIGHT HUNTERS: THE SEARCH FOR SUITABLE HOUNDS

I have enjoyed and, indeed, loved many of the field sports. It is surely true, however, that of them all, the one that has meant the most to me has been foxhunting. Much of my foxhunting education has been due to my association with Nashville's Hillsboro Hounds (established 1932, recognized 1960), the mastership of which I have been privileged to share for the past quarter century. Thus, it is inevitable that much of this book concerns the evolution of this pack and my association with it.

However, this book is more than a history of the Hillsboro Hounds. It is also about an important historical element of fox-hunting in America that provides many amusing moments and has, I think, great significance to our sport. I refer to the juxtaposition and interaction of the two types of foxhunters in America: the members of organized and, usually, recognized (by the Masters of Foxhounds Association of America) packs, and the night hunters and field trialers who hunt in settings that are more informal.

Mason Houghland

Mason Houghland, founder of the Hillsboro Hounds, described fox-hunting as having two cultures. One is that of the high-church

Brahmans in scarlet coats. The other, less obvious but vast in its popularity, is composed of the night hunters and field trialers who make sacrifices, if they must, to keep hounds. Houghland wrote:

> Fox-hunting is not merely a sport—and it is more nearly a passion than a game. It is a religion, a racial faith. In it are the elements that form the framework upon which beliefs are built: the attempt to escape from life as it is [to] a life as we would have it; an abiding love of beauty; and an unconscious search for the eternal verities of fair play, loyalty and sympathetic accord, which are so clouded in our mundane existence.
>
> It is a primitive faith; a "survival" the sociologist would term it, and harks back to the clear and simple outlook of our tribal gods. Through the years it goes on because, after the flush of many dawns, the thrill of never-ending pursuit, the sweet spice of danger, the simple tragedies of the field, and the weary darkness of long roads home, a few always become attuned to Nature's wondrous harmony of which they themselves are a part.
>
> Like all religions it has many sects. There are the very "High Church" hunters with carefully observed ritual, who need form to guard the spirit and ceremonial to nourish belief. It is these Brahmans of the chase who make the picture the world sees, the scarlet coats on green fields, the great leaps, the beautiful backgrounds. They play a great part and merit the recognition of great effort. But in shadowy outline beyond them, outnumbering them a hundred to one, are legions of Fox-hunters, like Franciscan Brothers, whose profession of faith neither poverty nor sacrifice can dim, some who must even deny themselves the necessities in order to keep a couple of hounds.
>
> On horseback, on muleback, or more often afoot, every night of the year, somewhere in every state in the Union, the horns of this great army of "hill-toppers" awaken the echoes of field and of forest.[1]

The interaction of these two cultures and the people who are part of them, which distinguishes American foxhunting and permeates the history of the Hillsboro Hounds, are the themes of these stories.

Field trials are competitions in which hounds are painted with numbers and then judged based on their performance in the field for hunting, trailing, speed and drive, and endurance. A champion hound is chosen for each of these categories and for the highest general average of all of these categories. The winning hounds are highly prized as breeding stock.

Mason Houghland left not only his classic book *Gone Away*, but also his hunting diary and his pedigree books. A copy of the diary was given to me by Mrs. Houghland after Houghland's death and the pedigree books were passed on to me by Vernon Sharp. Although all of these are instructive, it was the pedigree books to which Houghland confided his insights on hound buying and breeding and the colorful qualities of the foxhunters with whom he shared his adventures. The first pedigree book opens with the pedigree of Longstreet 1860. That hound was, in Houghland's words, "A perfect foxhound, and very fast—a hound who killed red foxes alone—sold for two hundred dollars in times of famine—thought to be the fastest dog ever owned by Birdsong."[2]

## Stump Prescott

Many foxhunters have endeavored to improve their packs by purchasing hounds. For example, a well-known hound man and field trialer from Dublin, Georgia, named Stump Prescott, sold a wealthy easterner one of his hounds after a protracted negotiation. The buyer, feeling rather expansive, said, "Well, I guess I bought the best hound in the South."

Stump shifted his cigar stub and said, "I couldn't say. There are probably a lot of people who have hounds in the South that I don't even know."

"Well," said the buyer, "certainly in Georgia. You know pretty well everybody who has hounds in Georgia."

"There again," said Stump, "there might be a man up in the mountains of northeast Georgia that might have a hell of a hound but never comes to a field trial."

The by-now exasperated buyer gave Stump an ominous look and said, "Well, for what you got me to pay, I better have gotten the best in this kennel."

Stump paused reflectively, repositioned his cigar stub, and said reassuringly, "Well, if you have, an honest mistake has been made."

Although the pedigrees of other famous hounds bred by such breeders as Haiden Trigg, E. H. Walker, Joseph White, Wash Maupin, Burell Frank Bywaters, Bob Rodes, Sam Wooldridge, and Joe Kirby, to name a few, are included in the pedigree books, it was after Longstreet 1860 that Houghland's most famous hound, Longstreet 1939, was named. There is a story that a man approached Ernest Hardison to see if he would help him buy Longstreet 1939 from Houghland. Ernest looked at him and said, "I know you have a prosperous drugstore and a nice farm on the edge of town, but what else can you throw into the bargain?" Thus was the esteem accorded Longstreet. Sadly, he was lent to Henry Bell Covington for use at stud and was killed coming home on the highway near Gallatin, Tennessee.

## Joseph B. Thomas

The most interesting part of these old pedigrees to me is the story they reveal about the activities of Joseph B. Thomas, who founded the Grasslands Hunt in Gallatin, Tennessee, and who was acknowledged by Alexander Mackay-Smith to be one of the greatest, if not the greatest, hound breeder in the history of American foxhunting. Joe Thomas bred the hounds with which Mason Houghland started the Hillsboro Hounds.

Let me go back a ways in the story. After the hound match of 1905 in which Harry Worcester Smith, with an American hound pack called the Grafton, defeated the English hound pack of Henry Higginson, called the Middlesex, it was commonly thought that Virginia, in the vicinity of Middleburg, contained the best hunt country in America. This area therefore attracted Joseph B. Thomas, who became the master of the Middleburg and of the Piedmont Fox Hounds in 1915. He lived and hunted on a lavish scale. He was also handsome, and so was a much sought after matrimonial prospect.

In due time Thomas became engaged to Miss Charlotte Noland, who controlled a large landholding in the Middleburg and Piedmont hunt countries. However, a beautiful and talented lady named Clara Fargo sustained an accident out hunting with Thomas and was taken into his house, Huntland, to await the doctor. She never left. The two were married, and the relationship with Miss Noland, which had been a consolidating coup for Thomas, rapidly deteriorated. Miss Noland, whose land became the campus of Foxcroft School in 1914, combined with Daniel Sands in 1919 to wire Thomas out of the country.

The result of Joe Thomas's retirement from the Piedmont and Middleburg was a huge increase in expenditure for improving the breeding of his pack, which is described in his great scholarly work *Hounds and Hunting through the Ages*.[3] In addition to those hounds he got from Burrell Frank Bywaters, the great Virginia market breeder, Thomas also acquired some Trigg hounds from the estate of the famous big game hunter and arctic explorer Paul Rainey. Indeed, Joe Thomas's lead hound was Rainey's Rattler, bred by Alanson Trigg and memorialized in the famous painting by Percival Rosseau.[4] The bloodlines of those original hounds are in the Hillsboro Hounds pack today, still providing thrills with their resonant cry.

Paul Rainey was a hero of Ben Hardaway's mentor, George Garrett, who wrote the interesting book *Fifty Years with Fox and Hounds*.[5] Late in the nineteenth century and early in the twentieth century, Paul Rainey had a huge plantation in Mississippi called Cotton Plant where camp field trials were held. Rainey sent his bird dog trainer Er Shelley to Africa with a pack of Trigg foxhounds that Shelley taught to run only lion. Shelley bought every horse that ran in the Nairobi Steeplechase that year for his string of hunt horses. Er Shelley's book, *Hunting Big Game with Dogs in Africa*,[6] is the greatest adventure book on hunting hounds I have ever read.

This book was given me by Bill Brown, who was said by Billy Haggard, the great equestrian sportsman, to be the best man to hounds in a wooded country he ever saw. Certainly, the field trialers thought so, as they had seen him jump barbed-wire fences to get to hounds; and they accepted his judgment without question, paying off big bets on Bill's opinion alone.

Bill had an albino horse named Clint that had a hard time seeing the wire if the sun was in his eyes, so Bill carried some Kleenex and would just put a tissue on a barb for Clint to see, if needed. Howard Stovall went around and asked everybody if they had heard about Clint dying. Of course, they were appalled. "Poor Clint. What happened?" they asked, taking the fly. "Don't know; maybe he got in a cotton field and jumped himself to death," Stovall would reply as he walked away.

Paul Rainey's Rattler became one of the lead hounds in Joe Thomas's pack, as did a hound called Bowler, which Houghland helped Thomas acquire from Joe Kirby. Here is how Houghland described it:

> "Bowler" was whelped at Bowling Green, Ky., in 1924, and was a "Trigg." His breeder Joe Kirby was the man who changed the Trigg color from the tan of the old Virginia to the ring-necked black white and tan that has long identified the Trigg hound. Joe ran a livery stable, and kept his running pack in some large mule stalls therein. In the winter of 1927, I think about November, I took Joe Thomas to Bowling Green (I had persuaded him to make a Trigg outcross) and took him to Kirby's stable. Joe and his pals were playing chequers by the fire in the stable office that night. We looked at all his hounds; but one, not in the stalls but lying in the office Kirby would not price. "That's Joe Bowler," he said, "I wouldn't sell him—besides you couldn't keep him in a pen." But Kirby was poor, Thomas was rich, and Joe Bowler left the livery stable, had his name changed to "Bowler" and became the great sire of the Grasslands pack in subsequent years.[7]

The Trigg crosses that Thomas obtained were successful at the shows and so predominated in the field that all the litters entered by him in 1930 and 1931 were by Trigg dogs out of Trigg bitches. This was astounding considering the volume he was producing and the access he had to July, Walker, and Bywaters hounds. Such eminence had the Thomas pack achieved that no fewer than thirty-two organized hunts in America used its blood. Many other packs were derivative users as well, and this at a time when access for breeding was infinitely more difficult.[8]

Lowry Watkins, the famous gentleman horseman from Louisville, Kentucky, accompanied Houghland and Thomas on the hound-buying trips that got Bowler, and he subsequently tried to get Thomas to move his pack to Harrodsburg, Kentucky, with its stone walls and bluegrass. However, Mason Houghland, and a pledge of one hundred thousand dollars by locals Rogers Caldwell and Luke Lea, convinced Joe Thomas that Gallatin, just north of Nashville, Tennessee, was the best place in America to have his hunt. He brought there in 1929 what was considered the premiere American pack of the day and founded the Grasslands Hunt. In Lowry Watkins's words in a letter to me:

> That is the story you should write before it is all gone. It was Joe Thomas's dukedom: hunting, shooting, falconry, racing, beautifully restored old houses and hunting boxes. I used to arrive in two cars, one for me and one with a jug band from Louisville—the famous Whistler. Joe Thomas's wife Clara's brother made a theatrical contract with them and took them to Paris. They got homesick in about two weeks and came home. Thomas wrote me about suing them. . . . I told him the Whistler's assets consisted of what he had seen him with the last time.

Now Grasslands was fancy doings with its stallion barns, its international steeplechase with the trophy given by the king of Spain, and its prominent members. It was top drawer as was indicated by what Joe Thomas once said to a dandy trying to borrow a white tie for his tails: "I had as soon see you at dinner without a tie as to see you, as I did in the field today, without your white boot garters."

## Con Thompson Ball

On one particularly festive evening at Grasslands, the guests included a young debutante, Con Thompson, from Nashville. She subsequently told me the story of being seated at dinner next to a gentleman in tails, who had arrived in his private rail car. In addition to the waiters, there was a liveried footman behind every seat. While the lively dinner was progressing, the gentleman leaned over and whispered to Con, "My dear, I saw you out hunting today, and I would give ten thousand dollars for your seat and hands upon a horse." "And how much would it be then for the whole thing?" she sweetly replied in a confidential tone.

Con Thompson Ball was a bold-riding field trial follower. That is how she came to be friends with Dave Ware, chief of the Osage Indians. It was a meeting of different cultures, as was apparent when Dave saw Mrs. John Sloan come out riding sidesaddle. Later in the morning, hounds were running, and one of Ware's buddies called to him, "Come on. They are going to cross down by the creek." "Go ahead," Ware shouted back. "I'm going to see that one-legged lady take a jump if I have to wait here all day."

Dave Ware's hound was winning the National Field Trial for Foxhounds one year in Bowling Green, Kentucky. Con chanced to hear some of the other contestants plot to get the Indians drunk so they would not cast their hounds on the last day. That night Con sat in the lobby of the hotel listening to the mayhem going on upstairs in the Indians' rooms. Finally, about midnight Con screwed her courage to the sticking place and went knocking on the Indians' doors.

"What do you want?" asked a half-naked brave who staggered to the door.

"David Ware," Con calmly replied.

"He might be here somewhere," said one of the brawlers.

They stopped fighting and appraised Con with a wary eye. Then they began to look under the wreckage in the room for the missing combatant. In due course, they surfaced Ware and delivered him drunk and battered to the doorway. "Come with me," said Con, and led him to the kitchen where she made him a pot of coffee. That was a mistake, she later told me, because when you give coffee to a drunk, you get a woke up drunk. So Con took Dave outside into a snowstorm and walked and weaved him around the hotel. He would fall in the drifts, wash his face in the snow, and then stumble on with her. Finally, before daylight, he began to recover, and they got him to the cast with his hound. As they were releasing the hounds, he looked at Con and asked, "What kind of flowers do girls like you like?" "Roses," she replied. Dave Ware's hound did not win the trial, but Con got a dozen roses for Christmas every year for the rest of her life.

I got to know Dave Ware while I was going around judging field trials with him. If he appeared to fall asleep during the scoring, I would give him a little dig in the ribs, and he would open one eye, look at me, and say, "Osage exercise."

It was Con Thompson Ball's friendship with Harry Hopkins, the advisor who enjoyed the confidence of President Franklin D. Roosevelt, that is credited with producing all the rock work done by the Works Progress Administration around Percy Warner Park and its Iroquois Steeplechase course in Nashville, Tennessee. Mason Houghland started the Iroquois Steeplechase in 1941 using most of the Hillsboro Hounds foxhunters as officials, owners, or contestants. His vision of the mutually beneficial relationship between steeplechasing and foxhunting endures today.

Grasslands' Failure;
Pack Split Half to Houghland's Hillsboro Hounds

Unfortunately, the Camelot called Grasslands was fated to be short lived. It was disbanded due to the Depression. By 1933, Thomas had sold half of his pack to Will Dupont for the Foxcatcher in Fair Hill, Maryland, and had given the other half to Mason Houghland for the Hillsboro Hounds. At the beginning of his Hillsboro Hounds pedigree book, Houghland took great care to describe the hounds he had received. Although there were many great ones, Houghland thought Dennis 1929 was the best. In 1955, he recalled:

> Dennis 1929 was bred by J. B. Thomas for his pack at "Grasslands" (Sumner County, Tenn.) but was presented to me when "Grasslands" collapsed following the Panic of 1929. He was a handsome big tan and white hound, ring necked, straight legs, fine head and muzzle, arched back & saber curved stern. He was one of the few hounds I ever saw that would cast himself perfectly at a check ie first a small circle with care, then a wide circle at a gallop. Most frequently he would hit off the line in style for his nose was very good, and his fox sense the same. He had a deep "chop" voice and gave it just right. I thought that he was the best hound Joe Thomas had bred during the years I knew him.

Dennis was by his Bowler '24 out of his Dinah '22.

I traded his litter-mate "Dealer" to Simpson Dean MFH the "Vicmead" (Wilmington, Del.) for $250.00 and gave Joe Thomas the $250.00 for the portrait of the Huntsman by Broadhead, which has hung in the library at Green Pastures for 25 years or thereabouts. "Dealer" was an excellent hound but not in the class of "Dennis."[9]

This hound Dennis was the greatest sire of Houghland's pack until Houghland purchased Longstreet from Eugene Torbett in 1939. Among Dennis's great offspring was a hound named Mischief, which was by Dennis out of Moonshine 1933, the latter also by Dennis 1929 out of Marion 1931. Again, let Houghland describe in his own pedigree book notes:

Mischief—by Dennis '29 Moonshine '33 was one of the best hounds I ever saw. He could find start and run his fox when other hounds couldn't own the line. He was fabulously fast and in Robertson County the Negro's [sic] called him "Pack Breaker." He broke the hearts of the North Cotswold hounds I imported the first day they ever ran with him. It was in Robertson County. We started (or *he* started the fox) upon one of my farms, and he ran 7 miles west down Red River then turned and came home with Mischief looking at him and the balance, footsore & weary, a half mile back.[10]

The point I am trying to make is that many of the competitive hound breeders of the day were line breeders. They bred close—a sire to its niece or a dam to its nephew. Who would not if it produces hounds like Mischief? Houghland noted when this hound died of pneumonia in the 1940 through 1941 season: "No faults, top hound, wonderful nose, lightning speed, good mouth: unusual 'fox sense.' Would only hunt on good scenting days."[11] He could have added: sire of Dennis II, another great Houghland stallion hound.

In other words, though not perfect, the line-bred Mischief was the fulfillment of a foxhunter's dreams. I try to keep that in mind when it is suggested that somebody has a hound we might try, although we have never seen it, and its ancestry is unknown. Something "of a troop of dragoons," Robert Burns would say.[12] In my view, many breeding programs suffer from excessive experimental outcrosses, to the detriment of the opportunity to improve the pack with careful selection of compatible candidates from within the kennel one knows best.

Ben Hardaway has told me that he would cross to a poodle or a rooster if it would help him chase coyotes. I told him that I did not see much commercial potential in the poodle cross, but that if he would give me some time, I could get up quite a crowd to pay to see that rooster thing. However, when one really examines Hardaway's hound list, it is apparent that he only experiments with a certain percentage while keeping his tried-and-true bloodlines intact.

The other thing one learns from studying Houghland's pedigree books is the value of realistic assessment and culling. Again and again in his notes, he stresses rather severe culling even when he thinks he has the best pack in the country and the best he ever had:

> The close of the season found the pack materially reduced. I drafted rather severely with the idea of making a real improvement in the pack. It is today the best pack of hounds I have ever owned, and I feel confident has few superiors in the South, or in the country for that matter.[13]

And Houghland reverts to this advice five years later. He stated in his pedigree book, "This is the best pack yet but would be better off if we drafted the bottom 6 couple of slower hounds, such as the N. C. [North Cotswold] dog hounds."[14]

Two other outstanding features emerge from Houghland's breeding program. The first is that one can do a lot of damage by a continuing commitment to a hound of impeccable credentials but apparently recessive genes. I have observed a huntsman make this same mistake with his master's acquiescence, breeding every eligible bitch to a flashy import and getting not one single useful hound. The other feature is that when bloodlines are well known, it is wise to breed at a young age to get the prepotency of the young hound, and to leave time to exploit the results if they prove satisfactory. Longstreet 1939's successful service with the North Cotswold bitches stands out as a classic case of this strategy.

## The Refugee Pack

Mason Houghland experimented with the great field trial blood of the thirties until he began going to England and visiting Bill Scott, master of the North Cotswold. The result of their tours culminated in the draft of thirty-seven hounds from the North Cotswold in 1938, which were split with the Vicmead Hunt in Middletown, Delaware. This pack was called the refugee pack because they were sent away from the impending war to avoid the fate of the many hounds that had to be put down in World War I due to food shortages.[15] Houghland walked this pack down Fifth Avenue in New York with the help of Joe Thomas, Joe Thomas's old huntsman, Charlie Carver, and Simpson Dean, master of the Vicmead, before putting the hounds on the train to Nashville. When Houghland got the hounds to their new home in Nashville, he wrote immediately to Scott:

Green Pastures
Nashville, Tennessee
October 24, 1939

Dear Bill:

The hounds arrived, and I went up to New York to unload them. You never could have devised a piece of propaganda as effective as this one was. No limpid-eyed movie star, staggering off the Normandie, burdened with orchids and rugs, could have ever brought as many cameramen to the dock! Newspapermen beset me on every side! And the next morning, all the principal newspapers of America carried pictures of the hounds and articles about you.

Had I known what a furor would have been raised, I might have done something really useful to the cause of Anglo-Saxon solidarity. But you did enough. This office is deluged with calls and letters from all kinds of people who are moved by your efforts to save your stock. I will send you some of the newspaper clippings under separate cover.

All the hounds arrived in perfect shape at the dock, ready to go places and do things. A pack of Bengal tigers would not have been more difficult to restrain. Each one had a chain, and each was determined to eat up the nearest Italian dock laborer that he could smell. Such a scene of pandemonium among the boxes and crates, you never saw!

The United States Bureau of Animal Industry had a representative there who insisted upon checking the descriptions, etc., and when it came to the longhaired ones, he demurred and wanted them listed as sheep dogs. I finally convinced him that you were an agriculturist as well as a foxhunter, and that these were dual-purpose hounds; in the summer they herded sheep and in the winter they hunted the fox.

I understand that the Baltimore Sun, one of our oldest and greatest newspapers, carried an editorial upon the shipment in Sunday's issue. I have written for it and will send it to you when I get it.

When I have recovered from the two thousand mile trip and have rid myself of the dirt, and of the docks, and the aroma of the Cotswold, I shall take time to write you in detail everything that has transpired.

In the meantime, be assured that all of America is standing guard over your hounds, and that unless I deliver them all to you in cotton wool upon your return from the war, I undoubtedly will be drawn and quartered.

Please give my love to Pam, who by this time is, I am sure, a proud mother.

Faithfully yours,

Mason


The Hillsboro portion of the draft was brought to Nashville and kenneled at Houghland's Green Pastures farm. Houghland immediately began a breeding program using his star stallion hound, Longstreet, by Sam Wooldridge's Buzzard Wings out of Eugene Torbett's Crooked Lena. This hound was crossed on three North Cotswold bitches: Beauty, Stainless, and Startler. These proved to be brilliant matches and produced the preponderant part of Houghland's pack. Houghland was very high on what he got and pronounced these crosses some of the great matches in the history of foxhounds. His pedigree book is replete with stories of their exploits in the field and at field trials. In one such story, he described the work of Beauty's get:

> This was another miracle litter, all top foxhounds. "Balance" proved herself to be one of the worlds top fox-hounds at Florence Ala. in the United States Open Trials where for two days she was top hound and then was lost. We drove 1500 miles searching for her but never found her. Dinwiddie [Lampton], Eugene Harris and I rode behind the pack there upon the greatest go of my life, with Balance leading and carrying the line for 40 minutes of the madest flight, with 50 of the top hounds of America trying to take the lead from her. I doubt if there have been many hounds ever bred that surpassed her. She and all the litter looked just as foxhounds should except that they had ears that were a little short.[16]

Imagine the excitement and satisfaction Houghland felt when one of his own breeding led the United States Open Field Trial for two days against the best in America.

Then, consider the despair he felt when, in one of those simple tragedies of the field, Balance was gone. Lost, never to be found, even though Houghland and friends drove over fifteen hundred miles looking for her. Disappeared, the best he ever laid eyes on, the stuff of his dreams, the culmination of his career as a hound breeder, vanished "leav[ing] not a rack behind."[17]

I am sure at that moment that the full weight of the tragedy did not sink in. After all, didn't he still have the fixings at home? Broken, a grandson of North Cotswold Beauty by Sam Wooldridge's Big Gene, had consistently run third during Balance's distinguished performance on the lead. But, for the next two years, a terrible blight of distemper swept through his kennels, prompting Houghland to write, "This epidemic set my breeding program back for years—in fact damaged it beyond complete repair."[18] Only after this assessment could the sweetness of triumph be compared with the bitterness of tragedy.

Many colorful characters competed in the United States Open (USO) where Balance had distinguished herself. Bill Brown of Columbus, Mississippi, was one. Bill Brown already had a long association with the USO when I first met him. In 1950, the year Halfback Pickett won it, that hound was so run down when the trial was over that Howard Stovall, riding Bill's albino horse Clint, had to take him up on the saddle to bring him back to the casting ground.

Bill invited Alice and me down to his Fox Camp where they were running the USO, and where I subsequently judged it. I was delighted to meet John B. Watson of Springfield, Tennessee, there. He was a very reliable and respected hound man who had the Seldom Fed Kennels. Alice and I became friends with his family. John B. was always a delight to come upon at the field trials because he gave out country ham sandwiches on homemade bread. The year his hound won the trial, he brought Bill a bottle of Tennessee whiskey in the shape of a hunting horn, which is still among Bill's souvenirs.

Then there was Tom Bridges from down around Nacogdoches, Texas, who had a hound called Chuck Ballot that scored the highest score ever made at the USO up to that time. Tom was part, if not all, Indian. His fellow foxhunting friends teased him about it until one year when the country was so dry that hounds could not run at all, the hunters started asking Tom if he knew any rain dances or chants that would bring rain. Of course, he told them he did not. You can understand their surprise, therefore, when he appeared at the USO banquet in full Indian regalia—leathers, beads, and feathers—and began to stomp, dance, and give incantations to the heavens. Well, of course, it broke up the crowd, who were giving their own boisterous imitations and catcalls, when someone heard an ominous rumble outside. When the revelers ran to the doorways and looked out, they saw lightning, heard thunder, and smelled the rain coming. With great hilarity, they told Tom he could stop, but he kept on, and, suddenly, a torrent of rain began to fall. The wind whipped and howled, shutters and doors rattled, thunder boomed, and lightning seemed to be running everywhere. Then they began to admonish Tom and even plead with him to stop. But it was too late. A real gully-washing, frog-strangling flood of rain was falling everywhere.

It was obvious that there would be no hunting the next day, and people began to strike camp, all the while hurling complaints at Tom such as, "Can't you take a joke?" and "Man, don't you know you have ruined the hunt tomorrow? I ain't never going to another field trial with you."

When I met Tom Bridges, I found him to be a very knowledgeable hound man with a kind of seriousness and dignity, although he freely admitted, if you had heard the story, that he had gone out of the rainmaking business to keep the attendance up at field trials.

It is no wonder that Houghland enjoyed the company of the field trial foxhunters, with their amusing antics and competitive natures. Certainly the loss of Balance encouraged him to try to duplicate her remarkable feat, and he continued his intense effort to breed National Field Trial champions.

However, Houghland's notes in subsequent years were often eulogies to canine athletes dying young. Although he tried on, and there began to emerge a pattern of line breeding employed by Houghland with brilliant success, the veterinary medicine of the day was no match for the deadly diseases that swept through the kennels. By 1945 distemper struck again and, along with depletion from losses and accidents, took a toll that continued from 1947 through 1951, killing with impartiality the field trial Walker hounds and the North Cotswold hounds.

Then Houghland decided to slow down his pack with more English hounds. He turned to Lord Yarborough, the Earl of Brocklesby, who sent him a draft of purebred English hounds in 1954. These hounds and their offspring were dominant in the pack until Houghland died in 1959.

Voltaire once said, "The best is the enemy of the good."[19] This certainly seems a fair comment on the history of the Hillsboro Hounds. Mason Houghland, its founder and master, was a man of great erudition with a felicitous pen and a charismatic personality. He was given half of the preeminent pack in America (the Grasslands pack of Joe Thomas) with a book of instructions, so to speak—Thomas's scholarly work *Hounds and Hunting through the Ages*. Nevertheless, Houghland proceeded to cross these famous Triggs, first with field trial Walker hounds, and then with the North Cotswold, a preeminent English pack. The resultant hounds he continued to cross with Walker field trial blood in a line-breeding program until age or desire to slow his pack caused him to switch to pure English Brocklesby hounds of a very different stamp from the North Cotswold. These Brocklesby hounds ultimately proved less suitable and were succeeded by Fell hounds of Ikey Bell's breeding or selection, which were acquired from Elsie and Tom Morgan of the West Waterford in Ireland after Houghland's death. However, that is another story.

## The Brocklesby Importation

The Brocklesby hounds from Lord Yarborough arrived in America on the *Queen Mary* in September 1954. They were English, of the so-called modern type, purebred with no Welsh crosses, which meant that they had neither the conformation nor nose to hunt to best advantage in the Tennessee woodlands and hills.

This brings me to my last lesson learned from studying Houghland's pedigree books. Do not go out and buy a pack that is unrelated in type, conformation, scenting ability, and temperament to the one you have spent a quarter of a century building and expect the new pack to fit right in. If it were that easy, the job of a breeder would be greatly simplified.

Houghland died five years after he imported the Brocklesby. His pedigree notes concerning the crosses he achieved breeding the Brocklesby imports become very terse or nonexistent. It is difficult to predict what his long-term reaction would have been to the unsuitability of these hounds, which, according to George Sloan, who hunted them for a season, were very hard on stock. I am sure Houghland had long since ceased to look at them with an owner's forgiving eye. He did, however, produce a very useful hound named Mixer by crossing imported Brocklesby Trouncer with 1950 USO champion Halfback Pickett blood. When Houghland's successors took over the pedigree book, Vernon Sharp described the pack as "pretty good," a far cry from the esteem in which Houghland held them through the first half of the forties when they were predominantly the North Cotswold-Longstreet crosses.

The new masters, Sharp and Sloan, immediately got an extremely favorable nick by crossing 1957 USO champion Bolt Action Howard Pickett to a Brocklesby dam named Alice (after my wife).

However, through the early sixties, the breeding program seemed to wander in search of a role model. I once asked Alexander Mackay-Smith why he had not put more about Mason Houghland in his great work, *The American Foxhound, 1747–1967*. He replied that it was because Mason Houghland took the greatest pack of American hounds ever bred (i.e., Joe Thomas's) and turned it into a nondescript pack of crossbred hounds, and that when he got to Valhalla he was going to ask Houghland why he had done that. Since I am not burdened with expectations of Valhalla, or any other part of heaven for that matter, I sought the answer to Mackay-Smith's question in Houghland's pedigree books.

The answer is that Houghland, for all his urbanity, loved the country and country folk. He liked to go down the highway to yesterday and turn off on the dirt road that follows the creek bed to the day before yesterday. There he found the adventure and enchantment that were reflected in his writings, his drawings, and stories imparted to young disciples like me, eager to follow his example. He was a man of tremendous intellect, fascinated and thrilled by field trials and by the culture and cunning of the great field trialers, such as Colonel Howard Stovall, Captain Sam Wooldridge, and others. Moreover, he was constantly amazed and amused by the accomplishments of those denizens of the country who, without benefit of much schooling or of many worldly goods, endured sacrifices to produce champion hounds. He began to breed hounds and buy hounds to compete in field trials. Thus, he turned away from the great legacy given him by Joe Thomas and began an odyssey of experimentation that ultimately proved to be highly successful, but then succumbed to an unfortunate outbreak of disease.

Houghland never sought registration or recognition for the Hillsboro Hounds from the Masters of Foxhounds Association of America. To the contrary, he considered becoming president of the National Foxhunters Association and then declined the position in a charming letter to Howard Stovall.

Dear Howard:

When I am finally called to the 'pearly gates,' to be given my choice of heavens, I have decided to petition Saint Peter for a sojourn at Columbus, Mississippi, instead of an eternity among angels. However, if you are in hell, I shall go on to paradise convinced that even Mississippi wouldn't be fun unless you managed the show.

I am indeed grateful to you for one of the most pleasant interludes in a mis-spent life.

Like Lawrence Jones, I realize that gratitude is really due that sweet 'Little Lonesome' Eleanor. Without her (and Will Timmons), you would be an outlaw.

After I finished talking to you yesterday, I reflected a good deal upon your offer to campaign for me to head the National. It was like you to want to take on a hard job for a friend, and I appreciate it more than I can tell you. However, there is very little I could do for field trials that you haven't already done in Mississippi. I believe that I would prefer to help you push that hunt along the lines you are going, than to try to be Moses leading a lot of foot people through a wired up wilderness. The job would be too tough for pleasure, and not high enough for glory.

Nevertheless, I would greatly enjoy going to the National with you and shall expect you on or before November 11th. The bench show may be Sunday night.

If we are not annoyed by politics and free to offer friendship to foxhunters, consolation to widows, whiskey to each other, and spurs to our horses, I imagine that we may have a laugh or two as we go. My love to Eleanor.

Mason


Despite this letter, Houghland relented and became president of the National Foxhunters Association in 1951. Moreover, his stamp on the National Field Trial for Foxhounds remains to this day in the Natural Carriage Class for hounds and in the Horse Show classes.

It is obvious from the letter above that Houghland held Stovall in great esteem, but there was a good-natured friction between them, a sort of competitive teasing that was always at the ready. For example, Houghland once arranged to meet Stovall in the manager's office of the Peabody Hotel in Memphis. Houghland arrived and was greeted by a charming young lady who said, "So you are Mr. Houghland." She invited him in and asked him if she could get him anything to make him more comfortable.

Later, as Houghland and Stovall were leaving, Houghland remarked on how impressed he had been with the attractive young lady, and how insightful she had been to recognize him when he had never been in the manager's office there before. Stovall listened to the observations and rejoined, "Hell, that's not so remarkable. I saw I was going to be late and I phoned the young lady. However, she said, 'Colonel, I have never seen this Mr. Houghland. How will I recognize him?' So I told her, 'Well, young lady, it's very simple. He has been around foxhounds so long that he looks more like a hound than he does a man.'"

The banter between Stovall, the warrior, and Houghland, the scholar, went on incessantly and was much enjoyed by their cohorts.

## My First Hound Exercise

Mason Houghland was very happy to see Alice, who already hunted with him, marry someone who wanted to hunt. I was very encouraged when he invited me, while I was in law school, to come out in the late summer to exercise hounds with him. I could barely control my exuberance until the appointed day when Alice and I arrived at the barn of Houghland's Green Pastures. To my surprise, there were some twenty-five or thirty riders mounted and ready to set off. Houghland was waiting for us and saw Alice aboard in his usual hospitable manner. Then he turned to me. I hardly noticed how quiet the riders became when he said, "Henry, I am afraid I have bad news. The horse I had for you is lame, and I do not have another available." Of course, I immediately said that was no problem, that I appreciated the invitation, and I would just climb a hill and watch.

"Well," he said, "there is another possibility."

"What is that?" I asked, barely able to restrain my transition from disappointment to enthusiasm.

"We have a mule if you would like to ride."

"Oh, that would be fine," said I, "thank you very much."

Whereupon Houghland nodded to one of the stable hands, who had apparently been instructed to follow the proceedings. Then, at Houghland's signal, the mule was led out to the mounting block. However, before I could seize my opportunity, Houghland pointed out that the girth was around the neck and not under the stomach. He explained that the mule had been saddled the day before to assure his suitability and had unfortunately developed girth galls.

I, of course, scarcely understood the subtleties being imparted, and I sprang from mounting block to stirrup expressing my appreciation and giving assurances that all would be well. Immediately I noticed a sort of rocking motion as the saddle listed from side to side, causing me to name my mount "Ship of the Desert."

We set off with me riding next to Houghland, who pointed out various things about the woodlands, meadows, and hounds as we rode along. Suddenly, to my surprise, hounds struck and went off for a short run. I smiled, expecting them to be brought back, when the master looked at me and said, "I wouldn't deny youth a little flirtation; ride your own line." There I was at the front of the field with hounds streaming away in full cry. What was I to do? Heeding the master's command, I loosed the lines and set sail on "Ship of the Desert."

All went well until we arrived at a post-and-rail fence. "Ship" hove up on his hocks and navigated the fence, with me going overboard like Neptune diving for the briny. When we arrived on the other side, I was still in the saddle but under "Ship's" bow looking up at the ugliest face I ever saw. When I got "Ship" stopped and myself back topside, I looked back at Houghland who was signaling me to come about and return to port. I did, only to find many of the field covering their faces or looking off into the distance. Then Houghland looked at me and said, "Henry, I don't know how it could have happened, but some of this crew did not see you take that jump. Could you please give them another look?"

By now hounds had lost, and the remaining entertainment of the day, obviously, was to see me put to sea and sail that fence again, which, in spite of some misgivings, I did. That prompted one of the lady foxhunters to swap mounts with me in order to experience the same adventure (or perhaps to please Houghland's eye). As we cruised back to the barn, Houghland invited me to come hunting whenever I could and promised to help me find a more seaworthy conveyance.

That summer, Houghland and his huntsman, Felix Peach, took Alice and me night hunting. We were having great fun until we heard a hound obviously in distress over by the railroad track. Felix and I ran over there to find the hound hung in a fence. While I was trying to take the pressure off its leg, the hound bit me in the face, right above my lip, which left a permanent scar. I was taken to the hospital, where, according to my hunting friends, the doctor did not do enough. They thought the doctor should have taken the opportunity to trim my ears a bit and reshape my chin.

Anyway, later that winter I was out with Houghland, and when the run started, he invited me to ride my own line. I did and bowled over a hound that was hidden on the other side of a solid jump. The hound made a terrible fuss but was apparently unhurt. If you kick a hound, kick a good looking one because you are going to see it the rest of your life. Then I looked back to the hilltop where Houghland and the field were watching. They had seen the whole thing.

Despite the fading cry of hounds, I turned around, jumped back to the side of the jump where Houghland had stopped to observe, and rode up the hill to take my medicine. My father always said that if you have to eat crow, get it while it is hot. "Master, I am sorry I struck and frightened your hound," I began. Houghland smiled, wiped above his lip with his thumb, and said, "You are a foxhunter, Hooker. I marked you myself. Have at it. But keep an eye on that hound; we may have to cull it for failure to hark."

In the late spring of 1959 in Nashville, during my spring break from Tulane Law School, Houghland took Alice and me hunting. It was pouring rain, and we drew blank for three hours. However, that time was not wasted. It gave Houghland the chance to extol for me the virtues of living in the wooded country of the Southeast and enjoying sport in the hills. He called New Orleans a polyglot of a place, and he was very keen not to have me settle there when I graduated from law school in June. That turned out to be Mason Houghland's last hunt, and Alice and I have often thought that he must have had some premonition of it. He certainly cut to the chase and discussed his priorities with us. Mason Houghland had an agenda for our lives, and he did not fail to tell it to us on our last hunt with him.


## Notes

1. Mason Houghland, *Gone Away* (Berryville, Va.: Blue Ridge Press, 1949), foreword. Reprint by The Derrydale Press, Lanham, Md., 2000.

2. Mason Houghland, pedigree book I, 1.

3. Joseph B. Thomas, M. F. H., *Hounds and Hunting through the Ages* (Garden City, N. Y.: Garden City Publishing Co., Inc., 1937).

4. *Ibid.*, 57–58, 66.

5. George Garrett, *Fifty Years with Fox and Hounds*, 2nd ed. (New York: Hobson, 1947).

6. Er M. Shelley, *Hunting Big Game with Dogs in Africa* (Columbus, Miss.: Becktold Printing & Book Manufacturing Co., 1924).

7. Houghland, pedigree book I, 8.

8. Alexander Mackay-Smith, *The American Foxhound, 1747–1967* (Millwood, Va.: The American Foxhound Club, 1968), 180–81.

9. Houghland, pedigree book II, 192.

10. *Ibid.*, 168.

11. *Ibid.*, 104.

12. Robert Burns, "Sodger Laddie," *The Jolly Beggars: A Cantata. Burns: The Poems and Songs.* Edited by James Kinsley (London: Oxford University Press, 1969), "Poems 1784–1785," 160.

13. Houghland, pedigree book II, 53.

14. *Ibid.*, 132.

15. Jane Ridley, *Fox Hunting* (London: Collins, 1990), 149.

16. Houghland, pedigree book I, 25.

17. William Shakespeare, *The Tempest* 4.1.168. *Complete Works of William Shakespeare.* Edited by W. J. Craig (London: Oxford University Press, 1914).

18. Houghland, pedigree book I, 29.

19. Voltaire, "Dict. Philosophique, art. *Art Dramatique.* The author has been unable to find a published English translation of Voltaire's *Philosophical Dictionary* that contains this particular article.

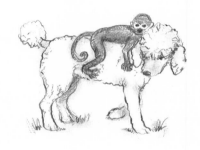

# TWO

# BILL AND JOYCE BROWN: A POODLE AND A SQUIRREL MONKEY

In the fall of 1959, Alice and I went down for a hunt with the Hillsboro Hounds in the Wartrace country, east of Nashville. Bill and Joyce Brown came up from Columbus, Mississippi.

Bill was a famous horseman and hound man and the judge most respected by the field trailers because of his combination of quickness, impartiality, and good judgment when scoring hounds. That was the beginning of a friendship for us that enriched our lives and has taken us to many exciting places, including to Alaska accompanied by a white poodle ridden by a green squirrel monkey. Yes, a white poodle ridden by a little monkey! If you want to get your picture taken, try a camping trip through Alaska with that movie star monkey riding into town on that little white poodle. Moose Pass, Alaska, had a population of thirteen when we came into town. All thirteen of them took our picture. In fact, there may still be a picture of the Browns' poodle, monkey, and us on the Moose Pass post office wall, just as there is on our wall.

Billy Haggard was also at Wartrace that time and he had as his guest Betty Shinkle from Saint Louis. We stayed at the Walking Horse Hotel. I remember Betty made a big jar of her special whiskey sours so we could have a drink before lunch. Then we went out exploring in the afternoon. When we got back to the hotel at dusk, it was strangely quiet, and there did not seem to be any staff preparing the dining room for supper. Betty went back to the kitchen and poured out some more of the whiskey sours, which she noticed had turned an odd color. Then she took the first sip and spit it out all over the room. "Somebody has drunk our whiskey sours and refilled the jar with grapefruit juice!" she screamed. Taking the jar for evidence, Betty advanced on the proprietress's office to announce the foul deed. However, when she opened the door, she found the proprietress resting her head on her desk and smelling like a lot of whiskey sours. There would be no dinner at the Walking Horse Hotel that night; the owner and her staff had run into a pollution problem.

### Frosty, the Dollar-a-Year Horse

From our first meeting with Bill and Joyce Brown, Alice and I began field trialing with them. Bill had a remarkable narrow gray horse named Frosty that soft-gaited on the roads and trotted in the woods. This horse was an incredibly accurate jumper, and he competed in the National Field Trial for Foxhounds' High Jump Class thirteen times and never finished worse than second. Since the judge always penalized Frosty for his way of going, this was an even more remarkable feat. Of course, Frosty usually won. He ultimately retired the challenge trophy, which had to be won three times.

How Bill Brown came to have this horse is typical of the lifestyle around his Fox Camp. One dreary rainy day not suitable for foxhunting, Bill went to the country store to sit by the potbellied stove and swap stories with the owner, who seasoned the tale-telling with some useful homemade whiskey. Suddenly the door opened and a local horse trader came in asking, "Anybody need a jumping horse?" The storekeeper and Bill did not reply so the horse trader went on to say, "I've got him in the pickup truck. I can't keep him in the paddock even with five-and-a-half-foot fences."

"Who in the round world would want a horse like that?" asked Bill before taking another glug of the whiskey.

"Well, I thought you might teach him to fox hunt," said the seller. "Ain't you got something you could trade?"

"Well, nothing but a pony," said Bill.

"What's he worth?" asked the seller.

"Not much," replied Bill.

"Well then I'd have to have something extra, like fifty dollars," the seller replied.

"I've only got twenty-seven dollars in my pocket," said Bill. "Take it or leave it."

"Don't you want to come look at him?" inquired the seller.

"No," said Bill, "you can take him around to my camp, put him in the empty paddock, and pick up the pony out of the other paddock with the mare in it."

The seller extended his hand for the twenty-seven dollars, helped himself to a swig of whiskey to celebrate the bargain, and took off for Bill's camp. Bill never looked at his new horse until the next morning when he found him in the paddock with the mare. Several years later, the result of Frosty's romantic visitation with that mare won the National Field Trial for Foxhounds award for Best Field Hunter. It was a horse appropriately named Oops by Joyce when it was foaled by the mare one day after the mare came in from hunting. Ironically, that same year Oops's sire Frosty retired the High Jump Class Challenge Trophy. Frosty was used as a hunt horse for twenty-seven years. That made him a dollar-a-year horse!

Vernon Sharp was very impressed with Bill's horsemanship and from time to time bought horses from him. The famous story is that Bill was at a field trial getting ready to go hunting the next morning by having a few drinks to get things in the right frame of reference. Mr. Sharp asked Bill if his horses would still lead over a fence. Bill said, yes, he thought they would, and Vernon said that he would like to take a look. So they went down to the stable together. There were, I think, about thirty stalls on each side of the aisle under a huge temporary shed, and there was only one lightbulb in the middle of the aisle. Vernon started going down the stalls looking for Bill's horses. But Bill said, "No, no, no, Vernon. You don't understand. You asked me if they would lead over."

Bill turned on the lightbulb in the middle of the aisle, leaned against the poles that held up the shed, said, "Frosty, Frosty, come out here," and clucked and clapped his hands. To Vernon's amazement, a gray horse came sailing over the door of the stall into the center aisle.

"Wow!" said Vernon. "That is the greatest feat of horsemanship I ever saw. How in the world did you teach him to do that? That is incredible!"

But Bill said, "No, no, Vernon. I told you, you don't understand. It's not hard to get them to jump out into the aisle, where there is light. The hard part is to teach them to jump back into that dark stall. Frosty, get around there; cluck, cluck, clap, clap, back Frosty."

Frosty rolled back on his hocks and went back over the door and into the stall. Vernon was still staring in speechless amazement when Bill turned out the light and said, "Come on, Vernon, they still lead over."

## WD-40

Now Bill's use of the barleycorn stood him in good stead when he took some horrendous falls and sustained terrible injuries. This was the price for riding in such a daredevil fashion. Alice and I saw some of Bill's falls and heard about many others. Bill was not a strong believer in doctors, preferring the pain medicine on the whiskey closet shelf at Fox Camp. He did seem to mend well. However, when he got older his right shoulder calcified from so many breaks, and he did seek medical opinions. These were not encouraging. Nevertheless, Bill seemed to improve in the use of his arm. So we asked him what was doing it. "WD-40," came the reply. "I saw a mechanic slide out from under a car and I heard him ouch about his knees. 'Forgot to use my WD-40,' he said, so I got him to explain how he rubbed it in and how it helped him move around without his bad knee hurting him." Bill did ask an orthopedic surgeon what he thought of the idea and to see if the stuff was poison. Bill got a "don't quote me" go ahead and use it. Well, it certainly seemed to work. Bill recovered some of the use of his arm, and his shoulder did not seem to ache him as much. For my part, I encouraged the young foxhunters to rub it on their heads. No telling how many Phi Beta Kappas would have come out that way if their parents had not squelched the program.

The Coyote Like a Possum

One year back in the sixties in Nacogdoches, Texas, where coyotes were considered a nuisance, Bill Brown had a long run at the Texas State Field Trial, and hounds drove a big coyote up to a cattle gate across a creek. The quarry backed under the cattle gate for protection. Hounds, about three hundred of them, were on the creek bank giving tremendous cry until finally they got up their courage and fell in there on the coyote. The water roiled. The hounds came back up off the coyote and maybe fifteen or twenty were injured and crept off. Nevertheless, the hounds built up and fell in on the coyote again, and there was another big fight. Just then, the hounds heard a different coyote off in the woods and about half of them left to run that other coyote which had come up and decoyed for the coyote that was in the water.

By now, it was getting down to a lot fewer hounds, and Bill was getting worried looking at that big coyote looking at him, so he decided to get a stick or something in case that coyote decided to come after him. Bill was all stove up from all the times he had fallen all those years hunting and all of the times he had medicated himself with Yellowstone bourbon instead of going to see doctors; so he was getting a stick when a couple of cowboys rode up and said, "Well, Bill Brown caught the coyote." Bill said, "No, I haven't caught the coyote; the coyote's pretty near caught me." They said, "Oh no, we're going to show you how you did it." One of the cowboys went to the fence that the cattle gate was under and he threw a loop over the coyote's neck. The other cowboy had that rope on his saddle, and his horse backed up and jerked that coyote right up out of the creek. Just then, the first cowboy dropped on the coyote, put a stick in its mouth, put a figure eight around it, and tied it off like a calf. Then the cowboys asked, "Bill, do you want to take this coyote back with you, or what do you want to do with it?"

Bill said, "Well, maybe I can take it back to Joyce and we can take it back to Mississippi."

"Fine, we'll just put it on your horse, and you take it back to the casting ground."

What they did not recognize was that Bill's horse was not enthusiastic about having that coyote put on it. It took Bill about ten minutes with a twitch to get that horse still enough to get that coyote up on it. When they started riding back to camp, Bill started looking in the coyote's fur to see where all it had been bitten—only he could not find any bitten places in there. The coyote was in good shape. Bill began wondering why the coyote was lying there so still on the front of his saddle, so he looked down there more closely. Then, suddenly, that coyote opened one eye and looked back at him.

"What did you do then, Bill?" I asked.

"I set the world's record for dismounting off a horse. And I didn't want to get back up there until they showed me that the tie on the coyote's mouth would keep it closed. I finally reluctantly got back in the saddle, but that horse and I felt about the same way about having that coyote up there. So we hurried on back to the casting ground, and as soon as we got there, I said to Joyce, 'Look what we have to take back to Mississippi.' And she said, 'You're not taking that smelly old thing back to Mississippi with me.' That's when my coyote catching days kind of ended up right there because Joyce had us turn that coyote loose. The only thing I can tell you for sure I learned out of it is that a coyote can sull up like a possum, so if you catch one, remember it may just be making plans for you."

## Fox Camp

This brings me to Mississippi, and Bill and Joyce Brown's Fox Camp. Not only were Alice and I invited, but the Browns encouraged us to bring our children and friends. We took advantage of this privilege and introduced the Browns to Ned and Nina Bonnie. Ned is the famous equestrian lawyer from Louisville, Kentucky, and Nina is the celebrated horse show rider. They loved the country and the simplicity of country life and soon became frequent visitors and great friends of the Browns. Their company added to the sport and merriment of our gatherings.

Fox Camp was in the hills between Lexington and Durant, Mississippi, about sixty miles north of Jackson. The soil was sandy and loamy, easy on horses. There were few natural hazards except for erosion ditches and quicksand bogs. We carried collapsible saws on our saddles so we could saw a limb off of a nearby pine tree, put it on a wire fence, jump over, and then pull off the limb.

It was about this time that I heard the story about the wood sawyer in Grundy County who noticed in the weekly paper an advertisement for a power chainsaw that would enable one to cut up to seven cords of wood a day. Well, the wood sawyer sat by the fire that night and figured on the back of a shovel how long it would take him to pay for this newfangled saw if he sawed seven cords of wood a day. He got so excited that he was there when the hardware store opened the next morning, even though it was not even Saturday. He got that saw, hit the woods at first light the next morning, and went to sawing, and he sawed hard all day. However, that night when he counted up, he had only sawed five-and-a-half cords of wood. He could not sleep that night either, and the next day he was there when the hardware store opened, even though it was not even Saturday. So in he went and put the saw down on the counter.

"What seems to be the trouble?" asked the proprietor of his agitated customer.

"Everybody knows I'm the best wood sawyer in this county, and if I can't saw seven cords of wood a day with that saw, can't nobody saw seven cords a day with it."

"Let's see," said the proprietor in a conciliatory tone as he pulled the little starter cord. Immediately the motor started with a brrrr.

"What's that noise?!" asked the wood sawyer.

After I told Joyce that story, whenever I went to work on anything with my little collapsible saw, Joyce would say, "What's that noise?" And when I dropped a fencing tool or did something else clumsy like dropping the steaks off the charcoal fire, Joyce would say, "I see what you mean, Alice."

Nina Bonnie certainly understood this sentiment because I noticed whenever she said, "That's a half nice horse," she meant it was a very nice horse. So I asked her one day, "Do all Virginians use that 'half' expression as a superlative?" "Most of them do," she said, "which you can tell even if you are half dumb."

## My First Pack

In 1963, Bill and Joyce Brown gave me my first pack of hounds. They were a couple-and-a-half of Trigg hounds. Sam Spade, Bullmoose, and Diamond Jim Brady were their names. They could find foxes, pack up, and run them. They were great fun for Alice and me. I took John Sloan Sr. hunting with them in the Hicks Bend, just the two of us. It was a small hunt, a couple of hunters and a couple-and-a-half of hounds. Sloan coached me on how to hunt them and then took over to show me himself. We had a big run and a big time. He asked me if I would like to try them in the Hillsboro pack, which I did in the Cooks Hills that Saturday. I got several crossings. Bullmoose was first, Diamond Jim Brady was third or fourth, and Sam

Spade was about seventh. I was invited to take them down to Cornersville the next week. When we got there, Granny Walker, an old man with an ear trumpet who rode a spotted pony, was there to hunt with us; so was Sehon McConnell, the Harwells' farm manager. If you told Granny Walker where you heard the hounds, he would tell you where they were going to cross. Then he heard Bullmoose coming across the ridge. "That's your big old Mississippi rolling mouth dog," he enthused. "He's looking at the fox right now." Well, one thing led to another, and I left Bullmoose down in Cornersville with Sehon so Granny Walker could hunt and hear him, and so Sehon could breed him. I do not know which one got the most satisfaction, Granny or Bullmoose, but we got a warm welcome in Cornersville after that.

Bill and I began to build up a pack together. He knew some trustworthy old Trigg breeders. We used them to great advantage. Bill collected and bred us a pack that ran to catch. Those hounds taught me to stay uphill or downwind if I wanted to live with them when they were running. Bill had a field trialer's technique. He would open the kennel and let hounds go in all directions. Then when there was a strike, he would cheer them together and ride like the wind.

I took my hounds out alone from time to time, which, of course, is not recommended. On one occasion when I was having a cracking good run, I carelessly galloped under a tree and was swept off by a big limb. I hit the ground hard as my horse, Mr. Fox, galloped on after hounds. I lay there wondering if anything was broken and trying to get my breath when I heard a sound in the woods. It was Mr. Fox coming back to look for me. When he found me, he stopped on the downhill side. I was able to pull myself up by my stirrup, and, with him standing stock-still, I hauled myself into the saddle. I was too dazed and sore to ride or do anything but hang on. Mr. Fox began walking towards home, now and then flicking his ears as hounds came nearer us, but he never broke out of that quiet walk. He very gently took me home and stood still while I slithered down off his back.

Sometimes I would go by the barn and hear our faithful old barn man sitting on a stool by Mr. Fox's stall door. He would be having a private conversation with the horse. Often it would go something like this: "You may be lookin' sassy now but Big Daddy is gonna hunt you Saddy, and when you come back here lookin' like somebody let the air out of your tires I be here waitin' to rub on you and fix your mash. So you know the world don't owe you nothin' when it come to that."

## Adventures with Bill and Joyce Brown

After a couple of years of this style of hunting, Bill sent all of our hounds up to Nashville so that I could keep them for the summer while we decided what to do about a heartworm problem. Dr. DeWitt Owen, our horse vet, found a vet in Miami, Florida, Dr. Knowles, who was an expert on heartworms, and he came up and prescribed carocide as a preventative. Moreover, he got American Cyanamid to give me the carocide in exchange for keeping records of its effectiveness. So I gave the hounds some carocide and started walking them. I took along some cheese, cracklings, or cut-up hot dogs. I would call a hound by name, and if it looked at me, I would throw it something. Soon the hounds started to get biddable (easy to control). Never forget what the old Blue Pye says: "For the huntsman knows what a hound can do, and he knows that I know that he knows it, too, and he knows my voice on a fox is true."[1]

Now there is a broke hound; there is a hound that is ready to go hunting with you—that knows you know his name, and knows that you know that he knows that you know it, too. The snack trick teaches you which are the most intelligent of the young hounds because those hounds will always be in the right place to get the snack. Great older hounds achieve a kind of dignity that causes them to disdain this play. Older huntsmen soon learn that dry chunk dog food works just as well as cheese, cracklings, and hot dogs.

That fall we took the hounds back down to Mississippi to get ready to go hunting. Bill had always just opened his kennel gate and let his hounds go, then when he finished hunting he would come in, and his hounds would come straggling in all afternoon and night. They would get up under the house and hide. You often had to crawl up under the house and get them out or try to catch them when they came in and put them in the kennel. I took our hounds down there at the start of the new season, and when we got ready to go hunting the next morning, I opened the kennel gate. However, this time the hounds just stood there looking at us. Bill asked, "What is this?" I said, "Well, when I call them they'll come on out, but they're not supposed to come out until I call them." So I called them, and the hounds came on out—I won't say perfectly, but it was pretty good. Bill started looking funny, but we went on hunting, and we had a big run. When it was over, I started blowing and calling for hounds, and Bill said, "You know, they know to come home. There aren't many hazards down here. We can just work our way back to camp." But I kept blowing and calling periodically, and by the time we got back to the kennel, we had pretty nearly every hound. The kennel door was standing wide open so we rode up there, and I said, "Kennel up!" and all those hounds went in there through that door, and I rode over and latched it shut from horseback.

Bill stared at them and me, and said, "Well, I'll be. I wish you hadn't done that." I said, "What do you mean you wish I hadn't done that?" He said, "When I think of all the years that I crawled up under that dang house to get hounds up there sleeping or something, and all those years I could have just been taking them out and putting them in the way you just did. What are you trying to do? Are you trying to ruin my foxhunting?"

## The Brown-Hooker-Bonnie Hounds

Bill, Ned, and I formed a pack of Triggs called the Brown-Hooker-Bonnie Hounds. One of these hounds, Trigger Bill, was always in the right place, but I could never catch his voice so I was afraid he might be running mute or might be stingy with his tongue. "No problem," said Bill, selecting two distinctively voiced veterans from the kennel that evening. To this duo, he added Trigger Bill and cast them into the woods down by the lake.

We had time to fix our drinks and get comfortable on the back porch before the trailing began. "That's Slide Rule," said Bill when his best bitch began giving her calling note. Soon she was joined by a booming voice of a lower register. "Shotgun," said Bill, who could immediately identify almost every hound in the pack, except for Trigger Bill, by its voice. Then the run began, and between the recognizable notes of Slide Rule and Shotgun came a fast chop, eager and packed in with the other two. They must have been on a red fox from the way it ran and the way they disappeared from hearing and then came back singing the joy of their pursuit in the night.

From that night on, I recognized Trigger Bill's voice, and I noted that the other hounds gathered themselves when they heard that chop because they did not want to get left at the station.

Bill taught me a valuable rule: only cheer to a voice you know. Otherwise, the hounds will find out that you do not know what you are doing. Knowing the voices of your hounds makes you able to take instruction from the pack. When you hear Pastor's voice and see all your hounds gallop off towards him, they are teaching you that Pastor is a reliable hound. Often when hounds are trailing, suddenly their voices change to a more acute note. Check your girth and shorten your reins: the fun may be about to shift into overdrive.

### Stopping for Mistletoe

I will say this about Bill. When he came in without one of his hounds, and somebody called and said, "Mr. Brown, I've got your hound over here," Bill would say, "Well, turn him loose, and if he's my hound he'll come home." That way Bill did not pay rewards for hounds all over the county, and neither did he teach his hounds to sit down and wait for him when they finished their run. You know, some people put their hounds up on their saddles after a run, and, pretty soon, the hound figures out that he runs, and then he gets a taxi home. I told one of those people, "You know, it would only take Johnny and Karen Gray [our hunt staff] about a week to train every hound we have got to lie down and get taken home." She did not seem to want to discuss it further after I said that.

The one exception I can remember Bill made was one year right before Christmas when we had a great run, and ended up way over in a place called Blackhawk. We had gotten back to Fox Camp, done our horses, and turned them out. Bill and Charles Berry had started on the milk punches when the phone rang, and a cropper over there at Blackhawk described our hound Big Un that had not come in with us. To my surprise, after a whispered conference with Charles, Bill told the cropper that we would come and get Big Un, and Bill and Charles got in the front of the truck and put me back in the bed of it.

We were going along the dirt road, which went the fourteen miles to Blackhawk, when Charles slammed on the brakes. "Hooker," he said, "here is the saw. Get up on top of the cab and saw the mistletoe off the limb of that big oak tree so we can take it back to the girls for a Christmas decoration." I got up on the cab, up on my toes, and started to saw, but just then Charles started the engine. Needless to say, I didn't lose any time getting down off that truck cab, and no amount of milk punch oratory could get me back up there. Anyway, we got Big Un, and when we got back to camp, I told the ladies about the mistletoe we almost brought them. The picture of me on my tiptoes on the cab of that truck got a strange reaction. I do not know if they were just taking pity on me, but we didn't seem to need that mistletoe after all.

## Haircuts

We happened to be down at the Browns' hunting camp sometimes when, by Alice's standards, I needed a haircut. To be agreeable, I offered to let Joyce go to the barn and get whatever implements she could find to give me a trim. She accepted and did a pretty good job—or so Alice told me. Nevertheless, that was not the end of it. There was a lot of talk, and some of Joyce's friends, such as Nina Bonnie, Dot Stephenson, and Poochie Berry got in on the act. They could hardly wait for me to get shaggy enough to need their services. Sure enough, the day arrived, and they brought their scissors and clippers out with great determination. I decided that they should each take a specific portion of my head, and then Joyce or Dot could even the whole thing up. Things proceeded according to plan but, to be honest with you, Alice did not seem too taken with the tradition she had started. In fact, when I asked her how she liked it, she suggested I let the barber around the corner from my office in New York have a look at it.

The following week, after some of my fellow employees discreetly inquired who cut my hair, I went to see Tony the barber. Even though it was his quitting time, he greeted me cheerfully. Then he took a closer look at my head. "Whatta happen?!" he exclaimed. I started to tell him. Before I could get him in the mood of it, he wrung a towel and blurted out, "Bossaman, pleesa, pleesa don'ta letta thema ruina my beesanessa." So ended the custom of free haircuts at Fox Camp.

## Coon Chile Saved

Bill Brown had permission to hunt everywhere. There were no posted "NO TRESPASSING, HIGH-POWERED RIFLE PRACTICE" signs as I have seen in some other countries. In addition, there were no "THAT MEANS YOU, SON OF A BITCH" painted on the back of "NO TRESPASSING" signs. There was dove shooting, quail shooting, and foxhunting until you were shot and galloped out. It was a great place to take the children, their friends, and their cousins. We often took our children to Fox Camp not only because they had fun there, but also because Bill and Joyce were such good role models.

One year, my daughter Lisa took Vernon Sharp's granddaughter, Trudy Caldwell (now Byrd) to camp with us, much to Sharp's delight. Lisa and Trudy made a big sign in the shape of a sunflower that said "HAPPINESS IS JOYCE AND BILL" and decorated the dining room for Thanksgiving with crisp colorful leaves under the table that made crackling sounds all during dinner.

The next morning Henrietta, who came to tidy up camp while we were tacking the horses to go hunting, swept up the decorations. She apparently did not see me in an alcove talking on the telephone. Henrietta was giving Joyce's pet raccoon, Coon Chile, her undivided attention. She was teasing it with the broom, at which Coon Chile was slapping, as she swept it toward the corner. Henrietta was laughing and Coon Chile was slapping when suddenly Henrietta pinned it with the bristles of the broom and said, "Ha, ha. I ets little things like you."

"Henrietta," I called from the alcove, "is everything all right?"

"Oh yes, sir," she responded, taking the broom away as Coon Chile made its retreat up a ladder to the space above the ceiling. "I didn't know you was in here."

"I am just going hunting so I will be out of your way," I said. "Keep an eye on Coon Chile, Henrietta. Miss Joyce is very partial to that raccoon."

Henrietta just leaned on the broom handle and looked at me as I went out the door.

641 Red Racer

Sometimes our son Timmy took his cousin Johnny Ingram to camp with us. Timmy had a little motor scooter that they used to explore the countryside. There was a country store two or three miles from camp called Con's Corner, and Timmy and Johnny would go there riding double on that scooter. The route was like a Mississippi Idit-arod to them with all its dangers and adventures. There was a man they called Drunkie who sat out on his porch with a big black guard dog overlooking the road. The dog would crouch down when he heard the scooter coming and launch an attack on the driver and passenger when they went by. Bill helped them with various defense mechanisms like a loud horn and water pistols filled with alcohol. These merely caused the black dog to recruit some of his running mates, and soon a bobbery pack awaited the boys when they tried the gauntlet. One time the black dog got Johnny by the pants leg, but Johnny was able to shuck him off into the ditch and escape.

It therefore came as a great surprise when the boys declared that they were ready to race Bill to Con's Corner. Bill had a red trac-tor with motor number 641. The boys declared themselves game to race "641 Red Racer" to Con's Corner despite the dangers along the way. The terms of the race were carefully negotiated. Bill was to get a head start, but he had to leave a mark at the bridge to show he had not left before the appointed time. The contestants had to get a Coca-Cola from Con's Corner to show they had indeed been there. The first vehicle back to camp with the Coca-Cola would win.

A contract between 641 Red Racer and the scooter team was duly signed by Bill, Johnny, Timmy, and assorted witnesses the night before the race. The next morning the boys had their scooter revved up and ready when Bill appeared from behind the barn with his old Volkswagen with a big new sign on it that said: "641 RED RACER." Timmy and Johnny were fit to be tied. There was a long renegotiation, and Bill finally agreed to use the tractor in exchange for a bigger head start.

Once the race was on, the motor scooter swiftly overtook and passed the tractor only to break down on the way home. Bill came upon the boys trying to make their racer run. Timmy and Johnny were about to wear the kick-starter out trying to get it to catch. Bill faked it like he was going on to Con's Corner but stopped a little way down the road. Then he came back to them, and there was a lively discussion about whether he must actually go on to Con's Corner and buy a Coke, or just take them home, be declared the winner, and go on fixing their scooter. This is how Bill arrived back at camp with the scooter on his bush hog, the boys on the back of the tractor, and their Coca-Colas up in the seat with him. I reckon the cousins learned a lot that day about contracts, sportsmanship, and dealing with the perils one meets along the way. However, their learning experience was not over.

## Snipe Hunting

Bill was commiserating with Timmy and Johnny when he mentioned how sorry he was they had not won the race because he had planned to take them snipe hunting as a prize. Of course, they immediately began to bombard Bill with questions about snipe hunting. He was very noncommittal, merely saying that a full moon like we were having was the best time, and that he thought the boys were good enough woodsmen to do it, although most boys were a little older when they went the first time. Maybe, he said, they could take Wilburn Hooker, whom we called Second Cousin, and who was coming to dinner with his wife, Mary Elizabeth. "What if Second Cousin doesn't want to go?" they added to their endless list of questions.

In due course, however, Second Cousin and Mary Elizabeth arrived. Although he was well fortified from a large plastic road glass, Wilburn picked up on the prospective adventure. He was a state senator and on the board of the Cotton Council, but he had never been snipe hunting, he said, and he was definitely up for it. He even paid me the compliment that he thought I was excellent with children, and he wanted his to be around me more. Bill, for his part, gave the boys and Second Cousin candles, grocery sacks, and an empty coffee can. He explained to them to get down out of the wind so the candles would not blow out and thump on the can in order to attract the snipe. Then, as the snipe came in, put them in the sack. "Don't try to catch them all at once," he admonished. "Just put them in one at a time."

I must say dinner seems to take a lot longer when three of the people at the table are asking every few seconds if it is time to go, if the moon is up enough, and so on. Finally, we gathered them up and walked down to the pinewoods by the lake where we repeated the instructions and took our leave back towards the house. They circled the lake and set off across the pasture with a big ditch in it towards the cover on the other side. Bill and I reversed our course as soon as they were out of sight and went back into the dark shadows of the pinewoods to await developments. We later learned that Second Cousin took a tumble in the ditch but undauntedly held up his plastic road glass and declared that he never spilled a drop. The boys observed to each other that the water in the mud puddle and Second Cousin's drink were the same color.

It took about fifteen minutes for the glass to run low, the candles to be useless, and the thumping of the empty coffee can to lose its promise, so the stalwart hunters pulled up stakes and started back for the camp. Second Cousin even put Timmy up on his shoulders to help him successfully navigate the ditch. Once on the camp side, they came around the lake with a few grunts from Second Cousin. Then, just as they passed close by the pinewoods, Bill stepped out of the shadows and asked in a very loud voice, "How was the hunt?" "Oh my God!" shouted Second Cousin, throwing his plastic glass in the air and staggering backwards into the lake. Both he and Timmy disappeared beneath the moonlit waters before popping up sputtering.

Timmy was laughing and giving Second Cousin a shove towards the bank, but Second Cousin fastened on me as the culprit. "Henry Hooker, don't you get near my children. You're the worst influence on children I ever saw. I'm going to tell my children not to listen to a thing you say." Whatever the merits of that accusation and course of action, I can tell you that it was withdrawn when we got back to camp, replaced the contents of that plastic road glass with some real good bourbon whiskey, and put its owner next to the fire. As for the boys, they seemed to like camp better than ever now that they were experienced snipe hunters.

## The Cackle Club and Beyond

We tried to make Fox Camp as entertaining as possible for the children and other guests. One of the ways we used to accomplish this goal was initiation into the Cackle Club. The children and others not in on the play were allowed to overhear some mention of the Cackle Club and its membership. We would say, for example, when discussing a good rider or woodsman, "He's been a Cackle Club member for years." Naturally, this caused curiosity and questioning that was treated very secretively. This led to more questioning, and, in due course, the prospective members would discover the existence of a secret honorary society in operation. An invitation to join this exclusive group was much to be desired. Moreover, there was usually an impediment to an invitation to join. The prospective inductee was too young, or too old, or had not been hunting long enough, or something. Then when the impediment was waived by the membership of the club in a secret meeting, the overjoyed prospect was invited to join and prepared for the initiation ceremony.

A chair was placed in the middle of the room for the inductee to sit in during the rite. A strong light, which was turned off, was placed next to the chair. The master of ceremonies was at the other end of the room with a bright light shining on him. It was explained to the inductee sitting in the dark that the Cackle Club was an honorary society based on merit, and that it got its name because its membership all learned about chickens so as to have a common body of knowledge as a bond between them. Then various facts about chickens were recited, and the names of kinds of game chickens and so on were told, repeated, and memorized by the inductee as part of the initiation. If the master of ceremonies was a little short on his chicken terminology or nomenclature, he just improvised and made up the missing information while the honoree seriously sought to memorize it all perfectly and to repeat it in exactly the correct order. When the secret ceremony was at the height of its solemnity, the inductee was asked if he or she knew what sound a hen made when she was laying an egg. Of course, the inductee replied that the hen cackled. "No, we mean the *sound*—how does the hen sound?" we encouraged. When the appropriate cackling sound was made, the observing membership expressed great support and suggested to the inductee that he or she flap his or her elbows and hop off of the chair to give more realism to the cackling imitation. When the inductee complied, the light next to the master of ceremonies' chair was switched off, leaving the room dark. Then the light was switched on next to the inductee's chair, which the hopping, flapping, and cackling inductee had just vacated. Applause would break out when the inductee turned around to see the vacated chair filled with eggs.

The Cackle Club initiations were a great success, and the secret was strictly kept so that new prospective members could be invited to Fox Camp to participate in this entertainment. However, there were a few glitches. During his initiation, Johnny Ingram was hopping, flapping, and cackling when he asked, "What kind of dumb game is this?" The members of the club howled and put his performance high on the list of great Cackle Club initiations. Alas, Second Cousin, despite his vow after the snipe hunt never to let himself get talked into anything again, succumbed to the bourbon and pump water, got wind of this secret society, and waged a successful campaign to be invited to join. To be fair to him, he did an excellent job of learning the chicken names and the fighting chicken strains. He even gave out enthusiastic cackles accented by flapping elbows at the appropriate time. However, when Second Cousin crouched to hop, there seemed to be a small equilibrium problem that manifested itself by his staggering back a step. In a coincidence of miraculous timing, it all happened at just the moment the eggs were placed in his recently vacated chair. It was the only Cackle Club initiation I ever remember where the inductee looked like he had an omelet on the back of his pants. Thenceforth, Second Cousin was a member of the Cackle Club with full toast-proposing privileges.

Other camp games included boo ray, crazy eights, and backgammon. The atmosphere of Fox Camp permeated our pastimes elsewhere, and the children were always ready for a game. Robin Ingram (now Patton) expressed it completely at age six when she was dealt four eights in a Christmas Eve crazy eights game at her house and went around the room showing everyone but me her hand, singing "'tis the season to be jolly." Robin certainly knew a fish when she hooked one. Later, when Alice, Lisa, and I flew to Vienna, Austria, with Robin and her parents, Bronson and Martha, Robin asked to sit by me and produced a little traveling backgammon board that she used to start her fortune.

## Honky-Tonk Gorgeous

One December we went to Fox Camp shortly before the United States Open Field Trial for Foxhounds was to be run. As we pulled into the driveway, we were surprised to see a strange camper parked not far behind the house. Of course, we wondered whose it was. Then, while we were unloading, a stranger walked up. Bill introduced him as somebody Brown. Bill explained that Brown had asked Bill's permission to stay at camp and acquaint his hounds with the territory for the USO while Bill and Joyce were away. While we were getting to know each other, another person with a lot of blonde hair piled on her head joined us and was introduced to us as "Gorgeous."

Gorgeous was quite a striking figure. She gave the impression that when she went to the beauty parlor she ordered the whole menu. Furthermore, her taste in fashion featured a photo-finish effect. It was a duel down the stretch to see if everything was going to stay covered. After surveying her assets and listening to her speak, I secretly nicknamed her "Honky-Tonk Gorgeous," a title that stuck when we were in the house and they were back in their camper.

As the field trial was not starting for two or three days, Mr. Somebody Brown offered to take me bird shooting the next day when we got in from foxhunting. I was delighted and accepted happily. When we got inside the house with everything unpacked, we quizzed Bill about his new friends. He was a little vague but said the man had some hounds to run in the USO, and Bill had agreed to let him give his hounds some practice at Bill's camp because everyone said the game would run right through there during the field trial. Bill did say, however, that Cousin Brown, as people were calling him in town, had irritated him a little by taking the camp door off its hinges and filling up the refrigerator with fish caught out of Bill's lake while Bill and Joyce were away. Then Joyce chimed in that Cousin Brown, who of course was no cousin at all, had done this or that, and I could see that Cousin's and Gorgeous's visit was likely to be eventful because the surest way to get on the wrong side of Bill was to irritate Joyce. I could tell that Honky-Tonk and Cousin might be heading down five miles of bad road.

Nevertheless, I went out quail hunting on foot with Cousin the next afternoon, and we covered a lot of ground, considering that I had been foxhunting since dawn. When we finally came in about dark, Bill was waiting by camp. After we put the dogs up, and Bill and I got back in the house, Bill quietly asked me about Cousin Brown's marksmanship. "Oh, he can shoot," I assured Bill. "He may not outwalk the postman, but his dexterity with a shotgun is without question." "Well," said Bill, "in his line of work he needs to be clever with firearms." "What do you mean?" I pursued his provocative statement. "Well, Stone Crane from over in Alabama called me while you were out hunting, and this Brown fellow may be wanted for bank robbery." I sank right down in a chair on the spot. However, there was no time for further questions because I looked up to see Honky-Tonk Gorgeous and Cousin Brown coming to the door. They looked like they were making a social call because she arrived dressed up in her Saturday night drinking-and-home-breaking outfit complete with beer in hand and wearing enough scent to lay a drag to Tupelo. When they knocked, Bill invited them in.

Cousin Brown immediately started telling Bill how much he liked Bill's lead hound Sugar Foot. He declared expansively, "She can trot the globe, Bill." He bragged on her, "She can mortally fly." "How do you know?" asked Bill, staring quizzically at Cousin. "Well, I ran her at night with my hounds while you were gone. You can hear her far-off lonesome wail like that night train to Memphis," Cousin elaborated, not realizing the meaning of that set to Bill's jaw. "She is a Dixie Flyer," he continued, although one could now see that Bill was not a happy camper.

Perhaps finally realizing he was in trappy country, Cousin Brown turned the subject to enhancing hounds' performance in field trials with drugs. That was certainly the starter button for Honky-Tonk Gorgeous, who began to express her opinion of the family lineage of anybody who would do that. "Doping dogs" as she called it was obviously the moral dividing line and subject of contention between Honky-Tonk and Cousin. She warmed right up to it. I think Cousin may have been needling her just so we could hear the verbal fireworks. Honky-Tonk could talk trash faster than those World Federation wrestlers. As she heated up on her subject, the number of cuss words per sentence progressed geometrically. As they say, she could cuss a blue streak. I'm talking deep ocean blue, Neptune's basement blue, bluer than blazes.

Finally, Bill stood up. "That's it! You'd better leave," he said, edging a word in between Cousin Brown's baiting and Honky-Tonk's cussing. "Right now, tonight!"

"What did we do?" they asked in a very surprised, offended, and disbelieving tone.

"Enough!" said Bill, opening the door for them.

Honky-Tonk and Cousin were never seen at camp again after we watched Cousin load his hounds and we made sure Sugar Foot was safe in her kennel.


## Ernest Hardison and Field Trialing

One of the most enduring memories I have of a field trial in the sixties was at the National in Camden, South Carolina, when Claude McCormick brought about twenty-five ladies from Memphis over to the trial and acted as their field master. The ladies were turned out very smartly with their black coats and buff breeches with double rows of buttons down the front. Bill Brown and I were judges. We were galloping for scores and passed McCormick's group in the pinewoods. They moved over to let us by, but just then the fox turned, and we had to reverse to go back the other way. It is a good thing we did because it gave us the chance to save Ernest Hardison from bad trouble. We heard someone galloping flat out down a dirt road, and we looked up to see Ernest racing towards us in overdrive with his hand over his eyes.

Now Ernest was known for riding steeplechasers, and this one was pretty shifty, but Bill cut it off and got it pulled up. Then we asked Ernest what had happened to get his horse running away with him. "It was Claude McCormick's ladies," he said, still shaking from his harrowing ride. "When the fox turned, I, as master of the field trial, turned with it and suddenly I found myself in the midst of McCormick's ladies, who were all off their horses making a pit stop. When they saw me, they dropped their reins, jumped up, and started squealing. Of course there was nothing I could do but put my hand over my eyes and give my horse his head and a kick to get out of there. I guess I overreacted because my horse bolted out of that circle of screaming indisposed ladies and milling horses." "You were a perfect gentleman," we assured Ernest, hoping to calm him, as we picked up our reins to get back to hounds. "Are you all right?" we asked as we departed. "I'm all right," Ernest assured us. Then as we rode off we heard his parting comment. "If I could just forget all those front flaps hanging down," he said. I knew Ernest for the rest of his life, and I can tell you he never did.

Some of the old-time field trialers told me that Bill had had a July hound named Truman that led the USO Field Trial for three days, only to break his heart running so hard in a race on the third day. When the fox was holed, Truman lay down across the den and would not leave it. That afternoon he was brought home to Bill in a pickup truck, but would not cast on the fourth day even after a day of rest. He never ran again.

There were a lot of tricks at those trials, such as people painting the same number on two or three hounds that looked exactly alike or tying a hound to a tree if it was ahead on the score sheet so that it could not come back to home plate and get scratched before quitting time. I am sure a lot of loopholes have been closed but others have been discovered as the years have passed.

## Note

1. "The old Blue Pye." Ascribed to Will Barnard, huntsman to the Fitzwilliam, in 1908, preserved by George Wells, a saddler, and passed to *The Field* by Mr. J. W. A. Smith, a vet in Peterborough, England. *The Field*, Vol. 233 November 18, 1971: 1107.

THREE

# ADVENTURES WITH BEN HARDAWAY

One morning about six o'clock, my good friend and fellow fox-hunter, Uncle Dudley Fort, showed up on my doorstep. He had a man named Ben Hardaway in tow. Ben was a great foxhunter, Dudley assured me, and we would have many good times together. I was a bit sleepy but summoned consciousness enough to invite them in and mumble some show of interest. Well, Uncle Dudley was sure right. I asked Ben to meet me at the National Field Trial, and he came over for a day and rode my horse, Mr. Fox. That got me invited back to Midland, Georgia, where I had a great time visiting Ben and Sarah in early 1965. My letter of thanks well summarizes our good times:

Dear Ben:

This letter is about how I am selling my house and farm and all the equipment and stock to try to raise enough money to move to Midland. Most people think I am doing it because I came back and told such big lies about your hounds that I am being run out of town. But the real reason is that I never had so much fun in my life. So I figure I better get down there before they put gates around it and call it heaven. Speaking of heaven, I never heard angels that could sing so sweet as that choir you are directing. What range, what a crash, what a chorus! When they got started, it sounded like all the symphonies and operas in the world were playing at the same time in the shower with me. I swear I thought my heart was going to jump out of my throat. It was whirring like a covey of birds getting up.

Then when I saw them coming through the woods, vying for the lead with each other like a pack of field trial champions, gulping down the scent and singing their fox eagerness, I thought maybe I had somehow gotten mixed up and ended up in Valhalla with Squire Osbaldeston hunting the lead hound from every pack since creation to now. Boy, you really said it right. That ya-ta-ta, ya-ta-ta, yayaya, screaming and meaming and slashing and dashing and racing and driving pack of hounds was the fire-eatinest, woods-bustinest, scent-gobblinest, fox-chasinest thing I ever saw.

Of course, they might have been showing off a little bit when they ran that fox down the railroad track and across those mud flats, across the highway three or four times, around that wide circle clean out of your country without ever losing it, but you can tell that little bitch, Wade, for me that I sure like show gals, especially when they are fast, pretty, and honest. Some other hound dogs think a lot of her, too, because they really harked when they heard her bringing that fox out of that swamp.

Well, there is no sense in me writing you about the finish because it would just get me excited.

The pad you gave me is hanging above Mr. Frost's stall, which I'll clear out for Sail, Wade, Drum, and their crowd because I am counting on them giving a real show in my country if the stinking violets haven't ruined scent. Everything is all set for Wednesday the 7th and Thursday the 8th. I'll have enough horses to go around and have arranged to put you and Jack up. I hope you can bring your wives because they are sure neater and nicer and sportier looking than you, besides which I would like to show Sarah the portrait that French lady did of the children.

Sincerely,

Henry

Ben and his brother-in-law, Jack Hughston, came and put on a wonderful show. Bradford got a holiday from school to be able to hunt with the famous pack. That fall Ben came to the National with Mel

Kaestler. Bill Brown and Billy Haggard were also there. We had a lot of fun competing while judging for speed and drive scores. There is nothing more frustrating than riding your horse at breakneck speed to get to a crossing, and then finding that you have dropped your pencil. There you are trying to repeat the scores to yourself so you will not forget them and asking every passerby if you can borrow a pencil. "Twenty-six, thirty-five, forty-four, eight. Have you got a pencil? Twenty-six, thirty-five, forty-four, eight. Has anybody got a pencil? Twenty-six, thirty-five, forty-four, eight." Well, you get the point. The only thing that comes close to being that frustrating is when you punch the wrong button on the tape recorder at a crossing, and you wind up dictating a deafening blank, or when you accidentally hit the erase button and lose the entire tape of scores. Alas, I am embarrassingly familiar with all these methods of scoring malfunction.

## Number 205

One year in the early sixties at the National Field Trial for Foxhounds in South Carolina, hound Number 205 was obviously a remarkable hound. Number 205 was hunting. Number 205 was trailing. Number 205 was speeding and driving. Number 205 compiled a tremendous score. Number 205 was just one hell of a hound.

Then on the last day, Chief David Ware, the home plate judge, came in and said, "Scratch Number 205."

"Scratch him? What do you mean scratch him? Man, that's the best hound in this trial. We'd swap our horses and the trailer they came in for that hound!"

Nevertheless, Ware insisted, "Scratch him."

"What for?" we chorused.

Ware explained, "Some of the boys had him over under a tree ten minutes before quitting time and they were breeding him over there."

"Scratch him, hell!" leaped up Hardaway. "Score him for endurance!"

That started an argument in the judges' meeting that broke out into the whole rank and file of the National Foxhunters Association.

People who were there and had been hunting with each other for thirty years were saying, "I ain't never going to hunt with you anymore. You ain't got no romance in your heart. You can't scratch that hound for doing that. That man shouldn't have had a bitch in season at the field trial; everybody knows that's against the rule book." However, the hound was finally scratched. This always seemed an injustice to me given the natural tendencies I have observed in foxhunters and foxhounds. However, I can tell you what settled the membership down and got old friends talking again.

At the height of the argument a man named Jack Smith from Milan, Tennessee, got up at the membership meeting and told about an evangelist preacher at a revival in his town who invited the infirm onto the stage for some faith healing. Sister Lizzie and Brother Horace responded to the call. Now, Sister Lizzie said she wanted to get rid of her crutches. The preacher put her behind a screen and asked Brother Horace what he needed. Brother Horace said he had always had a harelip and that he wanted to talk without any impediment. The preacher sent him behind the screen, too. Then after suitable praying the preacher told Sister Lizzie to throw her crutches over the screen, and when they came sailing over, the whole congregation "Hallelujahed" and "Amened." Then the preacher called for Brother Horace to say something to the congregation. "Sister Lizzie just fell down on her bottom!" Brother Horace said, still with his heavy harelip accent. The crowd at the membership meeting roared at this unexpected ending and it even seemed to cool down the debate over Number 205.

Some of my adventures with Ben Hardaway are in his book *Never Outfoxed*, which is a wonderful book. I have quite a few copies of it. But I do not know how much they are worth, because some guy has signed his name in the front of every last one of them.

## A Visit from Ben

It was not long after that field trial that Ben called me one day and said, "Hooker, I'm going to be in Nashville and I just want you to know that I'm not going to see you. So if you hear anything about my being there, just know that I don't have time because I got a tax matter that I want to talk about with a man up there."

I said, "Fine, Ben, but come on down and have a cup of coffee when you finish and just say hello. You're not here that often, so come on."

He responded in an unpromising voice, "I'll see what I can do."

Nevertheless, on the appointed day, he showed up at my office for a cup of coffee and we sat around and talked about hunting a little bit and I said, "Why don't you run out to the kennels with me and have a look at the hounds?"

"No," he said, "I don't think I'd better do that. I've got my men here studying on a big project. We're bidding on it with the Oman Company and my man Mr. Money has them over there now figuring on the bid."

"Come on, Ben," I urged. "We'll just go by and look at the hounds and you can speak to Alice, and then you can check on Mr. Money and go on about your business."

So Ben agreed, "Well, if it won't take too long."

We went out to the kennels. Peaches, our huntsman, was there and I said, "Peaches, draw me out some of these hounds and let's have Ben have a look at them." He did, and we talked about them and I said, "I'll tell you what, Peaches. Just hook that hound wagon over there up to my car, and put about ten couple in there and I'll go out hunting in the morning and maybe I'll get Ben to go out hunting with me, or maybe I won't. But I'll go out and have a little tingle and tangle." Peaches loaded up some hounds for me, Ben got into the car, and we went by the house to see Alice. We got there, and she was very happy to see Ben and said, "Why don't you stay for dinner?"

Ben called Mr. Money and he said their people were working away. So Ben said, "Hooker, there's absolutely no way I can go hunting with you in the morning; I want you to know that."

I said, "Well, I understand, Ben. But I'm going to try to get out of here no later than six o'clock, and so we could just take a little turn around and we'd be back in by eight o'clock and you could talk to your people and so forth."

We stayed up late talking and finally decided that we would go out the next morning. I lent him some hunting pants. My boots would not fit him, but he wore some long socks and we rode out into the Hicks Bend. We struck a big red fox there, and we had a gallop all the way around the bend and to Percy Warner Park and then back. The fox started to go into a hole down in the bend but we headed it, and so it went again all the way to the park and back again.

To make a long story short, it was twelve thirty in the afternoon when we came in from the hunt. Ben ran to the phone, called Mr. Money, and said, "You what? Did you put something in there in case anything goes wrong; did you put a contingency fund in there?" Mr. Money apparently answered him satisfactorily and Ben said, "All right, good luck. I hope it works out."

Ben turned around to me and said, "Henry, we just bid $135 million to build the Oroville Dam. That's the biggest fixed price contract in the history of the United States as far as I know. But I hope to God it's a good bid, because if it isn't, you're going to get blamed for it—shanghaiing me out there foxhunting." So far as I know, this huge project was very successful, and Ben Hardaway is one of the few men I ever met who could run such a big business by remote control while teaching me foxhunting. I do not know whether that was Mr. Money's real name, but I can tell you this: it was an apt description.

### Ben Gets the Horn

Not long after that, Ben invited me down to Butler, Georgia, for a hunt. He had a field trialer named Bill Smith, who had some hounds and was going to hunt with us. It was pouring rain but we went out anyway. Sound did not carry, but about once every half hour or so Bill Smith would say to Ben, "Ben, do you mind if I blow my horn now?" And Ben would say, "No, I guess it's all right." Bill Smith would extract from his homemade saddle scabbard a long automobile horn with a bulb on the end of it. He would squeeze that bulb and it would make a tremendous sound in the woods: "AH-UG-GA!" It absolutely made the leaves and the limbs on the trees tremble when he blew that horn. None of the hounds was very far away from us anyway because there was not any running, but Bill seemed to feel a lot better when he got his horn blown and it was about the only action we were getting out there. So we rode around for three hours with Bill periodically squeezing off noisy blasts.

The next morning, Ben said, "Hooker, we're going back to Columbus and lay out until it quits raining, and then we're going to hunt until we have to patch tack."

While we were all gathering up our stuff and getting ready to load horses and leave, I sneaked back there and caught Bill Smith by himself. I said, "Hey, Bill, I'd like to buy that horn."

He said, "You would?! You really like my horn?"

"Yeah, Bill. I could really use that horn. What would you take for it?"

"Oh no," he said, "I'm not going to sell it to you. I'm going to give it to you. I'm just so glad that you like it."

"Well, thanks a lot, Bill. I sure appreciate it. But let's don't say anything about it, because a lot of these other people might get envious."

So we went on out and loaded up and I had that horn in my suitcase where nobody could see it. We went on back over to Columbus.

That night we went over to Dr. Jack Hughston's house for dinner and had a big time, all in anticipation of the rain stopping and our getting to go hunting the next day. When Ben went out of the room for something, I said to Sarah, his wife, "Sarah, would you do me a big favor?"

"What is it?" she asked.

"Well, I've got this horn and I would like you to blow it for me. All you have to do is squeeze a bulb."

She looked at me appraisingly and said, "Well, where is it now?"

"I put it under the bed in your bedroom. Nobody knows it's under there, so when you go back there and Ben gets really sawing it off, and you're lying there trying to go to sleep, the thing to do is just briskly squeeze the bulb on that horn and after that I think you'll have plenty of time to go to sleep before he does."

So, sure enough, we went back to Ben's house and about one o'clock in the morning, I heard this God-awful blast: "AH-UG-GA!" In about a minute, Ben showed up in the doorway of my bedroom and said, "Hooker, you should have seen me. I was levitated right out like a magician's assistant. You could have passed a hoop all around my body. I was about two feet above the bed, straight out. I thought I had heard that horn enough over there in Butler. That thing is going to haunt me for the rest of my days."

"No, Ben," I reassured him, "it's not, because I got it for you. It's a gift from Bill Smith to you."

So that is how Ben got the horn, which he immediately put into permanent retirement. Bill Smith and Ben have been hunting and hound trading friends ever since.

## The Lesson

I should have known right then to go home; I should have known. But, noooo, I didn't go home. Ben took me out hunting the next day and we ran and had a big time. He let me ride up with his hounds. Everything was going well. He was staying back and directing me where to go. He was giving me the illusion that I was being the huntsman of his hounds when, all of a sudden, we came on a little clearing and there was a small church with a preacher in there with a congregation. I thought, "Oh my goodness! I've gotten into somebody's churchyard and I've got to get out of here!" So I was calling the hounds and blowing and leaving, and the preacher came running out and I said, "Oh, Mr. Preacher. I'm sorry I interrupted your service. I wouldn't have done that for anything in the world. If you'll just give me a minute, I'll get these hounds out of here."

But he said, "Oh no, young mister. Don't you be in a hurry. I saved the sermon for them; they're part of the lesson."

"What do you mean they're part of the lesson?"

"Well, ain't these here Mr. Hardaway's hounds?"

"Yes, sir, they are."

"Well, they says, 'How lonnnng, how lonnnng.' And then the others says, 'Not long, not long, not long.' Young mister, that's a lesson in the Bible. You better repent your ways and give Mr. Hardaway back these hounds that belong to him because we need them for our sermon."

I looked around and Hardaway and the field were right there laughing. They had heard the lesson before and no doubt thought it would do me good.

## Mischief at the Lake

Ben brings out the mischief-maker in me. One time Buck Allison and I went down to go hunting with Ben. Ben had a big crowd. We went out early in the morning. Hounds were sharp. We had a good run and hounds got their fox. Ben handed it to me to keep up with while we looked for another one. Nancy Steenhuis rode up to me and said in a worried voice that Ben had awarded her the brush. She was obviously concerned that I might misplace her trophy.

Sensing an opportunity for mischief, I asked her why she had not gotten the whole thing. She said, "Well, I don't know. Ben had already given the mask to Buck Allison." "Well, that's all right," I said, "Buck loves to dance and if you invite him and Bunny down to the Atlanta Hunt Ball, he will give you the mask and you can have the whole fox mounted for a centerpiece for your hunt table." This seemed to be a good plan to Nancy, who immediately went back to ride with Buck and talk to him about dancing. By the time we got in, Nancy had Buck's attention, which was immediately noticed by Buck's jealous Irish wife Bunny.

I realized that the subject needed to be changed or my role as a mischief-maker would be discovered, so I challenged Ben to a bet of twenty-five dollars on whether he could swim the lake just outside his house. "Sure I can," said Ben, holding out his leg for me to take off his boot. I replied, "There you go changing the odds. Who said anything about you taking off your boots?" He prevailed in this discussion and was soon changed into a bathing suit. Then I got to thinking about the omelet and lamb chops we had had for breakfast and how cold that lake had to be. What if Ben got a cramp? I would be out of the skillet and into the fire. I had better follow him or something. So I got a little boat and Jim Steenhuis and I followed along, with Steenhuis paddling, while Ben swam the lake with the hunters lining the bank. I waited until Ben got right in the middle of the lake to play my prank. I yelled, "Uh oh, Ben, here comes your wife Sarah!" even though there was no sign of her. "I'll hide under the rowboat," he quickly replied, not wanting to be caught perpetrating my silly scheme. "No, that's not her," I confessed, resigning myself to losing twenty-five dollars. And lose it I did because Ben finished his swim across the lake. So Nancy got her centerpiece, Bunny got her Buck, and I got out of town.

Plunder, the Honest Mistake

About that time was when Ben sold me a hound named Plunder. I got him home and found out that he would mark to earth and mark to tree. If it was a red-sided gray, he would mark it up a tree or he would mark a red fox to earth. Of course I was very pleased with this hound's marking trait; moreover, he had personality. He smiled at you and kind of minced around when you went to pet him. He was very personable. Then Ben called me one day and said, "Hooker, I need to find me a dog that will mark. I'm putting foxes to ground and up trees and I need a marking dog."

"Oh, do you really, Ben? I tell you, I know how you feel about that. I've got one of the best marking dogs I ever saw in my life and he's just absolutely added tremendously to our sport."

"You do? Where did you get him? I didn't know you had any marking dog; where in hell did you get him?"

"I bought him from a fellow."

"Well, that damn fool. He sold you his marking dog? What a mistake he made!"

"Yeah, he did. But I don't know. Maybe he didn't necessarily know; he has a lot of hounds."

"Well, where did you get him, no kidding? Maybe he's got another one."

"I got him from a guy down there in Georgia."

"You mean you got him down here? Who was it? Maybe he's got another one he don't know about."

"It was you Ben; it's that hound Plunder."

"My God! I had me a marking dog and I didn't keep it?"

"Well, I'll tell you what. I'll send him back to you."

"No, you won't."

"You mean you don't want him?"

"No, I didn't say I didn't want him. Of course I want him. But I ain't going to let you send him back because I know you want him, too."

So, Plunder stayed with me and retired to semi-housedogdom. The only vice he had was jumping in any car parked in the garage with a window open, especially if there was a thunderstorm and he had gotten good and wet. It would give me quite a shock when I came down in my business suit and opened the car door to find a wet foxhound in the driver's seat smiling at me.


Drawing for a Dear

Now, I do not want to digress too much with these Hardaway stories, but I do remember running into Sarah and Ben in London once when Alice and I were on the way to shoot grouse. They were having a big dinner party at the Connaught Hotel. They invited us to come. When we got there, Ben gave me my instructions in more or less these words: "Hooker, you are sitting beside one of the most beautiful women in the British Empire. Her name is Libby

Fanshawe. Now I want you to tell her about the time I did so and so. And you can tell her when I did such and such. And if you want to you can tell her about the time you were with me when I did this or that heroic thing."

Well, the dinner started and sure enough, I was seated by Mrs. Brian Fanshawe, who was a very beautiful lady indeed. I immediately let her in on the joke I intended to play on Ben. Several times during the course of the evening, I saw Ben looking over at us and I just smiled at him. Finally, about midnight when the after-dinner drinks were being served, he could stand it no longer and he came around the table to us.

"How's it going?" he asked. "Hooker, have you finished telling her about me?"

"Not yet," I replied.

"Well, did you tell her about the time I did so and so?" he asked.

"Not yet."

"Well then, what have you been talking about all night?"

He had taken the fly. "I have just told her about some things I have done. I haven't gotten to you yet."

Ben's face looked like hounds had checked in the middle of a great run. "Hooker, we are on the cognac already. When were you going to start?"

Then Libby laughed and started asking him about his exploits that I had recounted to her, which he seemed prepared to repeat freely. However, by then the party was over.


## The War on Deer of a Different Kind

Ben became concerned about deer; not the kind of dear that George Sloan built his tree house to show, but the kind hounds go crazy over. Ben was a proactive deer-proofer. He sent me the draft of a paper on deer-proofing. He explained the whole program to me. It involved using deer scent to entice hounds into a barrel and raising a noisy ruckus with them to give them an aversion to deer scent. Then he told me about his hound Wade figuring out these deer-proofing schemes. I, frankly, thought there might be a conflict between trying to breed smart hounds and this barrelizing technique. I think Ben thought so too because he took off his cap and said to Wade, "Please, ma'am, don't run no more deer."

I much preferred his next theory—that a dog can only count so high so that when you are housebreaking them, you only have to spank them for piddling in the house so many times, about five, before they figure out that they cannot remember all the places in the house where they are not supposed to piddle. That is the way hounds figure out about deer, Ben explained. They run Alfred and then Roscoe and then Sam and finally Jefferson and then they figure out that they cannot remember all the deer they are not supposed to run, so they had better just leave all deer alone.

Ben taught me something I still remember. "Hooker, if you whip a sorry hound all you get is a whupped sorry hound." "Well," I put it to him, "do these barrel schemes get the job done?" "I don't know," he gave me an honest answer, "but they won't go near no more barrels." It was about that time we got a white-tailed deer named Joe that lived in the kennel with our hounds and came to the horn and packed up when we walked hounds out. However, the Tennessee Wildlife Resources people made us get rid of Joe, and we were back to square one. Sometime later Mooreland Hunt master Harry Rhett's captive buck ran Rhett's huntsman, Tommy Haney, up the fence of its pen and kept him there for about five hours before Tommy could get out and get his rifle. That incident certainly enhanced my appreciation for the Tennessee Wildlife Resources people.

On one occasion, I went to the Essex Fox Hounds in New Jersey to hunt with Nick and Kitty Brady. Ben was there with his staff and his hounds. He had brought his hounds up there to break them off deer. He was hunting with the Essex huntsman, Buster Chadwell, and they were hunting Ben's hounds and the Essex together. The Essex were absolutely deer broke and Ben was giving his hounds, which he had already taught not to go near barrels and to count to five, a lesson in not running deer.

On the last day, Ben had all of his hounds in except his all-time favorite, Wade. Then he saw Wade coming down the road. He said, "Wade, come on. I just about left you; I'd just about given you to Jill," (referring to Jill Slater, now Jill Fanning, who was master of the Essex at that time). Wade came on down and they picked her up and put her in the hound wagon. But Ben said, "Wait a minute." He reached back there, and Wade kind of slunk back from him a little and he said, "Don't you cower back from me. You're never going to see me again, hound, because I'm getting ready to give you to Jill." He got the hound out, took her over, and gave her to Jill. I tell you this: it was a touching sight because I was watching a man give away his favorite possession in the whole world. It was a poignant moment and the meaning of it to Ben was not lost on Jill. Jill had to turn around and walk down the road and put her hands to her face before she turned again and came back to us. Even then, she wiped her eyes as she thanked Ben. However, Ben ultimately got Wade back and it is her portrait that hangs over Ben's fireplace in Columbus.

Actually, I got really worried about Ben on that trip. That last night after he had given away Wade, and we were having some drinks and getting ready to go out to a dinner party, Ben kind of got down. He said, "You know, Hooker, I've got to change my ways. Mr. Money is running the business all right but it ain't doing anything like it would be doing if I was spending my time on it. I've had all these guests from all over the world. It's been a perpetual house party. Sarah has paid a terrible price; she has to take care of people, make arrangements, and entertain them. It's just too much. I've got to change my ways and I'm going to cut back on the number of days a week I hunt. Maybe I'm not going to be as good a companion for you as I was before because I'm going to get back to concentrating on my business and let Sarah have a break from this terrible pressure I've put on her."

Well, I was so young I did not know where to get on the watermelon wagon. I just thought that poor Ben had kind of taken the vapors. I got back to Nashville, called up Vernon Sharp, and said, "Vernon, I'm really worried about Ben. I think maybe we ought to go down there to see him. He might need some attention you know, maybe try to cheer him up and get him a doctor or something. He seemed real depressed to me and I think we ought to do something about him because he's our friend."

Vernon said, "Yes, Henry, I know you would feel that way. I can understand that. But I'll tell you what I'll do with you. You call Ben and just ask him how he's doing and if he's still talking like that, you call me back and we'll get in the car and go down there right away."

I called Ben and got him on the phone. "Hooker," he said, "Come on down. I've got these guys coming over from England and we're going to hunt 'em out, Hooker. Sarah's putting on a big party and this is going to be one of the greatest sporting weeks you've ever had in your life. You just bring your good horses and come on down."

I said, "Ben, I'll see if I can do that. I sure appreciate your inviting me." Then I called Vernon and I said, "Vernon, I really think I was a little hasty in thinking how Ben was going to change. He seemed to me to be in very good cheer when I talked to him just now."

"That's what I expected," Vernon responded. "But I wanted you to hear it for yourself."

It was shortly after that that Ben invited me to go, in two weeks' time, to whip in for him in Virginia. He made it sound like all the girls would be prettier than movie stars, and we would get our fill of galloping over grass at last. But then Ben called to cancel the Virginia trip because he had taken his hounds out for a tune up and looked down in a very fast run to see the cloven hoofprint of the devil deer. "Hooker, it was awful. All my hounds were lost because I had been passing farms faster than a Manhattan subway. But then the phone rang and a gentleman at the other end said, 'Mr. Ben, are you missin' any hounds?' 'Yes, I sure am. I was afraid they were running deer.' 'Naw, suh, they ain't running no deer now,' reassured the caller. 'They's just rolling in the carcass.' Cancel Virginia, Hooker."

## Sojourning Down South

Ben and I had a lot of fun hunting together with Mooreland Hunt master Harry Rhett during his hunt weeks. Harry was a perfect Southern gentleman. He was, therefore, something of an interesting contrast to Ben and me. We might have tried to be gentlemen, but nobody accused us of being perfect. I will never forget the time we were having a big run there in Huntsville with Ben's hounds, and he and I went through a gate and got into a pasture that was bisected by a dirt road. The pasture was fenced up to the road on both sides. Hounds were running, so we looked all over for how to get out of there. It seemed like we were going to have to turn around and go back through that gate, although hounds were going in the opposite direction. However, a little creek ran through the pasture and under a little old wooden bridge across the road. The fence had been brought up to the edge of the bridge on either side and a cattle gate had been put down under the bridge so that the cows could not get down in the creek and walk under the bridge.

I was turning around to go back and open the gate for Ben when I saw him circle his horse down into that creek and jump off the creek bottom onto that bridge. He looked back at me and circled his arm like an organ grinder turning on the music for the monkey to dance, and shouted back, "Come on, Hooker, the music is playing!" I thought to myself that there is something peaceful about knowing you have to cooperate with the inevitable as I put Mr. Fox down into that creek and galloped at that bridge. Mr. Fox heard the music and he did not want to get left by Ben, so we got up on that bridge and skedaddled after hounds.

Ben has never quit providing me with amusement, entertainment, and sport when I am around him. Many is the cast he has made with me at a hunt ball, teaching me that time spent in reconnaissance is seldom wasted. I was at the Virginia Hound Show and I had the good fortune to run into a very pretty lady who gave me a kiss. The lipstick was apparently visible on my face because when I walked up the hill and ran into Ben talking to Alice, Alice looked at me and asked, "Who kissed you?" "A blind woman," said Ben, before I could answer.

## Getting Invited Back

Now, that kind of stuff will not get you invited back. How to get invited back is a very important thing if you go sporting around. I will give you an example. Wait until your host's favorite bird dog goes on point, then look at your host and say, "Look there, he's telegraphing heaven!" That will almost always get you invited back. Or if you are out hunting with somebody, figure out which one is their favorite hound or ask them. Then a few minutes later when things settle down, you can say, "You know, you're right. That hound has a real presence about him, doesn't he? I just love the natural carriage of that hound, you know, he just really knows who himself is, doesn't he?" That will get you invited back. I have been invited back lots of times on the strength of things like that.

The other thing is, when somebody gives you a foxhound or some good foxhounds, you always want to thank them because only a truly generous person gives away a hound already known to be good. Thank them genuinely and maybe you will get some more. I will give you an example. I had Nina and Ned Bonnie over there to the National Field Trials in Camden, South Carolina, and there were about a hundred riders. The hounds struck in a blackjack oak thicket, and we went in there and were tacking around in there in that blackjack oak thicket with our hands up in front of our faces warding off the limbs. Finally, the fox left the thicket and came out with hounds right behind it and us right behind the hounds.

We could look back and see all those riders arrayed back up on the road waiting to see which way to break. But we were living with those hounds singing and swinging down the long green declines, across the cotton fields, and into the edges of the swamps. That fox was running, and hounds were raving, and it was the greatest sport that ever happened. Finally, we saw the front twenty-five hounds go mute. They were so close to the fox that they were running it by sight and I got there just exactly the very second that they got the fox.

So I grabbed the fox back from the hounds and held it up to Nina and said, "Look here, Nina. How do you like that, Lassie?" But Nina had her eyes closed and she kept repeating, "Oh, wait until I tell Mummy; oh, wait until I tell Mummy." About that time, Bill Brown rode up on a horse named Wellington. "I saw you, but this horse doesn't have the foot to stay with The Black Crow," he said, looking at my ex-chaser and calling him by his stable name. "Do you know anyone who needs a nice quiet hunter?" Bill asked, as we rode back to the casting ground.

## Mrs. A. C. Randolph and Gifts from the Piedmont

Nina did tell Mummy and Mummy was Mrs. A. C. Randolph Sr., master of the Piedmont Fox Hounds. Nina and Ned got Mrs. Randolph to invite us to Virginia to hunt with her pack. We went and had a great time. The thing I will always remember about that trip, other than the great people we met and the friends we made, is the Piedmont huntsman, Albert Poe's, handling of hounds. We had a long run to a far corner of the country. It was getting dark and spitting rain. The cold night was settling in with a wind to give the chill authority. Albert pulled up and gathered his hounds. Then he turned to Erskine Bedford, the field master, and said, "Maybe I can hail a vehicle to take me back to get the vans." "That would be fine," agreed Erskine.

Wanting to avoid a long cold hack home, Albert then hailed the first pickup truck that happened by. It slowed, and then stopped. Albert asked the driver if he would take him and the hounds back to the casting grounds. When he received a dubious acquiescence, he turned to his hounds and said, almost conversationally, "Get in the truck." Immediately twenty-four couple surged like a wave into the bed of the pickup. Albert looked at the few stragglers and reiterated, "Get in," which they did. "Wow!" I said to him. "What a feat of houndmanship!" He looked back at me and said, "Well, it would have been easier if they had ever seen this truck before." Then he got into the cab and left to attend to his chores. I remember standing in the road savoring an indelible memory of how he managed the run, the night, the hounds, and Mrs. Randolph's visitors.

Mrs. Randolph was kind enough to give us some foxhounds. So this is the letter that I wrote her, and this letter was intended to thank her for the ones we had gotten and to make it possible for us to get some more if needed. Mrs. Randolph took a liking to me, I think, because when Nina was taking us over to another prominent hunt in Virginia, Mrs. Randolph said to me, "Henry, when you get over there, take a good look at that first whip." "Why?" I asked, innocently. "Well, I think she's a natural born home breaker," responded Mrs. Randolph, "and I just wanted your confirmation." "On her conformation," I thought to myself.

So here is the letter I wrote to Mrs. Randolph:

Dear Mrs. Randolph,

Having known Nina, Alice and I follow with a sense of participation the history and progress of the Piedmont. It therefore
seems a wonderful culmination of this interest to have a chance
to hunt the four couple that you sent with Ned and Nina and the
Bill Browns. Although most of my time this summer was spent
roading hounds and working on obedience, I did find an occasional irresistibly cool evening when the setting sun lingered on
the ponds and in the still woods. On several such evenings, I put
the entered Piedmont with our pack of Triggs and slipped out
of the kennel to join one of the children for that race between
darkness and good scenting.

We would gather our hounds and head into a hollow away from
roads, house dogs, and gasoline engines. There, in the lengthen-
ing shade, blackberry patches offered their ripe fruit to father
and child who picked the tasty berries from the brambles.
Hounds were eager. They hunted hard across the warm earth
through the briars. Horse and pony, wise to the game, watched
their quickness in and out of creeks, broom grass, and thickets.
We rode along talking, now and then tapping the horn. On one
such evening my youngest son, Timothy, and I halted to listen to
a far away owl. It wasn't a strike. Disappointed, we ambled on
through the gathering gloom. Some hound began trailing. The
first tentative openings were cursorily checked and then thoroughly investigated by the pack. Tacking together, they carried
their noses down and their sterns proudly, as they busily
searched for every trace of scent.

Then, suddenly, an acute, sharper, calling note gathered
horses, hounds, and hunters to the tingling din of the chase. Your
hounds needed no encouragement. Their excited voices made a
strange salient note among the familiar choir. The galloping,
cheering, and horn blowing didn't bother them. They had their
red-sided gray, had it to pour it on, had it to drive through the
briars into the forest depths, had it to pursue through the twilight
open places under maple groves, had it to lose and to find, to
exult over, to strive for, to burst in front of their cheering audience in the last light, to chase over dusky meadows and back into

the darkness of the woods, and finally, after an hour of singing thunder, to put to earth in the night.

I was so pleased with the hounds you sent us and so busy congratulating them at the earth that I did not hear him when he first said it, but he repeated it as I got back into the saddle. It was Timothy, then not quite nine years old, sitting atop his gray pony, Nibs, which had carried him stirrup to stirrup with me through the entire run. "It's nine o'clock, Pops, and black dark," he said. "We haven't had supper and neither has Nibs. You have us so deep in the woods that those hounds will need lights to lead us out. It's all right with me, Pops, but ladies worry when their boys get lost after bedtime." He was right, of course, so we picked up the hounds and headed straight to the kennels.

As we trotted home through the chill night, I thought of the crossings, of the beautiful wild grace of the fox, and of which hounds had been strongest at the finish. Then I thought of hounds from Canada to the Caribbean, running in the night and singing their joy. "It's all right, Timothy," I said, "a huntsman with his hounds is never lost."

Sincerely,

Henry

## A Hound Match

Shortly after George Sloan became joint master of the Hillsboro Hounds, he invited Mason Lampton to bring his Hardscuffle hounds from Louisville, and he invited me to bring the Brown-Hooker-Bonnie hounds to a hound match at his Panorama Farm. This venue was a real galloping country. Mason and George had competed with each other at point-to-points and steeplechases. They continued to do so at this hound match, producing some spectacular falls and causing George's groom, Sheila Davidson, to pronounce them both crazy—George for getting himself knocked out and Mason for laughing at him.

The clear winner of the match was a hound from the Brown-Hooker-Bonnie pack called Sly Eye. She was red with a white-ring neck and a white patch over one eye. Bill Brown and I had bred her out of his good bitch, Slide Rule. She dominated the match. Mason jokingly offered his pack and his horses if I would send Sly Eye home with him. His offer turned out to be prophetic because soon after that he married Ben Hardaway's daughter and moved to Midland, Georgia, and gave his pack, which was entirely derived from Ben Hardaway, to Brown-Hooker-Bonnie and Hillsboro to split. One other thing about Sly Eye was that she disdained participation in kennel quarrels or rough housing. Hounds were careful not to invade her space because they knew that if they provoked her to reach for them, it was a death sentence. I have seen other leaders of the pack have the same quality. They achieve a kind of dignity. They eschew quarrels and conserve their energy for the real work to be done.

### Jean Dupont McConnell Shehan: History Repeats Itself

The thank-you letter of all thank-you letters is the one I received from Jean Dupont McConnell Shehan when she gave the Foxcatcher hounds to the Hillsboro Hounds in 1980. This was a triumphant homecoming of the breed of hounds that Joe Thomas had made so famous and which the Foxcatcher had acquired in 1933. It was the same breeding that Mason Houghland got from Joe Thomas to start the Hillsboro Hounds. When I heard that Mrs. Shehan was going to give up foxhunting and that there were many packs trying to buy her hounds, I got Vernon to call her with me in an effort to retrieve the bloodlines so prominent in the history of the American foxhound. She was delightfully receptive and generous. She very kindly wrote me a note in which she said: "I cannot begin to express my thanks to you and Vernon for your consideration and interest in the Foxcatcher hounds. I am thankful they will have a fine next home and only hope they will do the job for you all that they have done for us."

Now I have gotten some gracious thank-you letters in my time and I have even written some passable ones, but this was the all-timer because Mrs. Shehan was thanking us for accepting one of the most famous and celebrated packs of hounds in the history of American foxhounds, the direct descendants of Joseph B. Thomas's hounds.

That day Mrs. Shehan sent us her pack. What a magnificent gift she made to us! Her relative, Mrs. Carpenter, and our old friends, the Vicmead, soon duplicated her generosity.

Lizmore

Now, lest you think I was cruising the countryside scavenging everything that crawled, wiggled, or walked that looked like a foxhound, let me tell you that we had occasion to give away a very nice hound named Lizmore. The story is that we went down to the Whitworth Hunt in Mississippi. They received us very hospitably. Longais de la Gueriniere, an old friend from New Orleans, came and prepared a fabulous feast in honor of our visit. It featured many kinds of game as well as other delicious dishes. I complimented him on a virtuoso performance and inquired especially about the venison. "Henri," he said, "it eez no problem. You just marinate zee side of zee deer in zee bathtube with zee window open to make zee refrigerator. It make zee deer so tender. But eef your wife comes home and goes to zee bathroom, Yi! Yi! Yiiiii!"

We had a great hunt with the Whitworth. However, when it came time to leave, we had one hound missing, a hound named Lizmore. We looked around the country, but we were unable to find any trace of Lizmore. So I went to Whitty Payne, our hostess, and told her that we were missing the hound. She immediately called her man Arthur over and explained to him that a very valuable hound had been lost on the plantation and that she wanted him to get in the pickup truck the next day and go to all the tenant houses and put out an alert that this very valuable hound had to be found. When he did find it, he was to put it in the kennel and call Bill Brown at Fox Camp near Durant, Mississippi, so that Bill could come back down and pick up the hound. I did not hear from Bill until the following Friday night. He called to say, "Henry, I have some good news for you."

"What is it?"

"Lizmore has been found."

"That's wonderful!" I said.

"Yes, but there's a problem," he continued.

"What is that?" I asked.

"Arthur got to thinking about what a valuable hound that was and how safe you wanted to keep it. He started worrying about their kennel fence and whether or not it was strong enough to hold that hound. So when he brought Lizmore back on Monday he locked him in the clubhouse with plenty of food and water. But he forgot about him until this Friday morning when he called me. Now, I want to tell you, Henry. I know this concerns you but they will be able to use the clubhouse again. Not this season, but some day, with suitable spraying and so forth, I mean, some day that place will be usable again. But it was just awful. It was one of the great disaster scenes I've ever seen in my life because that hound had gotten up on the back of sofas, on tables, everywhere, and marked territory and left calling cards and so forth."

I immediately asked him if Whitty had been told how bad it was.

"No," he said.

"I'll tell you what I want you to do. I want you to call Whitty and tell her that we had such a wonderful time down there that we just want to make her a gift of that hound, Lizmore. And we hope that he will be useful to her as a running hound and also as a stud dog. And tell her that we stand to do whatever we can to restore her clubhouse to usefulness in light of Arthur's extreme carefulness." So Lizmore stayed at the Whitworth and tended to business, as they say.

## Dr. John Youmans

Among these hunt visits, surely some of the greatest times we have experienced have been at Huntsville, Alabama, with Harry Rhett and the Mooreland Hunt. The first time Harry invited the Hillsboro down there to a joint meet, we were all excited and arrived in force and finery to the prehunt breakfast hosted by Harry and his wife Sharon at their house on the farm. Sharon served martinis and gimlets as the prebreakfast choice of cocktails. I regret to report that some of the Nashvillians were either overserved or incorrectly confident of their capacity. Among these was my colorful friend, Dr. John Youmans, who was famous for having an unusual tolerance for pain, which was demonstrated on a previous occasion when he fell into a wing while schooling a steeplechaser and then remounted and fell again.

He was taken to Vanderbilt Hospital and X-rayed, and it turned out that he had broken a different leg on each of the falls. He was then confined to the hospital with an array of pulleys, weights, and casts in a scene that would have given any cartoonist delight. Moreover, everyone at the Hillsboro Hounds had heard about the time in Holt's Hills when he cleared a big post-and-rail at speed, only to take the tree beyond with himself on one side and the horse on the other. As he was the newly appointed dean of the Vanderbilt University Medical School, he was rushed to the Vanderbilt Hospital emergency entrance. One of the senior nurses, a longtime friend of Dr. Youmans, was on duty there. When the ambulance drove in with the new dean, the nurse came out, looked at him in a questioning manner, shook her head, and said, "Well, John, it looks like old times, doesn't it?"

On this day in Huntsville, Dr. Youmans was riding from the breakfast to the cast with Sidney McAlister, a member of the Hillsboro Hounds, later to be a joint master. Sidney observed Dr. Youmans slam the car door on his hand, causing it to bleed copiously. When Dr. Youmans drew out his string gloves, Sidney expected him to make some kind of bandage out of them to staunch the bleeding. Instead, the good doctor began to pull a glove over his mangled hand. "Doctor, what are you doing?" asked Sidney, thunderstruck at what he was watching. "It's a formal hunt, isn't it?" replied Dr. Youmans, preparing to don the other glove.

There was an enormous run. I was first whipper-in enjoying the best seat in the house when they got word to me that Dr. Youmans had had a terrible fall and was laid out down in a drainage ditch by the road. I galloped back as fast as I could, dreading what I might find. When I got there, I found a small crowd assembled on the ditch bank. They were gazing worriedly down into the ditch at the doctor, who was laid out peacefully, his glasses missing and his top hat placed on his chest. I immediately dismounted and went to him.

"Look for his glasses, please," I said, as I bent my ear down to his mouth. "Doctor, where are you?" I asked, and strained to hear his answer.

"Give me a hint," he responded in a whisper.

"You are in Alabama," I replied.

"Oh yes," he whispered, "we are in Birmingham at the hunt ball."

"Doctor," I said, "Mr. Sloan's man, Eb Reed, will help you get in."

"I am going in with the hounds," he said a little more strongly as someone helped him put on his glasses.

"Very well," I said, signaling to others to help me get him up and into the saddle.

However, getting him into the saddle was an ongoing process, as he would immediately slip off whichever side was unmanned. Eb had to grab his arm or his coat to keep him more or less in the middle of the horse as they walked along. Moreover, he was holding his side and protecting himself in the fashion of one who has broken some ribs.

You can imagine our surprise that night at the party when Dr. Youmans arrived resplendent in his scarlet tails and proceeded directly to the dance floor. Alice went over to Mrs. Youmans and said, "Lola, John has had a terrible fall and has some broken ribs at least. Do you think he should be dancing?"

"Oh yes," Lola replied, "it's the way he wants to die. Wonderful isn't it?"

## The Day They Ran Off Collier Mountain

Through the years, we went to many of Harry Rhett's famous hunt weeks with their exceptional hospitality. One year, however, I was very concerned because he invited us to hunt our hounds on the final Saturday after the hunt ball Friday night. I was afraid that excess gaiety at the hunt ball might result in my being a somewhat inactive huntsman on Saturday. Well, we went to the hunt ball and Harry got up and made a long speech about what a celebrated pack of hounds we had to hunt the next day and what wonderful hunting they had enjoyed all week, all the marvelous adventures and so forth. The more he talked, the more I realized that we were going to have a blank day the next day, and that we were going to be greatly embarrassed by the Mooreland hounds that had already acquitted themselves so well. Moreover, one of my hounds, a hound called Ladybug, had lost her right hind leg in a fence and was sure to look very strange in comparison to the fancy bred performers of the previous days' exploits. When we finally got to bed that morning around two o'clock, I must confess I did not sleep well, as I knew the test of the morrow was going to be very embarrassing in light of Harry's flowery speech.

The next morning when we got up to get ready to go out to the casting ground, Harry came in and said, "Henry, I've got bad news for you. The wind has shifted around, it's out of the southeast, and we *never* have any scent with a southeast wind. I'm so sorry that this has happened, but it's just one of those things. We've had such good climatic conditions all week, the hounds have run so well, and they've accounted for their foxes. They've shown everybody such tremendous sport. I'm just so sorry this has happened to you." Well, I was lower than a toad in a ditch by the road, but what Harry came with next was even worse. He said, "Besides that, the temperature's gone up about twelve degrees. Instead of being in the low thirties like it has been every morning when we started, this morning it's about forty-two or forty-three degrees and it feels like a tropical heat wave out there it's so warm and sunny." Then he offered what I suppose he thought was consolation. "But maybe we'll be lucky and there won't be as many people out today since there was a hunt ball last night. Maybe you won't have as big a field."

With this scant shred of hope, I finished my breakfast and we went out to the meet. Johnny and Karen Gray were there with the hounds and the horses, and everything was ready. I prayed and prayed that the field would be minuscule but instead I got there and found there was a huge field; absolutely everybody from the hunt ball the night before was there and many others as well. I thought, "If only Harry won't repeat any of his speech, maybe we can get this over with quickly." Just then, Harry looked up and said, "Oh my God!"

"What's wrong, Harry?" I asked.

"There's Miss J. H. She's the worst jinx in foxhunting, an *infallible omen* of a blank day. We have never had a hound open when she has been hunting with us. She comes about once a year or every other year maybe, and she is absolutely death to fox chasing."

I thought, "Here we are with a southeast wind, a tropical heat wave, a long speech, and the jinxing J. H. What in the world am I going to do?" However, Harry was undeterred. He got on his horse, gathered up the field (there must have been eighty to one hundred people there), and gave the same long, impossible-to-live-up-to speech he gave the night before, all about a celebrated pack and so forth. I was absolutely about to dig a hole for me and my horse, when he finally turned around and said, "They're all yours." "All mine," I thought. "What the hell am I supposed to do with them?"

There is one hill in that flat Huntsville country called Collier Mountain, even though it is only about three hundred feet high. Harry suggested I draw the side of Collier Mountain on the way into the wildlife preserve. So I set off that way and was riding along wondering what in the world I was going to be able to do to show any sport, when suddenly somebody viewed a large buck deer with a quite handsome rack coming off the side of Collier Mountain. Just then I heard a hound open and I thought, "Uh oh, they're going to run that deer. In addition to everything else, they're going to embarrass me by running a deer right out here in front of all of these people who have seen these other fine packs and heard Harry's damn speech twice." So I was just about to blow the hounds back and call them to me when I heard Johnny Gray's voice, way off to the side, shouting a "Tallyho!"

I immediately turned and galloped to Johnny and he said, "These rabbit hunters over here saw the fox come by with Ladybug only about ten or fifteen yards behind it." I thought, "Hallelujah!" But I said, "Hike to Ladybug!" And hike they did. We came off the side of Collier Mountain out into the cotton fields right there at the edge of the reservation, and when I looked back I saw the hounds streaming across the cotton field and the buck deer crossed right through the middle of the pack, jumping hounds and, what luck, the deer was going one way and the hounds were going another. So I yelled to everybody in the field to see that the hounds were not running a deer, they were running a fox. I might as well have been whispering in a hurricane because the field was coming in a thunderous gallop.

Just about that time, the fox crossed the dirt road and went into the swamp. We rode over to the edge of a winter oat field and Tommy Haney, Harry's huntsman, who was up with me, said, "Mr. Hooker, the river goes around there in a big bend and if we get the fox out of that swamp into the reservation, it's ours because this is the only way out of the sack." I said, "Well, I'm going over there." "No," he said. "You can't take your horse across that oat field; the National Wildlife Agency doesn't like it." I said, "Who needs a horse?" So I jumped off my horse and ran over there. Of course, about the third stride, I had about a pound of mud on each boot but I finally got to that swamp, only to be greeted by a deafening silence. What in the world? How in the world could my hounds have lost that fox when they were that close up on it? I just can't believe this! What in the Sam Hill am I going to do now?

John Sloan, Sr. on Bank Robber

Johnny Ingram, Timothy Hooker, Orrin Ingram, Lisa Hooker,
Bradford Hooker, Alice Hooker and Henry Hooker

Ben Hardaway, Buck Allison and Henry Hooker

Alice Hooker on Mr. Fox

Henry Hooker on Our Big Girl

Henry Hooker on Macho, Bill Carter on Roan Mountain—Joint
MFHs of the Cedar Knob Foxhounds with Buck Allison (not shown)

Reau Berry, Timothy Hooker, Lisa Hooker, Alice Hooker, Joyce Brown (with Monk and Charles), Bill Brown and Henry Hooker

Alice Hooker, Jack McKinney, Claudine McKinney and Bill Brown with the Chireno Hounds in Texas

Felix Peach

Henry Hooker on Sky Lab with Hooker's hunting box, Hounds Ear, in background

Henry Hooker and Calvin Houghland  © *Brant Gamma Photography*

George Sloan on Spin the Top

Johnny Gray and Karen Gray with the Hillsboro Hounds

Vernon Sharp and Henry Hooker

(l. to r.) Sidney McAlister, Karen Gray, Johnny Gray, Henry Hooker and Bruce P'Pool

Alex Wade, Bruce P'Pool, Albert Menefee III and Henry Hooker, Joint Masters of the Hillsboro Hounds at MFHA–FCNA Performance Trial

Then I heard her way off in the swamp, "Auk, Auk-Auk, Auk." It was that three-legged bitch, Ladybug! Then Lavender, Larkspur, Lisa Lou, Sewanee, Harpeth Lassie, Heather, and Grit all joined in. I blew, I hollered, and I came running back and said, "Let me have my horse." Bill Carter, who was up with us, said, "We sent your horse back to the stable. We thought you were finished with it." I said, "Where do you have that horse hidden?" and I went over behind a bunch of people. There was my horse. I jumped up on him and we took out after that fox.

It was one of the greatest runs, with all hounds on in a country where you could gallop a horse like you were at the races. We would run best pace and then, if there was a little bobble, that Ladybug would come through there, three-legged and all. She would come through there "Auk, Auk-Auk, Auk" and Lyric, Hank, Hobo, and the gang would hark in there and they would get going again. Those big old Trigg rolling mouths would make the earth tremble with their cry.

Over and over, we could see the fox crossing the green oat fields, and hear huge flocks of geese getting up honking and hounds roaring. It was like that famous picture by Lionel Edwards called *Saint Gabriel's Hounds* because the geese sounded like hounds, the hounds sounded like they were flying, and the ruby red fox was right in front of them crossing those emerald green fields. We ran, and we rolled, and we slashed, and we dashed, until we saw the fox go to ground about ten feet in front of the lead hounds. I galloped up and jumped off my horse by the den, put my head down in it for a good whiff to make sure the fox was there, congratulated the hounds, stood up, turned around, took off my cap, made a deep bow, and said, "That, ladies and gentlemen, is the way we do it in a southeast wind."

I always thought that was a great run and a great time, but I was totally unprepared for what has happened since. Time and again, I have been in some far away place or going through an airport somewhere and somebody has called my name, come up to me, and said, "I was there the day they ran off Collier Mountain. What a run!" And for a moment, we stand and remember, caught up in the mysterious bond of venery that connects all hunters, whether their coats are of tailored scarlet wool or worn country denim.

So I give you wishes for great hunts, when everything goes right, even on days it shouldn't, with hounds all on, and the field all up. Then you, too, will know what it was like the day they ran off Collier Mountain.

FOUR

# THE MOST HUNTED

Bold fox who bursts before the pack
That must to live confuse the track,
This was your legacy from birth
To end who-hoop or gone to earth,
To flee before assassin hound
With deadly jaws to drag you down,
By scent in irony pursued,
A hunter who stalks his food
With savage stealth, no mercy given,
A driving hunter by hunger driven.
Far better to be broken and rolled
Than die from sickness, trap, or cold,
Amidst the pack and cheers to fail,
The hero of a stirring tale,
Deserving that fitting epitaph
Of fatal strife upon the path.
And, if by cunning you escape
The jaws which close upon you gape,
Enthralling legends we will hear
Of a daring fox's fleet career
By every bard your boldness sung
As to your life you coolly clung.

But, even in your haven found,
Remember well that charging hound
Who for your brush did strive and strain
And nearly then your life attain.
Forevermore awakeful keep;
Be sure to listen while you sleep.

Bold fox, you learn eternal truth
For which the histories offer proof.
It's true of all the world's host
Who hunts the best is hunted most.

—Henry Hooker

## Vernon Sharp, MFH: The Ultimate Diplomat

Elected president of the Masters of Foxhounds Association of America in 1973, Vernon Sharp proved to be both a colorful and diplomatic sportsman. His native South had long been well known as the source of many famous strains of hounds. The names Birdsong, Bywaters, Trigg, Maupin, Walker, Thomas, and Wooldridge establish the South's place in the development of modern American foxhound packs.

Harry Worcester Smith came to this area at the beginning of the century to collect the hounds that changed the course of modern American pack hound breeding. Moreover, at the time of Sharp's presidency of the Masters of Foxhounds, the Southeast, long the center of field trial activity beloved by the night hunter hill toppers, became a well-established and rapidly growing area in the country for organized hunt recognition. Because his sporting life had such a full measure of both of these sometimes contrasting but related cultures, Vernon Sharp's stewardship rallied to the causes of foxhunting a broad and sympathetic cross section of American sportsmen.

### A Disciple of Mason Houghland

The captain of the famous Vanderbilt University football team of 1927 would have been successful at nearly any athletic endeavor that attracted his interest but Sharp's choice of foxhunting is interesting because of the lady in the case. Sarah Sharp had hunted as a young lady with the Fort Oglethorpe Drag Hounds. She encouraged her husband to take up the sport and make it a part of the lives of all five of their children. So in 1940 Sharp became a disciple of Mason Houghland, then master of the Hillsboro Hounds. Their fellowship ripened through years of hunting experiences, field trials, and hound buying forays. Houghland immediately appreciated his young friend's most distinguishing characteristic—a kind of gentle humor at no one's expense but his own. *Gone Away*, the older master's famous book, contains the following anecdote so illustrative of the Sharp repertoire of animal fables:

> Foxhunters share with farmers and with fishermen a distinctive and noble phase of life in that their gain is no man's loss. And for this or other reasons, the men, women and children who follow the sweet cry of hounds are a most satisfactory kind of people. They are not, I am afraid, brilliant. They constantly see their hounds (and themselves) outwitted by a fox and so, quite naturally, come to assume that the hounds have little sense. The sincerity of this conviction is well illustrated by an experience my friend Vernon Sharp had some years ago at the forks of Lick Creek. It was late and cold, and he had ridden far when he came to the store there. He hitched his horse and went in to buy some sausage. Back by the stove there was a chequer board resting upon a nail keg. At one side of it sat the storekeeper and across from him a long-eared "Pot-licker" hound. Neither paid any attention to the customer, but he gasped with astonishment to see that the man and the hound were actually deep in a game of chequers, and almost held his breath until it ended. But when it did, he told the storekeeper that the hound must be the smartest dog in the world.
>
> "Pshaw," answered the storekeeper, very much annoyed, "he ain't smart—I don't lay claim to being a good chequer player but I beat him three out of four games myself."[1]

Houghland introduced Sharp to his sporting cohorts around the South and very soon the two of them were to be seen traveling to visit other packs, sometimes with Lowry Watkins, a widely experienced and constructive critic in the arts of hound and horse mastership. Moreover, Houghland took Sharp to field trials and bench shows to judge foxhounds under the discerning eye of one-suspender night hunters and hound breeders unwilling to suffer gladly a fool in their hounds' presence.

## Howard Stovall

Sharp's first such trial was judged in conjunction with Colonel Howard Stovall, a famous World War I flying ace, cotton planter, bird shot, raconteur, and foxhunter extraordinaire. They stayed and rode together at Sardis, Mississippi. Stovall brought his personal assistant Will Timmons, who, dressed in a black derby hat, cooked, cleaned up, stabled horses, cared for hounds, and mixed refreshments. Moreover, Timmons managed to cut through the woods and be waiting time after time, in his ubiquitous derby, under a tree to give directions to the two dashing judges when they rode up to a crossing.

It is said that one time Stovall went to the kennels and told Timmons to get hounds ready to go to Nashville.

"Will," he said, "Mr. Houghland wants us to bring the hounds to Nashville."

"Yas, suh!"

"Well. Will, when you get there, someone will ask you how many hounds you brought."

"Yas, suh!"

"That's the first thing to remember, Will. Call them hounds."

"Yas, suh!"

"And they count them by couples, Will. Someone will ask you how many couple of hounds you brought. Now a couple is two, Will, so you have to tell them the number divided by two."

"Yas, suh!"

"All right. Let's take all twenty-three of the running pack."

"Yas, suh, Cap'n . . . only it won't go."

"You are right, Will, so you have to say we brought eleven-and-a-half couple of hounds."

"Yas, suh, yas, suh. I tell them jus' that—'leven-and-a-half. Only them Yankees up to Nashville, they sho' goes to a lot of trouble countin' dogs, don't they?"

Wilbur Hubbard told me that Stovall was invited to speak at the Masters of Foxhounds Annual Meeting by some easterners who thought his accent would amuse the assembled. However, when Stovall told that story, it brought the house down and everyone wanted to be sure Stovall would be on the program the next year to continue the adventures of Will Timmons.

It was Timmons, when asked a decade later by Sharp how hunting had been, said, "Jus' fine, suh, and if we could keep Cap'n from goin' to all these wars, we could keep the foxes on they feet."

Shortly after the Sardis adventure, it happened that the Mississippi State Field Trial was to be held on Minnie Vaughn's plantation outside of Columbus, Mississippi, on the banks of the Tombigbee River. Stovall served as master and recruited the mounted judges. In contrast to the sometimes plow-marked horses furnished to judges, Sharp brought his own Thoroughbred hunter with him. Hounds were cast as usual at daybreak. They struck immediately and raced in full cry directly toward the river, which was swollen to the top of its banks and very swift. The judges, field, and master galloped after them, confident that the fox would turn and provide a great thrill across the river-bottom cotton fields.

Instead, hounds plunged straight into the torrent and were washed violently downstream. All riders, except one, pulled up their horses and watched the spectacle of hounds emerging, bedraggled and wet, well down the river to hit it again and disappear in full cry. A lone horseman rode the line. It was Sharp. He never checked. In full view of hound owners, field, and judges, he put his horse straight into that angry river. He was washed uncontrollably through the swirling water. Now and then, he would disappear, only to bob up again further downstream.

Finally, he gained the opposite shore and continued after the running pack. A great cheer went up from all assembled, who had despaired of his safety. Stovall, never at a loss for words, turned to the group who had witnessed this feat and shouted, "What's the matter with you lily-livered judges? Can't you see hounds aren't turning? Have I got to have a man come all the way from Nashville to show you boys how to cross a creek? Get in there and score those hounds!" Not a rider moved but one man had the pluck to answer, "I don't know where you got him from, Howard, but he's all right with me. Any score he brings to the judges' meeting, we'll count."

## Master of Field Trials

The next year Stovall called long distance and asked Sharp to come and serve as master of the Mississippi State Field Trial. Though flattered, Sharp was somewhat hesitant and asked Stovall how long a man had to think it over. "Well," said the Colonel in a brisk business tone, "that depends on the importance of the man I'm asking. In your case, I'd say about half a minute." So began a career as master of foxhound field trials that included the Tennessee, Mississippi, and Kentucky State hunts and two National Field Trials.

The second National Field Trial, of which Sharp was master, was held at Sevierville, Tennessee, in the foothills of the Great Smoky Mountains. It produced a still celebrated story. The area was renowned for some rough customers and word soon passed around that one denizen of the territory had threatened to shoot any foxhound seen on his place. This caused quite a stir of apprehension among the hound owners, who feared their hounds might wander into the menacing blusterer's whereabouts. Sharp set out to clear up their fears. Finding the man and his son standing beside a road, he saw that both were armed with shotguns. The master casually rode up to the pair and, introducing himself, proffered his hand. Both the mountain men raised their weapons without a word. Although fixed in their deadly bead, Sharp continued his undaunted apology for any damage hounds might have caused and offered to have the National repair it. Finally, he was able to elicit some conversation from the aggrieved landowners. As the discussion warmed, the guns came down. Whereupon Sharp turned his horse around and rode slowly away with his back to the touchy marksmen. Later, when he was asked about the incident, the courtly

Sharp, in his usual self-deprecating manner, merely remarked that the barrels on those shotguns looked like about the cleanest he had ever looked down.

Of course, the incident was soon well known to the local gentry, who regarded the master as something of a curiosity to be studied. They lost no opportunity to be with him, as they expected his sojourn on this earth might be short. A case in point occurred the next day. Sharp and his friend Ernest Hardison were galloping down a logging trail in hot pursuit of hounds. They came upon another mountain man with a sled of firewood hitched to a mule. At the sight of the hunters, the mule bucked out of his trace chains and took off at a gallop, strewing the sled and firewood all over the trail. The man, for his part, generously swore in local idiom.

The riders were dismayed at the havoc they had caused. Hardison chased after the runaway mule, while Sharp tried to make peace with the enraged man. The mule was soon caught and returned. Sharp identified himself and began regathering the firewood. The woodsman set the record straight that he was not cursing the hunters at all. The mule was the object of his genealogical description and the intended beneficiary of his directions. After all, "It wasn't the fust time that cussed mule had heard them kind of dogs runnin'. Come to think of it, the ole lady has a plenty of firewood to last till tomorry anyway." The man evidently understood Henry Bell Covington's advice to the would-be foxhunter that he had a chance to make something out of himself and not to waste it working. An invitation to hunt was issued to the mule owner and was quickly accepted. Trace chains were thrown over the recalcitrant mule's back and a gunnysack was produced for a saddle. In no time, the trio was on its way, scrambling after hounds in high spirits.

## The Diplomat

Such was Sharp's wide reputation for diplomacy that he was often chosen to extricate a hunt from some difficulty with landowners. On such occasions, he seemed to agree with nearly everything

the landowner had to say, but at the end of such an exchange, the hunters were always cordially invited back anytime. A broken rail, a carelessly left open gate, a gallop across an unharvested field, whatever the transgression, Sharp was always selected to plead the case.

The choice was wise. Most listeners would have marveled at how abjectly he accepted bitter denunciations of foxhunting, hounds, riders, his friends, and city folks in red coats. However, most of those conversations ended with the farmer offering to pen up his stock the next time and suggesting, "That old rail was rotten anyway." As to the field, he had had a cow get in there a week ago and that did not seem to hurt it. Almost every time Sharp departed as the man's friend, to be welcomed anytime.

There was, however, one occasion when it took Mrs. Sharp to soothe the situation. It was at a National Field Trial in Starkville, Mississippi. A hard-riding group had completely smashed a fence and Sharp was attempting, along with Bill Brown, to repair it, when suddenly the farmer's wife appeared in an implacable rage. She had seen the whole thing. She hollered for them to get out of her pasture. Her fence was ruined. She did not want them on her property.

Sharp's customary charm was wavering before this tirade when the impeccably attired and veiled Sarah Sharp leaned forward from her sidesaddle and, in a shy voice, asked the irate lecturer if she would be so kind as to let her borrow the outhouse while the discussion and fence building were completed. After a double take, the answer was, "Why, of course, honey." From that moment, the only reason she had not wanted them in the pasture was a mean mule. The fence was nothing to worry about. She had been after her husband to fix it anyway. She could tell them the short cut to get back where the dogs had gone. Her well had sweet water and she wanted them to have a cup because they might be thirsty from working on her fence. As for Mrs. Sharp, she was treated to a special wave goodbye and, "Come again, honey."

Joint Master of the Hillsboro Hounds

Vernon Sharp's and John Sloan Sr.'s mastership of the Hillsboro Hounds continued the traditions inaugurated by their predecessor, Mason Houghland. They welcomed visitors who were foxhunters and found horses for them. They provided hounds for the foundation of new packs, the most notable of which was Harry Rhett's Mooreland Hunt in Huntsville, Alabama. They encouraged children to hunt and to ride their own line to hounds wherever the country permitted. They never lost the guiding insight that foxhunting should be fun. Perhaps most important of all, they fulfilled Houghland's dream of opening up to the Hillsboro Hounds a great galloping country away from subdivisions, asphalt, and railroads. While not able to repeal the invention of wire, which would have satisfied Houghland's fondest hopes, they did sprinkle chicken coops over the wire fences for rapid transit.

However, heaven was not meant to be obtained in a single leap, and the two masters had a short period when hounds did not provide sport up to their high standards. Some experimenting with imported hounds had produced a pack with insufficient cry and nose for the thin-soiled hilly country of the Hillsboro Hounds. The masters talked it over and Sharp secured some of the strain bred to hunt in such country, the descendants of Tennessee Lead. Six-and-a-half couple of Walker pups were brought to the pack. They proved to be tractable as well as game. By the end of their first season, they were strike hounds. From this infusion, a pack of predominantly Walker and Walker-Fell crosses was developed that could rock the hill country of Middle Tennessee with reverberating cry. In spite of the abundance of limestone holes, they managed to catch foxes.

Triple President

In addition to his activities as joint master of the Hillsboro, Sharp served during this period for three years as president of the National Foxhunters Association and for two years as president of the American Foxhound Club before becoming president of the Masters of Foxhounds Association of America. It was during his presidency of the American Foxhound Club that the Club sponsored the publication of *The American Foxhound, 1747–1967* by Alexander Mackay-Smith. This scholarly book makes a great contribution to the literature of the sport and is already a collector's item among serious students of the art.

As if this did not keep him occupied, Sharp visited kennels all over the United States and Europe and continued to judge hounds, from Bryn Mawr to the tobacco barns of his native region. Moreover, with his fellow master, the redoubtable Ben Hardaway, he hunted with many Irish packs, an adventure that suffers from neither one's description. All these endeavors, in addition to his successful business and civic careers, did not, however, make him too busy to open a gate for a child or to help teach a balky pony to load in a trailer. Although this interest in children was manifested in his long and signal service as the president of the Nashville Children's Museum (now the Cumberland Science Museum), it was in Pony Club and foxhunting that you could see it most frequently displayed.

I held Sharp in great esteem. Thus, I was very keen to help him in his quest for the presidency of the Masters of Foxhounds Association. I could see that the stream of distinguished visitors had thickened when Harold Ramser, Fife Symington, Sherman and Peggy Haight, and Harry and Josephine Nicholas showed up to augment our usual visitors such as Ben Hardaway and Harry Rhett. While he was entertaining Harry and Josephine Nicholas, Sharp brought them over to see my kennels and the private pack of hounds I owned with Bill Brown and Ned Bonnie.

Unfortunately, just when we got to the kennels, a terrible thunderstorm put all the lights out. There we were in total darkness, lucky to be in out of the driving rain. Then a lightning bolt lit everything up for an instant, and I pointed out a hound: "Look at that bitch," I said, and waited for another bolt. It was a kennel tour by lightning flash, and Harry and Josephine never forgot it. Wherever I would run into them, Harry would emulate me. "Look at that dear bitch," he would point and say and then howl with laughter.

When Ned and Nina took us to Virginia that Thanksgiving to stay with Mrs. Randolph and to hunt with the Piedmont, the Orange County Hunt, and the Rappahannock Hunt, I naturally tried to interest Mrs. Randolph in supporting Vernon for president of the Masters of Foxhounds Association. She would not hear of it. She was going to support Bunny Almy for president and thought that Nashville was the great unwashed West. She thought some of our friends were too loud and self-promoting, and she proceeded on the way to the Rappahannock to give me her opinion with great candor. When she paused for breath, I countered that I knew the people in the South better than she did, and I liked them enough for both of us and she should not talk bad about my friends. "Good enough," she said, looking me straight in the eye. When we got out of the car Nina said, "Oh, Mummy is so happy. Not many of the men in Virginia talk to her like that."

At the Masters of Foxhounds Association Hunt Ball in New York two months later, I introduced Mrs. Randolph to Vernon and he asked her to dance. I watched as they drew the periphery of the floor, so to speak, and I saw Vernon as he chatted her up and gave her response his rapt attention. Then I saw he was headed towards docking her back with me, so I sprang up to greet them. Vernon thanked her for the dance and with an understated hint of a bow, took his leave. I stood with Mrs. Randolph in silence as Sharp disappeared across the floor. As soon as he was out of earshot, she turned to me and fixed me with a level gaze. "We must support Vernon for the presidency," she said. "Are you doing all you can?" "Yes, ma'am," I said, "and I know your opinion will be influential in Virginia." "Leave that to me, young man, and go along about your business," she said as she proffered her cheek for a good-bye kiss. Sharp's accomplishments as president of the Masters of Foxhounds Association were, I am sure, a great source of satisfaction to Mrs. Randolph.

## A Letter to Joint Masters Sloan and Sharp

Vernon Sharp was the first to encourage me to write descriptions of hunts. I wrote one for him and John Sloan Sr. when they were away at the Masters of Foxhounds Association Hunt Ball. Later, when Sharp, Sloan, and I were at Collierville, Tennessee, attending the National Field Trial for Bird Dogs, Sharp told me he had read my account quite a few times.

Mr. Vernon Sharp, MFH
Mr. John Sloan, MFH

Gentlemen:

Please do not attribute to youth, nor yet to audacity, the enthusiasm which prompts me to give an account of Saturday's sport. Because I know that you have for some time carefully and eloquently chronicled the accomplishments of the Hillsboro Hounds and also that you are prevented from your usual service in this regard by having cast a most promising covert at the Masters Hunt Ball in New York, I put aside apology in the hope that my description might somehow or somehow else catch the dash and drive of those fleet warriors whose stirring battle cry chased across the grass and into my dreams.

Dawn on Saturday, the first day of February 1964, silvered small puddles were still standing on the wet grounds from a day of unseasonably warm rain. However, a mild morning confirmed the clearing and absorbed much surface water, so that by noon the fifty-degree temperature and clear skies were being welcomed as harbingers of spring. The day was not windy, yet it was not still. Perhaps only a foxhunter would have noticed the cooling breeze wafting from the western slope.

Even the fourteen or so couple of hounds being roaded from the kennels across the railroad bridge and into Cooks Hills gave no indication of exceptional scenting, and most of the field must have expected to see more pileated woodpeckers than foxes.

Felix drew the country without particular hopefulness until about two o'clock when sporadic bumping developed on that cedar hill behind the Kennon tenant farmer's house. Never were trailing hounds urged and cheered more steadfastly than by our huntsman. First around to the north, then back west they trailed. Each loss seemed shorter than the last; each find seemed to include more hounds. Holds were shortened on listening horses as that tingling first din of a race began. Then hoof beats, hound music, and cheering horn melded and swelled into a ringing confirmation across those hills.

No more tacking through the cedars pursuing that chorus. The fox turned south through the woods, came around the hill, and headed left-handed under the power lines. Still no view, but hounds were running well together and singing their joy from chest height as they sped across the valley and climbed into the woods on the ridge, high above the tenant house. There Felix, cheering hounds as they entered the woods, saw his quarry drive just in front over the ridge. With never a check the race ran a long course towards Ravenswood. For a moment George Sloan and I, who had by now galloped to the east slope of Margaret's knoll, feared they would cross the pike and leave the country with only our ears to follow them. Then they turned, and far along that country's easternmost ridge we saw them driving. By now, they were a long thin line, but driving still and throwing back their music. Across the ridge they sailed, their speed and drive flashing through the broom grass, and, for two men watching from the opposite slope, their flags unfurled were a braver sight than so many corsairs in battle line. Then I saw a dart of red so quick it seemed a glint of sunlight. There, down the slope by a briar thicket below that big dead tree. "Look at it jump," said George, and as suddenly as we saw it, it seemed to vanish like a magic haze before our stare. Had we seen it, or did imagination animate some blowing leaf? As if in answer to the unarticulated question, that line of corsairs came about and swept down the hill through those very briars. Hounds were in the valley, the leaders beginning to start up our side when I heard it. It was maybe ten yards away and coming straight. It was as red as an apple. Its mouth was open, its tongue perhaps a little out. Its brush, though not dragging, was low. It was excitement coming on swift feet. It saw us then and with wild grace changed directions in a single bound. Scarcely away down the slope had it gone when hounds drove into view. We watched the first five one-by-one as they overran the turn and started to hunt the lost thread. The next three or four hounds that we turned gave such exultant tongue that the overrun leaders harked immediately. The second flighters might be accused of running a covered line; but that scopey fox had been afoot a full twenty minutes and four ridge crossings were made in its first burst east.

As to the overrun, I can only surmise that the fox's scent temporarily abated when it saw George and me. Although it had crossed within a few yards upwind of us, we could not smell it. You will recall that Joe Thomas refers to this phenomenon in his chapter on scent in *Hounds and Hunting through the Ages*. This must have been a perfect example. Although scenting conditions were excellent and hounds had pushed their fox hard, we could not smell it there with the wind blowing right across it at us. Moreover, when hounds were turned onto the line, they found not more than twenty-five yards away and were gone with a crash.

I have never seen gamer quarry. Once more, it assaulted that farthest ridge and, crossing it, made a deep right-handed cut into newly opened country. There it stayed out some twenty minutes more without a check, leading a tour of the Menefee coops, and "Niver a foiner parade sparkled in the sun."

Felix now gathered ten-and-a-half couple of his charges and carefully sought to steer them through enticing sounds that beckoned from the nearby woods. However, like Odysseus, he failed to plug those ears to which the sirens' song was sweetest, so at last he let Sweetmeat confirm the authenticity of those seductive sounds, calling him irretrievably away from the road home. Sweetmeat's familiar voice relayed the clarion call. "Hoick to Sweetmeat!" They were off and, slapping spurs to horses, we were close behind on a twisting, darting turn through that reverberating tangle. Then a straight spurt took us out of the cedars and back to Margaret's knoll where hounds were picked up at the first check.

There, where earlier Reynard and I had our confrontation, the gloom was settling on Cooks Hills. Only atop the ridges did the faded orange of sunset burnish the golden broom grass. The huntsman's mournful horn mingled in the chill with the far-off trailing of hounds. His plaintive chant, carrying through the hollows and across the still evening, drifted further away as he began to move part of the pack kennelward. The horn, though fainter, continued to call away home. Not without a long last listen and a lingering look at a shadowy patch below the silhouette of that big dead tree did your correspondent begin to pick his way back from the solitude of that place.

The hills now were comforting shapes in the dusk. As my musing drifted back over those dusky hills to the first strains of the night lullaby, I thought, "This is not the best country, perhaps, not the legendary Melton Mowbray, but a good country, our country, and may the exciting pageant of foxhunting never be lost from these Tennessee hills."

Sincerely,

Henry


T. Chatsworth

Perhaps Mr. Sharp's multiple reading of this account encouraged me thereafter to write a tongue-in-cheek letter about the Hillsboro Hounds, signed by the fictitious T. Chatsworth, which many of the members of the Hillsboro, including Mrs. Sharp, took seriously. Some of them even claimed to have met Mr. T. Chatsworth. Sharp called me and said he appreciated the compliment about the Hillsboro Hounds, but he was going to wait a while before telling Mrs. Sharp that she was mistaken about having met the fictional and satirical Mr. T. Chatsworth, who got his name because I thought it would be worth a chat at a tea.

November 27, 1967
Mr. Alexander Mackay-Smith

Dear Sir:

The most complimentary letter concerning the Hillsboro Hounds opening meet in yours of 17 November 1967 is at hand and constrains me to reply. Having unsuspectingly hunted that country, one feels compelled to set the record straight.

Of course, the Hillsboro Hounds' refusal to charge a capping fee is some forewarning of the emphasis placed on running foxes to the exclusion of club activities. However, one is unprepared for the attention given to the pleasure of children. They are invited to hunt and to tea, just as though they were adult members. Moreover, they are shamelessly encouraged to converse with the older members, who seem to enjoy their company. Perhaps this is explained by the behavior of the joint masters, who are free and open with everyone, even permitting the children to laugh and ride with them in a very independent and fun-loving fashion.

You must imagine my consternation when I have seen one or the other of the masters actually dismount to open a gate or otherwise assist a child across the country. This, coupled with their habit of stopping to visit with landowners to inquire about a son or daughter helped into college or to invite some lad to catch his barnyard pony and come along, would be quite disconcerting were it not for their practice of allowing the members of the field to ride their own line to hounds.

You may be surprised when I tell you that such behavior resulted in not less than ten families appearing in the field on a recent hunt. Furthermore, the children soon become imbued with an interest in such old-fashioned values as courtesy to others and respect for individual ability. I fear this may result in their being affable and self-reliant throughout life, but surely my concern is outside the purview of this reply, and I only mention it to set the stage for other peculiarities of the Hillsboro Hounds.

For all their pleasant banter with the young while riding across fields, I must report that the activity of the masters when hounds strike is even more unusual. They seem to forget protocol altogether and, making no effort to keep the field from seeing hounds, ride boldly through the country at a slashing pace. And what a country it is! Places are filled with a horrible thorn tree called mock orange or bodock, which clutches at one's face and finery. It is not uncommon to see several members of the staff and field come in at the end of the day thoroughly raked and bleeding from an encounter with these devilish devices. The re-weavers in Nashville do a brisk trade. It must be said, however, that the natives seem to ignore their wounds and dash on to hounds.

The hounds themselves, for all their bench show reputation, are an unusual pack. They hunt out loose, drifting through the country with their huntsman, who seems to delight in the woods and briars where foxes likely lurk. I have actually seen the huntsman riding through the woods without a single hound visible, although one could hear the sound of their movement in the leaves. Then, when a strike is spoken, hounds appear from everywhere and the galloping, cheering, and horn all burst into sweet bedlam. The field taking their best lines, the hounds roaring and driving, and the children leaping big panels, all make a sight quite informal and irregular. Many a visitor has been heard to gasp an involuntary "Good grief!" as he strove to keep the young entry in sight.

Out of a sense of abundant impartiality, I observe that huntsman and hounds give consistently good account of themselves. I say this to assure you that my perspective has not been prejudiced by the more formal hunts to which one is accustomed.

Having been a guest in their homes, I would indeed be ungracious if, in my zeal to be strict in my standards, I failed to describe the conviviality and warmth of the after-hunt parties of the members. One finds one forgetting oneself and talking animatedly with a youngster who took a daring wall and viewed the fox, or one of the lovely hunting ladies whose big and shining eyes always make one feel most welcome.

Sincerely,

T. Chatsworth

Sharp accepted his satirization gracefully. He did not publicize himself as the figure in the letter, but he always gave me a knowing look when the action turned to the subjects observed by

Chatsworth. As Bill Brown would say, "We always knew we were going the same way." Sharp had me as his biographer, which he acknowledged with a twinkle in his eye and the quiet smile of one who was keeping a satisfying secret.

John Sloan, Sharp's joint master, liked the portrayal of his longtime friend and asked me if I would give him similar treatment. Of course, I was appreciative of this sincerest form of flattery. The following is the result.

## Note

1. Houghland, *Gone Away*, 2–3.

FIVE

# STEEPLECHASING

The Hunting and Racing Career of John Sloan Sr., MFH

After forty-two years of official service with the Hillsboro Hounds in many capacities, John Sloan Sr. retired from the joint mastership he so ably and vigorously discharged from 1959 through 1974. On his retirement, the elder Sloan was presented a portrait of himself in hunting attire. It provided an appropriate opportunity to tell something of the legend behind the picture.

John Sloan Sr. started hunting in the fall of 1931, the year that Joe Thomas's Grasslands Hunt folded. The Harpeth Hills was then the hunt in Nashville. Sloan soon became a disciple of the Harpeth Hills master, Mason Houghland. In 1932, they took hounds to Wartrace, Tennessee, a rural area with extensive snake-rail fencing. Sloan arrived with the hounds in a furniture van owned by his family's department store, Cain-Sloan, to find Houghland entranced by the rail fencing. The master painted such word pictures of the galloping country that awaited them on the morrow that Sloan could not sleep. Every time he closed his eyes, he would see visions of what he imagined to be Leicestershire. It was a pattern to be repeated in country after country as Houghland and Sloan traveled to Leiper's Fork, Greenbriar, and finally back to Brentwood, always in search of that super shire with rolling pastures, rail fences, and stone walls, which

Houghland could conjure in a foxhunter's dreams. Instead, they very often found briars, wire fences, and mock orange thickets that Sloan managed to navigate with such daring and proficiency that Houghland was constrained to celebrate it with a poem by Warburton in his diary:

> Give me a man to whom naught comes amiss,
> One horse or another, that country or this;
> Who through falls and bad starts undauntedly still
> Rides up to the motto; be with them I will.[1]

Not all the Nashvillians, however, were as enthusiastic as Houghland about finding a wireless heaven. So during one of Houghland's famous sorties in 1932, Mrs. John Branham called a meeting of the Harpeth Hills Hunt and complained bitterly that Houghland was ruining the fun because his only interest was foxhunting. Houghland may have seen the irony of her complaint but he was not amused. To express his ire, he resigned immediately as master and started a new pack with Sloan, Ed Potter, and James Stahlman. Sloan suggested the pack be named the Hillsboro Hounds.

They had a country and foxhunters but they needed an essential ingredient. Therefore, the master sent his honorary secretary and first whipper-in, Sloan, to scour the countryside for hounds. Since Grasslands was disbanded, Houghland cannily located some remnants of the Thomas pack. Seven couple of the famous reddish brown strain were procured. To these Sloan added some Walker hounds from Cookeville, Tennessee. Thus began a hunt that has, from the first, attracted noteworthy visitors both real and fictitious. An early arrival among the former was Joe Thomas himself, who must have been quite amazed at the backwoods hunt country complete with stills for making moonshine whiskey.

From the first, Houghland began to cross Walker and Trigg hounds into the pack. His friendship with Sam Wooldridge, Howard Stovall, and other field trial foxhunters, along with his uncommonly eloquent storytelling by voice and pen, continued to attract the interest of young sports such as Sloan. The latter had a horse named Saab that was very much a favorite of Houghland's for having departed from the astonished field over various brush piles and large farm gates at the urging of the first whipper-in. Houghland told the story that Saab was responsible for the size of Squire Sloan's family in that Sloan had to keep his beautiful bride, Margaret, busy having children so that she would not be able to hunt Saab during the winters. Whatever the inducement, the Sloans had four sons, all sportsmen, all exceptional horsemen.

## Bank Robber

Throughout the late thirties Sloan campaigned his hunters in pasture races. One such hunter, Bank Robber, met with notable success and went on in the forties to finish with a first (compulsively cheered by its owner), two seconds, and two thirds in the Iroquois Steeplechase. Perhaps my favorite memory from the Iroquois Steeplechase, which has provided so many memories since I attended the first one in short pants, is the year when Ernest Hardison rode Bank Robber. Sloan was announcing the race that day for WSM radio. When the horses came to the last jump, Bank Robber was challenging and Sloan was overtaken with competitiveness. He began screaming into the microphone, "Come on Bank Robber! Come on Bank Robber!!" and so he cheered him down the stretch. The crowd, including me, roared with excitement and then laughter as we realized the announcer was bringing home his own horse, the winner.

In 1959, when the Volunteer State Horsemen's Foundation was formed, Sloan became its vice president, a job he held for the rest of his life. Calvin Houghland succeeded his father, Mason Houghland, who was also the founder of the foundation, as president. This result reflected Sloan's understanding of the mutual benefits hunting and racing derived from each other. It befitted Sloan's unremitting interest in racing that his sons George and Paul should have come on to ride the Grand National at Aintree and that George won both the coveted titles of Leading Amateur Steeplechase Rider in America and Leading Amateur Steeplechase Rider in England.

In 1965 and 1966, the Hillsboro Hounds imported Fell hounds from the West Waterford in Ireland. Later, a generous portion of Walker was added back to produce a pack predominantly white in color, very tractable, but with nose, speed, cry, and hunting instinct suited to the thin hilly soil of the Cornersville hunt country. An

English lad from the West Percy, named Bob Gray, was brought over to understudy Felix Peach as huntsman. Bob became huntsman upon his predecessor's retirement. Thus, Sloan left as the legacy of his joint administration of the Hillsboro Hounds a good country, an excellent pack, and a well-trained staff.

The greatest legacy of Sloan's participation in the Hillsboro Hounds, however, was in the minds of its diverse followers of forty-four years. Each remembered something different: a personal kindness, a daring ride, or an evening of fun and laughter after a good hunt. Some of the ladies doubtless remembered him best for the Wartrace shuffle, a dance of Sloan's invention characterized by energetic movement of the elbows to the tune of a lively street band. Some of the old guard's sentiments were best expressed in the remarks of Mason Houghland. In his dedication of a volume of *Gone Away* to his protégé, Houghland wrote:

> To John Sloan, Esq.
>
> The greatest hunting comrade I ever had, the best man behind hounds I ever saw, and the truest friend, best father, and soundest citizen I ever knew.

However, Houghland's grandson, Mason Lampton, capped it for many. His tribute to Sloan came after a long run on a Cornersville red fox with the retiring master leading the field over mile after mile. All who had followed Sloan arrived on steaming horses at the fox's earth. None disputed Lampton when he remarked appreciatively of Sloan, "We had better not cull the old dog yet."

This tribute to Sloan was not an ending but merely a flag in the race run and continued by his sons, one of whom, Tommy, ably whips in yet today for the Hillsboro Hounds. He is like his father in so many ways that stir the memory.

## On to Aintree

In the spring of 1969, George Sloan and I both ran horses in the Grand National at Aintree, the most famous and, perhaps, most punishing steeplechase in the world. The youngest of the Sloan boys, Paul, rode my horse. Alice and I took my mother and the children over a few days before the race. We went down to Lambourne to visit Fulke Walwyn, as I had a couple of horses with him. He and his wife, Cath, made us very welcome. They were full of stories about the American Crompton Smith winning the Grand National on Jay Trump and how he had protected the horse from the cough that had gone around the stables where many of the prospects were in training.

Then the conversation somehow got to Cath's nephew, Andrew Parker-Bowles, a noted polo player, who had taken a dare that he could not make it around the course at the Grand National. Andrew had had the cleverness to borrow a good chaser named The Fossa, which belonged to Aunt Cath. Apparently, The Fossa had the distinction that he had never fallen in a steeplechase, so Andrew was relying on him for safe conveyance. This dare had attracted a lot of attention and many of the younger female race goers had vowed to go see Andrew meet his fate. Parker-Bowles had a fiancée who came along with the entourage to see his courageous feat. Her name was Camilla. They later married.

On the morning of the race, I saw Andrew sitting alone in the dining room of the hotel with his breakfast in front of him. As I stopped to speak and wish him good luck, Fred Winter and Dave Dick came up. They were two of the greatest and most successful jockeys in the history of the race. Observing, as they must have and as I did, that Andrew's fork was moving the sausage, tomato, and egg around on his plate but never to his mouth, they immediately reassured him. "Parker-Bowles, old man, that's all the wrong breakfast. Kippers. That's it. You should be having kippers. Then when they autopsy you, they can identify you immediately. Adelphi Hotel— worst fish in England." Parker-Bowles managed a laugh which, considering his light green pallor, I thought to be a good show. Then Winter and Dick pressed on, offering to walk the course with the jockeys in the room and give them tips on how to ride the race.

I was very flattered to be included in the invitation and repaired with them to the course. I noticed as we went in the gate that Dave Dick took a police sign and hid it under his coat. The first fence was fairly low and inviting relative to the rest and our coaches did not spend much time on it, but at the second, bigger, more imposing fence, Fred Winter began talking about riding around the inside where the jumps are higher but the way is shorter. "If you don't have a horse that will jump the inside, you are not going to be there at the finish anyway," he told them. Then he turned to Dave Dick, who was standing by me looking at the fence. "What do you want to tell them, Dave?" he asked. Quick as a flash, Dick fished out the police sign from under his coat and propped it on top of the fence. "I'd read the bloody sign," said Dick, pointing to the legend: "NO PARKING, ORDER OF THE POLICE." For the first time a few of the jockeys laughed and pushed each other. Then we walked the course step by step with two of the greatest recounting their experiences and recalling the historic events of races past, always mixing in their advice and wisdom. It was a great education, but I kept thinking, "Andrew, why the hell did you accept the dare of those guys and promise you would do this?" However, Andrew was looking better. Somehow, the coaches and jockeys cheered each other. They were all in it together. I did not see a police marker that said "NO U TURN," but it was there in their resolute faces.

That afternoon George and I went to the paddock to see our horses saddled and to wish the jockeys a safe trip. There was a tremendous number of horses, like thirty-five or thirty-seven as I recall. What a magnificent sight when they broke for the start and came down to the first jump, their hooves sounding like a hundred drums. Then I saw Parker-Bowles's disaster as his horse pecked and put in an unexpected short stride sending Andrew into a launch right out over the horse's neck. Andrew would have been a goner, but some kind and quick thinking jockey in that swarm around him reached out a hand and grabbed him by the pants. This caused Andrew to drop down on the horse's neck, from whence he could struggle back into the saddle.

Frantically feeling for the stirrups, he was heading with the pack for the imposing second fence when he heard a jockey nearby admonishing him, "Look under your seat." And there it was. Parker-Bowles fished out the stirrup, dropped it, and clapped his foot in it just as The Fossa took a tremendous leap over the second jump. The rest of the story is that Andrew finished eighth in the Grand National on his first try. This was certainly better than George and I did: George had a fall and my horse, ridden by Paul, twisted something in his back and pulled up.

There was a tremendous celebration that night as all the young women who had come to see Andrew's demise instead celebrated his survival. Somehow, in all of this gaiety, Alice and I invited Camilla to come and visit us in the United States. She did come for our steeplechase a month later. She was a very vivacious and pleasant guest.

## George Sloan Succeeds His Father as Master of the Hillsboro

In 1974, George Sloan replaced his father, John Sloan Sr., as joint master of the Hillsboro Hounds. He brought great enthusiasm to the office, opened a new hunt country around his Panorama estate, and inaugurated the Hillsboro Hounds point-to-point races. The races are a major fundraiser for the hunt as well as a great fun event that occurs at the end of the hunting season.

## The Jubilee Sportsmen

George Sloan was a very successful amateur steeplechase jockey in the United States but he aspired to be more. In 1977, he came to me to tell his secret ambition and his willingness to sell his farm to finance it. He wanted to be the only person to win the Leading Amateur Steeplechase Rider ranking in both the United States and England. When he laid out this scheme to me, I suggested we form a syndicate to buy the necessary horses. We would call ourselves the Jubilee Sportsmen, I suggested, in honor of the Queen's Jubilee.

We rounded up friends from all over. Each member of the syndicate invested a set amount that gave him an interest in eight horses. By investing this way, rather than acquiring outright ownership of a single horse, the members of the syndicate were likely to see some of their horses running somewhere in England. I bought an extra horse for good measure. His name was Mr. Know All. I knew nothing about the horse except that George and his English trainer, Josh Gifford, thought he would be useful.

Shortly thereafter George called me from England. He was so excited he hardly needed long distance. Mr. Know All had run a good race and finished high up against a class field at Cheltenham. "I told them that heart murmur didn't mean anything!" George shouted. "That what?" I interrupted. "That heart murmur," he replied in a considerably softer voice. As it turned out, George was right. Mr. Know All had a lot of wins and good finishes that helped George achieve his goal. Furthermore, I sold the horse at the end of the campaign for enough to recoup some of the cost of the adventure. I think the horse went on to help a subsequent owner compete for the amateur championship as well.

Jane Kidd wrote a delightful book, called *The Race for the Championship*,[2] about George's quest. It tells the story of the Jubilee Sportsmen. George gave me an autographed copy in which he inscribed:

> To Henry Hooker,
>
> Without whom there would have been no 'Jubilee Sportsmen.' Many thanks for your support and friendship, which have made many things (especially this) possible.

George made many friends in racing on both sides of the Atlantic, and he has since pursued a career as a steeplechase promoter. Many luminaries of foxhunting and steeplechasing have come to hunt with the Hillsboro Hounds while visiting George. These include: George Fairburn, master of the Tyndall; Tina Gifford, the top English three-day rider; Josh Gifford, four-time leading jockey in England and the trainer for George Sloan's Race for the Championship; Bob Champion, the contract jockey for Josh Gifford and winner of the Grand National on Aldaniti; John Thorne, master of the Warwickshire and winner of the famous race, the Foxhunter (run on the Grand National Course in Liverpool) on Spartan Missile; Dick Saunders, master of the Pytchley and winner of the Grand National on Grittar; Peter Greenall, now Lord Daresbury, two-time leading amateur rider, master of the Wynstay, and president of the Masters of Foxhounds Association of Great Britain; Jane Starkey, former British Three-Day Eventer; Nickie Henderson, trainer for the Queen Mother, three-time champion trainer at Cheltenham Festival, and trainer for Andrew Lloyd Webber; Jim Wilson, last amateur rider to win the Cheltenham Gold Cup; Peter Matson, field master of the Limerick; Jane Kidd, head of dressage discipline for Europe; and Nick and Valda Embericos, owners of Aldaniti, the winner of the Grand National Steeplechase.

There are stories about all of them. One of the most striking involves Bob Champion, who came here on an American tour. After going about the country and encountering several attractive young ladies, he ended up in Miami with a lady veterinarian, who urged him to have a medical examination, which he did. Unfortunately, her intuition was correct, and he was diagnosed with cancer and given a very guarded prognosis. After surgery, Champion began a rigorous training program. Not only did he survive, but he went on to win the Grand National on Aldaniti and, unexpectedly, to rear a family. All his friends were greatly cheered by his survival and accomplishment after being saved by the lady vet.

A few years later, the then governor of Tennessee, Lamar Alexander, called me and told me that some movie producer wanted to make a movie about Bob Champion and use our farm and house in the Cornersville hunt country as the backdrop. I checked with Alice who said, "No way. These farmers think you are crazy enough now without bringing a lot of Hollywood types in here." Although disappointed, Lamar went on with plans to make the movie elsewhere.

I called a few of the ladies with whom I had seen Bob on his earlier tour and asked them if they knew about the movie. I let it drop that I was concerned that the actress playing each was not, in my opinion, as pretty as she. Naturally, each of them immediately wanted to meet the producer and director and let me know that she was available to play herself. Of course, each ultimately found out that she was not among the characters in the movie, but each forgave me when I told her that if she had been among the characters in the movie, whoever was cast to play her could not possibly have been as attractive as she.

Speaking of the movies, I had two friends who met an Academy Award–winning actor at a tennis ranch and invited him foxhunting with me. He came hunting and confirmed the following story. My friends were very excited when the actor offered to put them in a film that he was directing. They were quite flattered and secretly harbored illusions of being discovered. The actor told them to meet him in New York City where the scene would be shot. At the appointed time, my friends set off on their adventure with extravagant expectations. In due course they arrived in New York to find the actor busy directing the movie. Suddenly they got a whiff of serious business and, for the first time, they began to question their own qualifications.

"What exactly do you want us to do? Where are the lines you want us to learn? Shouldn't there be some coaching?" they asked.

"Don't worry," the director replied. "We'll shoot it in the morning. I'll show you everything. I am a great director. Just do what I tell you."

"But what do we do?" they asked as the cold fear began to make its presence known in the pits of their stomachs.

"Just laugh," the director replied.

"Laugh?" they asked. "What if we can't?"

"Then I'll blow a lot of money because I am right on budget with this film and this scene has a number of extras in it."

"Extras?" they asked incredulously as the apprehension settled completely over them.

"Don't be late," the director admonished, turning away to his directorial duties.

My friends spent a very fitful night before arriving at the scene of the shoot quite early the next morning. They were completely unprepared for the hundred extras, the cameras and crew, the lights and technicians, the makeup people, the arrangements scribe, the wardrobe assistants, the director's assistants, and the spectators and passersby who crowded the rather narrow street where the scene was to be shot. Laugh? How were they going to laugh when their mouths tasted like unripe persimmons and their stomachs felt like anchors had been dropped into them?

The director moved with alacrity to dispatch his staff and set up the scene. "You stand here and watch me. Do what I tell you to do and you will be fine." Then he called for lights, camera, action, roll it, take. All eyes were on the director, dispensing orders, when suddenly he turned his back on the scene and our friends, dropped his pants, and yelled, "Laugh!!"

Laugh? People could not stop laughing. The crews were laughing, the hundred extras were laughing, the spectators, the passersby, everyone was laughing. Our friends were holding their sides laughing. They could not stop laughing. The director simply said, "Print it," and, looking at my doubled-over friends, said, "I told you I am a great director." My friends could not reply because they were laughing too hard and savoring the relief of an actor with a satisfactory scene "in the can," so to speak.

## The Foxhunters and the Iroquois Steeplechase

Through the years, the two Middle Tennessee equine institutions founded by Mason Houghland and John Sloan Sr. endured and prospered. This was undoubtedly because of the caliber of the men involved—Calvin Houghland, John Sloan Sr., and Vernon Sharp, who succeeded Mason Houghland to the responsibility of managing those institutions. It was also in part because of the natural relationship that exists between the hunt for the fox and the race for the finish line.

In the early years, the hunt furnished many of the horses and ponies that competed on race day, and the steeplechase, with all its beauty and pageantry and horses jumping and hounds parading, presented the Hillsboro Hounds in a most attractive setting. Calvin Houghland, chairman emeritus of the Iroquois Steeplechase Race Committee, has remained throughout his life an unflagging supporter of the hunt, and the masters of the Hillsboro Hounds have been equally supportive of the race. Two of those masters, George Sloan and I, came up with the suggestion that the Vanderbilt Children's Hospital be associated with the race as its beneficiary. Calvin Houghland, chairman of the Volunteer State Horsemen's Foundation, and my wife Alice, then chairman of the board of Vanderbilt Children's Hospital, approved of this plan and made it work. For Alice, it was an extension of her life-long commitment to children's advocacy, which caused her to be a Pony Club district commissioner, a horse show mother and aunt, and a life trustee of elementary and secondary educational institutions. Her many collaborators in these matters, such as Margaret Lindsley Warden, founder of the first U.S. Pony Club, and Catherine Norton, Alice's district co-commissioner, were highly respected at our house.

The dedications in the Iroquois Steeplechase programs through the years detail the progress of the race, the hunt, and their relationship, which are also celebrated in the thank-you notes that I, as chairman of the Race Committee, write every year to the officials, owners, trainers, riders, participants, and other supporters. The Iroquois Steeplechase remains a great sporting and social event, the beneficiary of the power of the skillful volunteers who work so hard putting it on. The fact that it has raised over five million dollars for the Vanderbilt Children's Hospital adds to the fun and strengthens the friendships formed among the officials, competitors, and spectators.

Celebrating Friendships on Heart Break Hill

Festooned with flags, covered by crowds, and shimmering with springtime, the Iroquois Steeplechase is run on the second Saturday in May. Through the combined efforts of dedicated professionals and volunteers, the Iroquois has become more than a race; it has become one of the centerpieces in the culture of Middle Tennessee. The celebration of each running gives occasion to look back at some of the colorful history and characters of this popular event.

Since May 1941, the Iroquois has attracted most of America's leading amateur steeplechase riders. They have come to compete with their peers in this, the heartland of amateur racing. Of course, fierce rivalries and enduring friendships have resulted from the testing. These relationships add a special piquancy to the races and a special poignancy to recollections of them. For the riders, the owners, the trainers, and the officials, the beautiful Iroquois course is filled with memories of sportsmen like themselves, who have come there to participate in the great pageant, to taste its sweet danger, and to savor the exhilarating elixir of winning.

The picturesque Iroquois course is in a natural amphitheater where spectators have a clear view of all eighteen jumps in the feature race. However, two times around the mile and a half track, under one-hundred-fifty-eight pounds, is a long and grueling test of fitness and heart, accentuated at the end by the famous Heart Break Hill coming up to the finishing stretch. It is here that horses and horsemanship come to their ultimate moment of truth. Here they look their counterparts in the eye and summon whatever is left to find out if they can be champions that day. The drama of animal and jockey giving their last vestige of effort in the final desperate challenge of that long and arduous odyssey is what makes the Iroquois such a thrilling event for spectator and competitor alike.

In the first Iroquois in 1941, Dinwiddie Lampton Jr. showed the way and spurred the competitive zeal of the likes of Lowry Watkins, who subsequently went on to become a three-time winner. Watkins, because of a back injury, once rode the race in a corset, which kept him from being able to sit down on the horse. Soon John Sloan Sr.'s Bank Robber began to challenge, ridden by Ernest Hardison Jr., proving that even Phi Beta Kappas are willing to risk their necks for sport. Calvin Houghland, on Frederick II, battled and bested Hardison at the finish of the 1942 running. The useful Bank Robber, so often a finisher in the money, came back the following year with the colorful Hardison to claim their place in the records and to give Sloan a lifetime of stories. Perhaps the love of racing and taste of victory provided by that strikingly named campaigner inculcated in the next generation of the Sloan family that spirit of competition which has done so much to draw top horses and riders to the event in later years.

By 1947, another exceptional horseman, Austin Brown, came on to begin his hat trick and, incidentally, a career in racing management. Soon after Austin's back-to-back wins on Bluish, Dr. John Youmans's Storm Hour came to the fore. This great horse was always an early finisher and won the Iroquois twice for his remarkable owner. Jarrin John, a big-hearted winner in his maiden effort, was a powerful black horse whose ground-eating stride was ratable by the strong hands of Howard Tilson. However, it was in 1956, after he had become the property of Dr. Paul Dent, that Jarrin John gave Iroquois watchers one of their greatest thrills. Caught and passed twice by two-time winner Ginny Bug on Heart Break Hill, Jarrin John summoned himself for a third anguishing effort to edge the speedy mare at the wire.

Following the tradition of Sloan and Youmans, Nashville owners have always been supporters of the race, encouraging their friends to come and try, but with horses "better than an empty stall." Guilford Dudley Jr. participated in the race as a competitor and as a winning owner. Margaret Henley, shrewd horsewoman and gracious hostess, and Calvin Houghland have been frequently in the winner's circle to collect the beautiful Lorillard trophy. Moreover, they have provided the opportunity for some of the meet's most steadfast participants to ride their first winners. The initial wins for Ned Bonnie, Dwight Hall, and George Sloan, all popular sportsmen, were the products of this intense local support for the race. Through the seventies, however, it was in large part the friendship and rivalry between George Sloan and George Strawbridge Jr. that characterized the tradition of sporting competition at the core of amateurism celebrated by the Iroquois. Between them, they owned no fewer than seven of the winning horses during that decade. Nevertheless, in a gesture of sportsmanship and generosity, in 1982, the injured Strawbridge brought his favorite to the Iroquois and named his friend and rival Sloan to ride it in the race in which the two of them are the only jockeys to have ridden four winners. Another Iroquois family has emerged to claim its place as champions. The popular Johnny Griggs, as owner and trainer, and his son, Kirk, as jockey, have won three times and have come on in a manner that their patriarch, Henry Griggs, who finished in the money so many times in the forties, would have loved.

Beginning in the eighties, D. M. (Speedy) Smithwick Jr. and Blythe Miller earned their families' place in the records with three wins each. During this decade, two remarkable horses dominated the running for five years between them. Mrs. Michael Sanger's Uncle Edwin won the Iroquois three times under the masterful hand of Speedy Smithwick and the brilliant Census won it twice for different owners. No history of the race would be complete without mention of the great Flatterer, who was brought to Nashville by his owner, William Pape, so that the spectators of the Iroquois could see this leading steeplechaser in America.

The nineties brought a change that allowed professional jockeys to participate in the races. During the nineties, there were three horses that doubled. Back-to-back winners were Bill Lickle's Victorian Hill, R. D. Hubbard's Mistico, and the popular Vesta Balestiere's Rowdy Irishman, an old warrior who succumbed to a heart attack in a try for a third trip to the Iroquois winner's circle. Rowdy was buried on a hillside in a meadow overlooking the scene of so many of his triumphs.

Thus, one comes to the second Saturday in May. Steeplechase owners, trainers, and riders around the country who aspire to leave their names and accomplishments among the legends of the sport gather to test their mettle and that of their steeds against their peers on Heart Break Hill. Everything possible will be done to see that they will have a good trip.

## Calvin Houghland, Successful in Many Facets of Steeplechasing

Since his victory on Bright Hour in 1932 in the Tennessee Timbers at Overton Downs, Calvin Houghland has been a participant in the many phases of steeplechasing. Success has characterized his endeavors as rider, owner, organizer, official, and sponsor. Following in the footsteps of his illustrious father as president of the Volunteer State Horsemen's Foundation, he was the guiding force in the Iroquois from 1959 through 1991 when I, his understudy, succeeded him. Calvin knows how it is to win the race, having done so as a jockey in 1943 on Frederick II and three times as an owner (twice with Local Run and once with Hidden Chance). However, his contributions to the Iroquois and to steeplechasing go far beyond his support and participation as a competitor. His unwavering attention to every detail of the day is reflected in loving preparation year after year of a celebration of life on the second Saturday in May. Other cities in our region, some larger in size, have seen their era of racing come and go, but the Iroquois has gone on as the anchor of steeplechasing in the Midwest because of the sustained interest and exceptional leadership of one sportsman, Calvin Houghland.

All Gong: From Ringworm to Winner

In the spring of 1999, Bruce Miller called me to see if I would be interested in buying a horse for him to train. He knew that Alice and I had had some useful chasers through the years, including Hiawassee Star and Spin The Top. Nowadays, the purses in the Novice Division would give an owner a chance to come out, Bruce reasoned. We chatted along for a few minutes. Then I told him that I knew someone who would be a good prospect for him but he would have to change his presentation. "The person I am talking about," I told Bruce, "wants to win the Iroquois. Never forget that. Everything else is ancillary. I have stood by him year after year and seen him take the disappointment of watching his horse lose with the graciousness of the genuine sportsman he is. So don't try to sell him one horse; sell him two in case one of them has a setback." Bruce must have known from my description that the prospect was Calvin Houghland, who had had a horse in all but one of the runnings of the Iroquois and had won it three times as an owner and once as a rider, but who had not had a win since 1964. Still, Bruce declined to call him because Calvin already had other trainers. "Why don't I call him then and get him to call you if he is interested?" I asked. That suited Bruce, who only knew Calvin by reputation. I did call Calvin and we discussed Bruce and his two superb family jockeys, Chip and Blythe. Calvin called Bruce and bought two horses for Bruce to train: one from England, All Gong, which Calvin picked out of the pasture, ringworm and all, and one from France, Duc Moriniere. All Gong won the Atlanta Cup, was second in the Iroquois, won the Breeders' Cup at Far Hills, and was third in the Colonial Cup, on the way to the Eclipse Award. It could not have happened to a greater sportsman or to an abler steeplechase trainer, Bruce Miller, and his exceptional rider-daughter, Blythe.

In February 2001, Calvin was inducted into the Tennessee Sports Hall of Fame in recognition of his achievements in the sport of steeplechasing. The induction ceremony was a very festive occasion for the foxhunters, steeplechasers, and Vanderbilt Children's Hospital supporters who celebrated Calvin's well-deserved honor. In May 2001, Calvin brought All Gong to the Iroquois Steeplechase to contest with the New Zealander Rand and Rowdy Irishman.

Although Rand looked good in the paddock, knowledgeable horsemen observed that he had been shipped from his homeland to the Grand Jump in Japan and then on to Keeneland before coming to Nashville.

Calvin was encouraged by this daunting itinerary and was even more heartened by Rand's trainer's assertion that "We all wonder how he will handle three miles." However, just as Calvin's hopes soared, he overheard the finish of the trainer's remarks: "He loves four."

Perfect sportsman as he always is, Calvin, who watched the race standing next to me, saw All Gong finish second to the New Zealand wonder horse and observed in farewell as he left the viewing tower, "That *is* a nice horse at three miles."


Rob Banner


Calvin's honor was reported, as elsewhere, in *The Chronicle of the Horse*, which has followed foxhunting and steeplechasing for many generations now. It was in his capacity as editor and publisher of the *Chronicle* that I first got to know Alexander Mackay-Smith. Mackay-Smith was succeeded as editor by Peter Winants, author of *Steeplechasing: A Complete History of the Sport in North America*,[3] who also was president of the *Chronicle*. In 1985, John Strassburger succeeded Peter as editor. Robert L. Banner Jr. became publisher of the *Chronicle* in 1991. He invited me to speak to the Horse Publications Convention and gave me permission to speak on foxhunting or steeplechasing as I saw fit.

He was surprised, I am sure, when I gave him this counter introduction to the kind words he said about me:

> As for being introduced by my good friend, Rob Banner, I have had some experience with his introductions because I see him at race meets, invariably with an entry that looks like you should tie her for conformation. Then he introduces me to this deep-chested, wasp-waisted, flat-bellied, fine-flanked, big-eyed filly, tacked out and ready to run, and before I can gather my reins, he calls me 'Mr. Hooker' about six times in the next twenty seconds. Now this is like taking a ten pound allowance, so I am telling him in front of all of you: Rob, when you introduce me, just pull up your stirrups, take a good wrap, and drop the flag.

Rob later wrote me back: "Go ahead and pull up your stirrups and drop the flag. Those big-eyed fillies kick up a fair amount of turf. Don't forget to pull down your goggles!"

## Notes

1. Houghland, hunting diary. Quoted from *Quæsitum Meritis*, stanza 7, *Hunting Songs*, R. E. Egerton Warburton (New York: Scribner's, 1925).

2. Jane Kidd with John Oaksey, *The Race for the Championship* (London: J. A. Allen, 1979).

3. Peter Winants, *Steeplechasing: A Complete History of the Sport in North America* (Lanham, Md.: The Derrydale Press, in collaboration with the National Steeplechase Foundation, 2000).

# HEY FOR BOOT
# AND HORSE, LAD

When all the world is young, lad,
And all the trees are green;
And every goose a swan, lad,
And every lass a queen;
Then hey for boot and horse, lad,
And round the world away:
Young blood must have its course, lad,
And every dog his day.

—Charles Kingsley, *The Water Babies*[1]

When I graduated from Tulane Law School, Alice and I decided to return to Nashville to live. We wanted to hunt the woodlands and meadowlands of the mid-South. Bidding farewell to our New Orleans friends, we made for home. Mason Houghland had just died but his successors as masters, John Sloan Sr. and Vernon Sharp, were waiting to encourage us to join the hunt in the fall of 1959. Alice gave me Good Enough, a Thoroughbred hunter, for Christmas. Good Enough was well named. A big, dark bay horse with a not-so-good way of going, he was a bold and accurate jumper, a real packer for his green rider. He instilled confidence; he was a long-galloping, tough kind of a horse.

## The HooDoo Fox

A year after I got Good Enough, hounds met one morning at seven o'clock at Dr. Jackson's farm at Wartrace. Felix Peach, whom we affectionately called "Peaches," was the huntsman. The field had hardly shortened their girths when hounds struck. Peaches whooped and flashed by me heading straight on the line. Seeing me hesitate, I suppose, and wondering about the whereabouts of the field master and the whippers-in, Peaches stood up at the gallop and waved me on. Thanks to Good Enough, I was soon in Peaches's pocket as we crossed straight through the country with its snake-rail fences. We viewed our red pilot more than once and soon surmised that we had interrupted a courtship. Whatever its amorous exploits, the fox had suddenly developed a fondness for its home grounds, which lay way beyond the perimeter of our Wartrace hunt country.

Soon Peaches and I were in strange unpaneled parts, putting limbs on the top of barbed-wire fences and cutting cunningly down dirt roads when they headed in the fox's direction. We were saving our tired horses when we rode up on the little town of HooDoo, warming in the noonday sun. "Shall I call them off?" asked Peaches, surveying his field of one. "Suits me," said I. The words were hardly out of my mouth when hounds turned and headed back towards that wired up wilderness we had just crossed. Seems our quarry must have left something behind because, brush sagging, it turned and followed its back track. Hounds were blown, horses were cooked, Felix and I were lost and exhausted, but the run, now down to a fast walk and an occasional trot, continued with fox, hounds, horses, and foxhunters unwilling to quit.

We got back to the scene of the cast about four-thirty in the afternoon. Many of the field had been out looking for us. They were full of questions. "Where did you go? How did you beat us? What happened to these horses?" Peaches answered them with a mysterious smile. When he had their curiosity at fever pitch, he said, "We ran the HooDoo fox." "What is HooDoo?" they asked. "We never heard of it." "Well, it's not exactly around here," Peaches smiled again and looked at me. "But Hookerman and I have been in downtown HooDoo this very day." Then to prove his point Peaches got a map when we got back to the Walking Horse Hotel in Wartrace and found the little village called HooDoo. It was nineteen miles as the crow flies from the cast, one way. From that day on, Peaches, whenever he saw me, would laugh, "Hookerman, we ran the HooDoo fox." Through all those years of slashing and dashing and waving me on as his first whipper-in, he repeated, "Hookerman, we ran the HooDoo fox." Even when he was old and sick, with heart troubles, banged up from falls, walking with a cane, and with a voice that was just a whisper, he always made me bend down so he could whisper in my ear, "Hookerman, we ran the HooDoo fox."

## Mr. Fox

Good Enough gave me three good seasons before he became lame from sidebones sustained from scrambling up and down the rocky hillsides we hunted in those days. Alice, who has always been more observant than I, began to look for a good replacement—for Good Enough, not for me—thank goodness. The Tennessee State Horse Show was held in Nashville that summer and Alice's radar was fairly beeping when we watched the classes. Soon she zeroed in on a sixteen three-hand gray Thoroughbred hunter that was winning on the flat but seemed a bit sour in the jumping classes, frequently chipping in or stopping if the pro riding him out of hand did not see the perfect spot. Alice and I went around to the barn that night, and at her encouragement, I went in the stall and petted the big gray beauty.

The next day he came to our farm on trial. I rode him and found him to be very nervous, jigging and fidgeting and stopping on even low fences. He certainly did not seem to have the temperament to take me hunting. Moreover, I had our friend Billy Haggard, a United States Olympic Team rider and very discerning horseman, come and ride him as well. Unfortunately Billy's experience was similar to mine, and he pronounced the horse unfit to make a hunter and not worth the money as a show horse. I was crestfallen but glad to have the expert advice of a horseman infinitely more qualified than I.

However, that night I dreamed that I was riding the horse and that I let him go off the bit. I even dreamed that we went around the farm jumping the rail fences, stone walls, and whatever else presented itself.

The next morning I went down to the barn where they were preparing to load the horse to send him back. "What about one more little try?" I said, and we saddled the horses. Alice rode out with me. I rode the horse on the buckle. He jigged at first, but after a while he settled down. Then we tried a few jumps. When he jumped, I held his mane to prevent possibly hitting him in the mouth. With Alice's coaching, we were soon flying over jumps or trotting over them—he did not care which. Incredibly agile, he had a beautiful way of going, with an automatic transmission; he was totally responsive to the aids. That afternoon I called my banker and told him I wanted to borrow the money to buy a horse. He sounded perplexed until I told him he could tether it behind the discount window and just give it some oats and hay every day. Then he started laughing and asked, "How much do you want?"

I bought the horse, whose name was Mr. Fox, and he had a distinguished career for me, earning championships as a hunter, a show horse, and a combined training eventer. I was the first whipper-in off of him. He was a very elastic horse. You could take him up and let him out over short distances, which made him very quick in the woods and at trappy places. No wonder he won the Best Field Hunter at the National Field Trials after going six days as a judge's horse and competing in the horse show on one of those days as well.

## The Young Entry

As our children got old enough to take an interest in hunting, they went out with Alice and me on the front of our saddles. Then they went on their ponies on lead lines. Bradford, the eldest, had a pony named Chocolate Chip that was not entirely satisfactory because, despite a checkrein, he could put his head down whenever he wanted to eat and would pull Bradford off balance. Chocolate Chip had his way even though Bradford hung in there with him. Then one Christmas Bradford got a pirate's outfit. That afternoon he wore it out riding on Chocolate Chip and something miraculous happened. The pony stopped and put his head down, pulling Bradford off balance as usual. However, this time Bradford pulled on him, brandished his plastic pirate's sword, and gave the bad pony a resounding whack. The pony's head immediately came up, and he set off as instructed.

Right then and there, the relationship changed. Bradford became the boss. No more lead lines were needed out hunting—just a plastic sword that was soon exchanged for a crop and Bradford was galloping and jumping right behind me. He might occasionally draw a toy pistol from beneath his coat and shoot a few imaginary bad men, but the horseman and the hunter were born in him on his well-behaved pony. This gave the lead for his sister, Lisa, and brother, Timmy. All three children became elegant riders but, more importantly, they became observant, humane owner-riders like Alice. It was a great pleasure to see them advance, as they did, to larger and more talented horses and more intense competition. They all three campaigned with their mother and sometimes with me on the horse show circuit. Bradford represented the United States in Canada on the Junior Olympic Team and Timmy did the same in Cuba. Lisa was a consistent qualifier for the indoor circuit. I was very proud of our group not only for their accomplishments in the horse world, but also because they always kept their studies up and whenever there was any conflict, school always came first.

## A Horse-Shopping Tour

When Mr. Fox got older and had to go on bute to lessen inflammation and soreness, I began to look for a replacement and enlisted Billy Haggard to go on a flying tour with Alice and me to see some prospects. With each horse we looked at, Billy would compliment the horse and then say to me privately, "No, not that one." Finally, late in the afternoon, we ended up in Montgomery, Alabama, looking at some horses belonging to Dr. Llewelyn, the famous vet. Billy praised every one of them but privately told me,

"No." Then a handsome young gray was produced as an "also available." Billy immediately found fault with the horse and pointed out in a nice way his shortcomings and potential problems. Llewelyn said, "Well, that's the lot," and went in the kitchen to get us a drink before we left for the airport.

As soon as Llewelyn was gone, Billy said, "That's the horse." We bought him partly because he was a half brother to Mr. Fox. His name was Mr. Frost and he was a beautiful, talented horse, but he never lived up to his potential because of early sidebones. Mr. Frost did one thing for me that was beyond price. Because of him, I sought out the owner of his sire, Mr. Fiske. This led me to Mrs. Parker Poe of Shawnee Farm in Harrodsburg, Kentucky. It took me an hour on a long distance phone call to her, during which I told her about my father (who as U. S. special prosecutor convicted Jimmy Hoffa), to get her to let me send our mare Hiawassee Star to Mr. Fiske. It was the beginning of a great sporting friendship with Mrs. Poe that endures in my mind and memory. I will tell you about it when we get to the feathers.

## The Suicidal Rooster

I am not going to take you through all the horses I ever owned, but I have been fortunate to have Alice pick horses for me and take wonderful care of them. We soon had the nice cozy old barn full of horses and a few cats and some game chickens thrown in, courtesy of my brother-in-law, Bronson Ingram. Unfortunately, hounds met the day after Christmas one year and Bronson's prize rooster, the one he was going to fight that Friday night down at Mayfield's, came afoul of the pack. "Uh oh," we all thought. "This is going to be viewed by Bronson as a major tragedy."

Then Vernon Sharp, with his legendary diplomacy, saved the day by accosting Bronson as soon as he showed up. "Man, have we done you a great favor," Sharp told the owner of the dead rooster. "You know, you had a suicidal fighting cock. No telling what that rooster would have cost you down at Mayfield's." Now, I will not say that beguiled Bronson of his bereavement at losing his rooster, but

he did smile at the ingenuity of the defense. As for me, it made me want hounds that I could walk, without mayhem, through a barnyard full of chickens, goats, pigs, barn cats, and other miscellaneous critters. Come see our kennels situated among just such a menagerie and you will see what I mean.

Well, I had best not get ahead of myself, so I will hark back to those days in the early sixties when we still went to Wartrace, Tennessee, for special fixtures. On one of my first trips to Wartrace as a rider, John Sloan Sr. let me ride with him and things were going good until he galloped under a guy wire. It was a horrible looking thing but, to my astonishment, Sloan jumped up and commanded me to catch his horse. "Hounds are running," he said, as he took the reins and sprang to stirrup. I had been in awe of him enough already and that performance certainly cemented my admiration.

## Peaches

When I was made honorary secretary and first whipper-in of the Hillsboro Hounds, I had the opportunity to hunt right with our huntsman, Felix Peach. I had a lot of fun with him while he was teaching me the lore of the hounds. Peaches was a great hound man and a fast man across country. However, he rode strictly by balance. Sometimes he would ride into a briar patch, and, if the horse dodged, Peaches was left still sitting but with no horse beneath him. He went down like he had caught an elevator. I know I was not supposed to laugh, but seeing my friend disappear into the blackberry patch did give me some concealed chuckles while I was catching his horse.

Peaches and I had great communication. He would just point to trouble, and I would gallop off to deal with the problem. One day we were having a big run in Cooks Hills when I saw Peaches urgently pointing. I looked into the indicated valley. There was trouble all right. The fox had run through a herd of goats with hounds in close pursuit. The bleating goats headed for the refuge of an abandoned tenant house. I swung off my horse as soon as I got there and began cracking my whip to keep hounds out of the house. However, the goats in the house ran up the stairs and jumped out of the second-story windows. It was raining goats. The hounds were waiting for the goats when they landed and ran them through my legs back up the stairs. I was recycling goats faster and faster. I was starting to perspire. I was nearly popped out. I was starting to wonder how many pops could a pooped popper pop? I began to wonder why there were so many hounds still there in spite of my vigorous whip popping. Then I looked up and saw Peaches. He was off his horse, whip cracking, too. "Peaches," I said, "get on your horse and call these hounds or we're going to have a two-year supply of this farmer's goat meat." Peaches got back on his horse, blew his horn, and rode off with the hounds. I sat down on the porch to catch my breath. The goats came out of the house and crowded around their sweaty savior with thankful bleating and evident signs of relief.

Shortly after that, I was in Knoud's Saddlery in New York getting some tack and I saw some of their fancy waxed whip crackers.

"How are these selling?" I asked. "All right," came the reply. "Well, then, you need a testimonial from me," I said. "These will bring them out of the goat house," and I proceeded to tell them the story. Thereafter, I was always offered waxed whip crackers immediately whenever I went in Knoud's.

## More Peaches

I will never forget one late afternoon when we had hunted at Sloan's Maple Grove Farm and had a great gallop, through some country being mined for phosphate, to a place called Holt's Knob. Here Peaches and I stopped at sunset to gather hounds as it was a long way, but equidistant, to either the kennels or the casting ground. There were only the two of us left from a field of sixty-five, including staff. Peaches was blowing and calling when suddenly, without warning, he turned to me and said, "Hookerman, I'm awful disappointed in you."

"What for, Peaches?" I asked, wondering what he was going to put up.

"Well," he said, "I always thought you was going to be a fox-hunter."

"I am trying to be a foxhunter," I replied. "What makes you think I'm not going to make it?"

"Well," he said looking at me hard in the gloom. "I heared you took up bird hunting."

"Well, I have done a little bird hunting, Peaches, but it was just because I needed to learn something. I needed to learn how to talk to women."

"Well, what did you learn about how to talk to women?"

"You talk to them just like a good bird dog on point. Close, close in here, careful, careful, whup, whup," I answered in my confidential bird-dog voice.

"Why sure. That's the way you're supposed to talk to them," said Peaches. "What have you been doing up to now? How have you been talking to them?"

"Just like these foxhounds—Hike! Hike! Hike!"

---

Peaches laughed until his eyes watered and then squinted, indicating he was making a mental note. "Hookerman, it's going to be dark when we get home. I reckon you learned what you needed to know out bird hunting so you come on back foxhunting."

I did not have the heart to tell him that I had been reading *Jaybirds Go to Hell on Friday and Other Stories*[2] by Havilah Babcock. I figured he had heard enough about bird hunting and me for one day.

It was about that time that Peaches began to have real trouble with his teeth. Indeed, the dentist declared that he needed a set of false ones. I undertook to raise the money for the procedure and the dentures. Peaches was quite happy with the result but there was a problem. He could not blow his hunt horn with his beautiful new teeth in his mouth. The only way he could make much in the way of a note was to try to blow out of the side of his mouth. It was while he suffered from this predicament that we had a good run on a red-sided gray at Vernon Sharp's Inglehame Farm. Seeing that his side mouth calls were not going to work, I suggested to Peaches that he take out his teeth and clamp them to a limb so he could properly cheer and blow for hounds. "What if I lose them?" asked Peaches about his precious new possession. "Tie your stock to the tree," I said, "and it will mark where you put your teeth."

So he did. With the horn work now rallying hounds, we closed on the fox and accounted for it. Then the search began. It was amazing to me how turned around we had gotten and how hard it was to find that tree, much less the store-bought teeth. However, after about thirty minutes we lucked upon them. Peaches was elated and so was I. He was all smiles as we rode in with our gaily sterned pack and the trophy across my saddle. During the years when I hunted hounds, I never thought my horn work was all that good, but I never considered taking out my teeth as a way to improve it.

Peaches's Retirement

Some time later, Peaches rode under a limb that squashed him down on his horse. I could see he was in terrible pain, but it never occurred to me that he would hang up his spurs. However, I think he knew best because soon after his retirement he got much better. I will never forget his coming back to see us and telling us he was in the honey-do club—"honey do this and honey do that"—but we all knew his lovely wife, Lillian, so we did not buy it.

"Well," he admitted, "I've really gone back into dog training."

"What kind of dogs?" I asked.

"Right now I'm working on Lillian's little Pomeranian."

"What are you teaching it to do?"

"I am teaching it to go potty like a proper housebroke dog."

"How's it coming?" I asked.

"Not so good. I can get her up on the little seat, but I can't seem to get her to reach over with her little paw and push that lever down."

Peaches never lost his interest in hounds or in showing them. When he looked at the Brown-Hooker-Bonnie hounds, he offered to take Alice to the One Gallus Show at Eagleville, Tennessee, to show them. They went and the hounds won first place and every other place in every class in which they were entered. Alice was accepting congratulations when Peaches came to collect her.

"We are leaving right now," Felix told her.

"Oh no," Alice protested. "What about the last class?"

"Come on," Felix insisted. "A friend just told me that it will be the last class these hounds are ever in if they go in that ring." Upon hearing that, Alice hurriedly helped Felix in their swift departure.

When Peaches died, the Hunt Servants Benefit Foundation of the Masters of Foxhounds Association of America asked me about Lillian. This foundation has paid Lillian a stipend, which it has adjusted for inflation, ever since Peaches's death. Thank goodness for this worthwhile organization, which is so ably run by its executive trustee, Richard Webb, MFH, a humanitarian with a wonderful sense of humor.


## Bob Gray

Peaches was succeeded as huntsman by Bob Gray, who came from a family in hunt service in England. He was a hard rider and a lot of fun. Here is a story about him and one of his favorite hounds.

The hard winter and high pelt prices had taken a terrible toll on foxes in parts of Tennessee. Poachers with squealers and spotlights had lured and shined the hungry foxes, wreaking decimation on our game population. Accordingly, only a small band of the hard-riding nucleus braved the flash flooding to meet at Jim Burns's Foxlea farm for a one o'clock cast. Richland Creek was over its banks and across many of the roads and bottoms. Rain that had fallen so copiously for a day and a night was still threatening, although the clouds overhead seemed to be racing to another destination. With so much water standing on the ground, the rather warm day did not seem to promise any game except some web-footed straggler late to leave for a summer place in Canada.

Nevertheless, ten-and-a-half couple of eager hounds were soon on their noses settled to a long afternoon's industriousness. For two hours they tried, cheered by their huntsman and eager at their work, while the field found ordinary coops turned into splash jumps.

Only the irony of hunting can explain the day. When there is so little chance, sometimes the wild creatures appear and reward the hunter with an unforgettable thrill. So it was when Bardo spoke in Sharp's pine thicket. Not some predictable long trail up on an old line with hounds picking their way to get on terms, but a sure bitch with a respected tongue to start the dance with a reel. Hounds laid on with a clamor, causing the red to burst left through Lady Leonard's and down towards Buford Station Road through a muddy sea of a barnyard full of dairy cattle, pigs, and assorted chickens. Hounds carried right through the barn itself. For one moment the fear arose that our scarce quarry might have made the fatal error of taking refuge in that barn, but Bardo emerged to work it out in the pasture and lead hounds back through Upton's and into Sharp's again. There hounds lost it. The huntsman cast them through a long check. Nothing. Sadly, he announced his conviction that the fox had beaten them. Hounds were collected, except for a few, while the field relaxed to give their horses a congratulatory pat. However, suddenly Jonny Harwell galloped back from his forward whipper-in's post and yelled, "Bob, do you have Mighty?" "Not yet," answered Bob Gray, who knew, without looking again, exactly which of his charges were missing. "Well, then Mighty's got the fox!" hollered Harwell.

Everyone galloped like blazes to Hopkins's where the pack harked to Mighty and brought the fox around the hill to a large brush pile on Warren Wilkerson's where it went safely to ground. By now, the sun was shining and horses were fairly blown by their fifty-minute pursuit of the cry.

While the hunters were adjusting tack and inspecting the fox's haven, a rabbit came out of the brush and hurried away down the hill. John Sloan asked Bob if he was sure it was the fox and not a rabbit he had viewed going to ground. Bob answered him very definitely, much to the amusement of everyone, including Sloan. The sunny day, the unexpected sporty fox, the budding trees, and the blue skies of spring were all a sweet combination. Easy smiles quickly turned to merriment.

Warren Wilkerson, seeing the fox was so close to his house, invited everyone down for a toast to its health. He soon found that putting an icebox with a cold beer for each of them in the custody of hot and happy foxhunters could be like leaving a lettuce garden to be guarded by rabbits. When it had all been guarded to the last drop, the hunt was over.

## Here Came the Judge

In 1968, I was judging the Kentucky State Field Trial for Foxhounds when I had a terrible fall galloping across a concealed woven wire fence buried under some leaves. I was lying there in the woods unable to get up or crawl away from my horse, which was lying there beside me. Then I heard a truck coming and Judge Jimmy Richardson emerged to check me out. He and his friends laid me on the bed of the truck, took me to the hospital, and took care of my race mare, which was all right after all.

This, of course, made me take a great liking to Judge Richardson and I was very glad to see him later that fall at the National Field Trial for Foxhounds. He was certainly in fine fettle, as his dog had just won the Futurity, a victory that he was celebrating with one of Kentucky's best-known products in generous portion. Then his friends reminded him of his promise to go in the hotel's outdoor pool if he won the Futurity. He said not a chance because the temperature had dropped to freezing. However, his friends persisted as he took on more liquid cold-temperature repellent. Not long after, somebody came running through the door shouting, "He's on the diving board! He's going to do it!"

The whole crowd emptied out of the cocktail room and stood outside to see Judge Richardson carefully walk out on the diving board and survey the freezing cold water below. Suddenly someone shouted, "Hey, Jimmy, that's my hat!" And someone else said, "Hey, you've got my tie!" Then someone said, "He's got my coat!" Now there was a chorus: "We didn't mean it, Jimmy. Don't do it! You'll ruin my shoes. I need those pants to wear home!"

However, the judicious figure on the diving board raised his arms for silence and the shivering crowd hushed. "Well, you boys drive a hard bargain, don't you?" he said. "Now I have been to every one of your rooms and I've got something of everybody's, from the underpants out, including this watch which you left on the dresser."

"No, no, Jimmy!" came the anguished pleas. Nevertheless, undeterred, the good judge walked straight off that diving board and disappeared into the water. Of course, his friends hauled him out to get their things. So far as I know, the judge's intentions have never been questioned since.

## An Effort to Cheer Sharp's Recuperation

Vernon Sharp was not at the National in the fall of 1969 because he was recovering from a stroke, so I wrote him a letter with great big type so he could read it easily. This is the letter, which he seemed to enjoy. It may not be politically correct nowadays, so just think of it as a bit of history.

November 21, 1969

Dear Mr. Sharp,

For the last several weeks, I have been following your progress through Mr. Sloan and others, whom I have asked to give you my best wishes. Since I am told you are coming along in good shape, but that it is too early for rowdy visitors such as I, it seems best to write you something of the experiences we might share.

The Hillsboro Hounds have benefited greatly, I think, from the recent rather generous culling. The West Waterford bring the noble heritage of Isaac Bell and the redoubtable Morgans to their quest. Although scent has been somewhat spotty in keeping with the season, their steadiness on stock and general tractability result in a pack much more convenient to hunt. The few runs we have had were, to use Beckford's phrase, "short, sharp, and decisive."[3] This will round out into one of our better packs by the time the weather knocks down in January, and those romantic February dog foxes will have some rapid transit on the long way home. Next year promises to be a real girth shortener with one of the ying yangingest packs ever to set these Tennessee hills reverberating with that sweet thunder that gives man and horse the gift of lightning.

I am hopeful that one of the pack then will be a full sister to this year's National All Age Champion.

The way around is kind of a story. Let me tell you what happened. Three years ago when they last held the National in Camden, a hound named Hornet won the Futurity, but there were two gyps I liked better that were pushing all the way. One of these gyps was second, the other well up in the top ten. On awards night I introduced myself to the owner of the number two hound. He was a man named Buck Edmonson from Pikeville, North Carolina. We hit it off pretty well at first, and of course, great after he met Alice.

Moreover, he used to be a tobacco warehouseman from Gallatin, Tennessee, so he didn't regard any Tennesseans as strangers. Well, after I told him how many times I had seen his gyps on the front end and flying, he got a smile on his face like somebody brought hot biscuits to the breakfast table. Right then I said I thought his hound should have won the Futurity and I would like to buy her. He didn't take offense. In fact, he said that Alice and I should come to Pikeville to hunt. He said they make a mark for every fox they account for on a different fence post so at the end of a season they can count them. Seems they had accounted for one hundred and two the year before, all in the daylight. The latter is important because he knew I needed to see to keep up with Alice. Now with me standing there drooling, he proceeded to say that if we'd come he'd get his buddies and put on a fox catching party with all the fixings including fence posts, paint, and brush as well as the moving parts. Then he allowed as how he would sell me one of those gyps, but that he would have a hard time getting his partner to part with one. The gyps were named Zip Code and Molly B. Well, Bill Brown has a hound named Zip Code that can really deliver the mail and doesn't truck with the postal employees union, so right away I told him what a coincidence it all was and how much I'd like to come hunting and hound shopping. Underspoken as you know me to be, I suppose it will flabbergast you to hear that I told him that it wouldn't surprise me to see one of those gyps come back and win the All Age. Of course, he smiled tolerantly at Alice. Then he took out his pencil and wrote down his address and phone number. I carried that name and address around in my wallet for two years, but I seemed too lazy or too busy to go to Pikeville.

This year Alice saw Buck Edmonson at the National. When she passed him, she said, "You look mighty happy, maybe you deserve some congratulations." The crowd around all laughed and said, "Lady, he sure does! This here is the man that had the first and second All Age dogs." You guessed it. Molly B. and Zip Code! Moreover, when Buck saw me, he came over and said, "Well this is the man that picked the All Age winner three years ahead of time out of four hundred dogs." Then he got telling me how Molly B. had been lost and he bought her back for twenty-five dollars. While that price was fresh in his mind and hoping that he thought maybe I brought him some luck, I asked him again if he might not help me get some of that blood. He told his partner the whole story and said we had to have a full brother or sister to Molly B. or Zip. He indicated he had a litter with the same sire and dam that hadn't started running yet.

Remembering about Stump Prescott saying that if a fellow bought his best running dog an honest mistake had been made, I always look for hounds that haven't started yet. So he was singing my song. After no deliberation, I suggested to Alice that she call Mr. Edmonson and trade for that hound well before Christmas so Santa wouldn't have to fret about my stocking. Things were going pretty good until I got to Nashville and bragged to Felix about the odds against a man picking the All

Age winner with his first prediction three years in advance. That was when Felix said the gyp sure would look sporty in the Hillsboro Hounds kennel and, who knows, she might even marry into Irish aristocracy someday.

Next year you, Mrs. Sharp, Alice, and I will have to ask Buck the story at the National because he tells it much more colorfully than I. Besides, you can see then how I look when they bring in hot biscuits at breakfast.

Yours,

Henry

Sharp's health improved, but we took our hound program in another direction.

It was about that time that Ben Hardaway imported Gladstone from Tom and Elsie Morgan at the West Waterford in Ireland. These hounds, assembled with the advice of Isaac Bell, the great American hound man who had had such an impact on British hound breeding, were white Fell hounds from the north of England. They were very tractable. Moreover, their promotion by Ben Hardaway soon enhanced their desirability. Buck Allison, a faithful member of the Hillsboro Hounds, and his wife Bunny were soon traveling to visit the Morgans and importing hounds from the West Waterford. By 1971 Buck had founded the Cedar Knob Hounds. The pack was predominantly West Waterford. The Cedar Knob was a hard-driving pack and some of its blood is evident in our pack. Interestingly some of that blood typically produces black hounds, going back to an excellent white dog, Black Eyes, and his daughter, a very good black-backed bitch named Calamity, in which the dominant gene was asserted.

We subsequently imported some Fell hounds from the Milvain in the north of England, a country similar to ours in some respects. These Milvain hounds were unfortunately not bred soon enough to make a lasting contribution to the pack. However, our subsequent cross to Milvain Swimmer produced a prepotent line of top hounds. Right then I began to realize how difficult it is to sustain a great or even a good pack of hounds. There are so many traveling salesmen offered you, so many exceptional hounds that are not recognized and bred until it is late and litters are small. Even if one is given some great hounds and, indeed, some great packs, as I have been, blending that excellence and homogenizing those packs to produce a level pack of descendants is not easy. I especially came to respect hound breeders with small excellent packs, such as Bill Brown and, currently, Dr. Charlie Walker of the Woodford Hounds. It is one thing if you have the resources to breed sixty pups a year, quite another if you are breeding ten. Bill taught me that if your breeding program is working, you should be producing great families of hounds, not just great individuals. In other words, a high percentage of the litters should turn out to be useful.


## Making Friends in Nacogdoches

When the National Field Trial for Foxhounds moved, we followed, first to Laurinburg, North Carolina, then to Nacogdoches, Texas. We hired a blacksmith named Mack Anderton to drive our rig to Texas and look after the horses. Everything seemed to be going fine. He had the horses well turned out and well tended. Then some of the city leaders came to see me. "Does that Anderton fellow work for you?" they inquired.

"Part time," I said. "He's really a very good blacksmith who does our horses."

"What do you know about him?" they pressed on.

"Well, I know some people who have known him a long time and they say he is all right. Why do you ask?"

Then they told me the story that Mack had gone to the pool hall during his off time and made a bet with some of the local sharks. It seems Mack ran the table three consecutive times in eight ball. That cleaned the locals out. Someone said, "Lock the door and let's teach this boy what we do with pool hustlers." Mack waited for the door to be locked and then spoke earnestly to his audience. "You boys have made one mistake already," he said. "Please don't make another one." Then to emphasize his point he calmly picked up one end of the pool table and stood there holding it. "Unlock the door!" someone shouted, starting a mass exodus.

Naturally, I spoke to Mack when I saw him the next morning with our horses. "We are guests here," I reminded him, "and we don't want to make trouble." "Don't worry," said Mack. "I was just making friends with those boys."

Jack and Claudine McKinney

Nacogdoches turned out to be a place of many adventures for us because Bill and Joyce made friends with Jack and Claudine McKinney, who had a hunting place there called New Camp. The camp was in some vast piney woods full of Texas coyotes. We took our hounds down there many times to run coyotes in Sam Houston country. Jack and Claudine were great sports and great people. Jack had only one arm, but he skied, shot, and rode very well; he acknowledged no handicap. If you tried to pick up his case for him, he would knock your hand away. He would look at me while he was putting his boots on and say, "Hell, I'm too old to die young."

Late one night at New Camp when I was foraging in the kitchen, I was surprised to see Claudine come walking into the room in her sleep. She was completely unencumbered by any clothing. I had the presence of mind to turn my back to her, open the refrigerator, and rattle some bottles, which woke her up so she could disappear with her dignity. I certainly would not have embarrassed that great lady, but it was a close call. Later she said to me, "Henry, you are more gentleman than you claim to be." I did not pursue that remark.

We had many an adventure at New Camp chasing those plentiful big Texas coyotes. But perhaps the best show of all was a fight between a Jack Russell terrier named Kinlet and a big coypu (nutria). A coypu is a sort of big water rodent with fur that was at one time used to make young ladies' fur coats (called nutria coats). That caused some overexuberant fur rancher to import coypu to the United States, and they survived down there in that area near the big thicket.

The thing about coypu is that they are very lethal to dogs. They have razor-sharp teeth and razor-sharp claws. They either eviscerate a dog with their claws or they bite him through the neck with their teeth. The Jack Russell terrier belonged to our English whipper-in, Jeremy. Of course, we told Jeremy not to let Kinlet loose because we did not want Kinlet killed by a coypu. However, that was, unfortunately, like advising me of the dangers on the dance floor. So sure enough, we had been down there just a few days when a coypu was sighted near the pond in front of Jack's. Jeremy immediately let Kinlet out. Kinlet ran down and engaged the coypu in a circling maneuver from which he attacked and caught the coypu behind the ear. This was not so good because Kinlet could not get far enough up on it to dispatch it, and he could not let go of it because, if he did, the coypu would get him with its feet. For a number of minutes that seemed like hours, they were locked together in a weird sort of a circling motion, the coypu trying to reach Kinlet with its feet to eviscerate him and Kinlet trying to get a better purchase on the coypu's neck to shut down on it.

Neither was able to gain the advantage until the coypu stumbled from the weight of the dog pressed against it and, with lightning quickness, Kinlet reached up, grabbed the coypu's neck, and killed it dead as a hammer. This was the cause of great excitement around the piney woods, as nobody owned or had heard of a dog that had killed a coypu. So the next day pickup trucks began arriving, spewing dust as they came up the dirt road, and guys would get out and say, "Hey, we hear there's a man got a dog here that killed a nutria."

"Yeah, that's right."

"Man, I'd love to get a dog like that. Where is that dog?"

We would point to that little terrier and say, "That dog right there."

"Oh, man, don't tell me that. I've driven a hundred seventy-five miles to come down here. I want to see—what are you talking about—that little ole dog—that little ole cut-up dog right there?"

"Yep."

"Oh, man, you sure wasted my time." They would jump back in their truck and throw gravel all over the place getting out of there. But we would just sit there and wait because we knew that in about ten minutes they would come back, jump out of their truck, and ask, "How much would it cost me to get a puppy by that dog?" I think Jeremy and Kinlet would have made a fortune out of that part of Texas if we had not gone home to Tennessee at the end of the week.

Our friendship with Jack and Claudine grew. We went to England and then to Scotland grouse shooting with them. On the trip to Scotland, Jack was the most amused I ever saw him. He was a great proponent of British Railways. When he heard that Alice and I were going to fly to Edinburgh from London, he was horrified at our poor taste and stupidity. When I did not change our reservations to ride on the train with Claudine and him, he was amazed by my stubbornness.

On the appointed day, Alice and I left for the airport and told Jack and Claudine we would see them at the moor. However, it did not work that way because we missed the plane and had to skedaddle over to the train station barely in time to catch the Scottish Clipper. Of course, we were seated right with Jack and Claudine. I never saw a man think anything was that funny. Jack not only laughed through breakfast and lunch, not only through meeting our friends in Edinburgh, but through the shoot and for years afterwards. He would say to somebody, "Do you know how Henry goes from London to Edinburgh? He misses the plane, then hurries back to the train station and books a seat on the club car."

Jack had, and was having, a fascinating business career. Among other things, he had consulted for DeBeers (Claudine had an eight-carat uncut diamond she had been given by DeBeers in appreciation of Jack's services to them) and had built the foundation for the first atom smasher to Dr. Einstein's specifications. He found a German company after the war with the technology to freeze mine shafts in front of the augur, which allowed mines to be developed in some regions at a fraction of the time and cost. He built McKinney Drilling Company into a highly regarded global foundation contractor.

Some years later, Claudine's jewelry was stolen when she was on a trip to London so she went to the great jeweler Harry Winston to have something made up with her DeBeers stone. When Claudine produced the rock, the place freaked out. Guards turned up. Champagne was uncorked. The chiefs were summoned from the depths of the establishment only to be shocked by Claudine's determination to have the stone cut into two diamonds so as not to be ostentatious.

Jack's company had worked all over the world, yet he and Claudine, their children, and their grandchildren were completely down to earth and unpretentious. The Chireno Hounds, then hunted by their daughter, Mary Ann Bussa, and now hunted by their granddaughter, Libbey Duggar, still have a lot of the Hillsboro Hounds bloodlines. The Chireno Hounds' colors, with which they presented Bill, Joyce, Alice, and me, are a denim coat with an orange collar.

## Harry Rhett's Visit

During the seventies, Alice and I continued to visit Miss Pansy Poe in Thomasville, Georgia. She had the Alexander Mackay-Smiths there. Alex encouraged my writing and suggested that I write a book with Vernon Sharp and Lowry Watkins about Colonel Howard Stovall and Mason Houghland. Although this project never got off the ground, I did write an account for *The Chronicle of the Horse* of Harry Rhett's visit to the Cornersville country with his hounds.

"What a day for kite flying," said ten-year-old Timmy as we set off for the ten o'clock meet of the Mooreland and the Hillsboro Hounds. Indeed, Warner Park was already festooned by a dozen high flyers whipping in the chill March wind. With master Harry Rhett's chargers on from Huntsville, the Hillsboro masters Sharp and Sloan had hoped their Cornersville country would yield a straight-necked fox, but the Friday coverts had been disappointing. Now with conditions difficult, the huntsmen, Ray Cochran of

Mooreland and Felix Peach of Hillsboro, would have to produce some legerdemain venatica.

Nevertheless, a field of seventy riders watched as the joint packs moved off to quest among the hills for a morning fox. A brave sight they made. Riders wearing slickers beside those in black and scarlet presented a variegated pattern against the green fescue and dull gray woods. Here and there around an old house site, early buttercups resolutely waved their golden promise of warm days to come, but the forty-four-degree temperature, carried on a north wind with its trace of mist, made these advance sentinels of spring shiver in the chill.

For an hour, the huntsmen drew the country. They were not rewarded by even so much as a tentative whimper. Hounds, frustrated and bored, required an occasional admonishment as they worked through goats and sheep temptingly close to foxless woodlands. The huntsmen's smiles tightened as the second hour brought no respite from the deafening silence. Felix, bringing hounds out of a disappointing thicket, cast me a grim look and said in a low voice, half a prayer, "Let's don't shoot them a blank." One glance at Ray showed how devoutly he shared those sentiments.

A huntsman communicates with the earth through his hounds. To him they tell its story; tell it with their sterns, the angle of their heads, how widely they range, whether partner hounds hunt together, the way they move, and, sometimes, when scent is right, they tell it with that thrilling thunder that causes even the most casual follower to understand they are "speaking." With so many senses involved, it is no wonder that weaving the delicate thread between earth and hound and huntsman is an art to be studied by many but rarely mastered except by those who spend their lives hunting a pack composed of hounds known and loved as individual stars of a team. For two such huntsmen to work a pack of strangers under difficult scenting conditions advances greatly the use of protocol. To do so for long hours with three masters, assorted field masters, various important guests, and the fields of two hunts riding expectantly close behind them elevates manners to diplomacy. Ray, used to hunting a matchless country, watched his counterpart sift the sparse soil. However, pride perseveres sometimes in defeat. Hounds never quit trying. They soldiered on. They searched vainly for a fresh track in the lee of a hill, on a damp place in the shadow of a ledge, or at a crossing protected by some cedar woods. Always they continued to try. Finally, his face set in a granite smile, huntsman Felix Peach dismounted and walked hounds below a knoll and into Pinkston's Valley. There they found that for which they had lusted through the long morning.

It was sporadic, a spotty, patchy, tentative thing. They trailed it, worked at it, only to lose. Then they tried back. They harked to Felix's cheer and picked it up again with a pluck. So out the ridge they came picking and plucking. A light rain had begun to fall. The temperature may have moderated a bit or maybe it was just that the wind laid. However, they had it better. Here and there, a bass joined the flutes. Then suddenly the orchestra was done tuning up and the overture began. Felix came running up the hill. Ray had his horse. Hounds were charging now, both packs singing their unpent joy. Two huntsmen who had shown they could handle hounds, much to the interest of those who hunt to hunt, now showed the rest they could ride. Whatever the deficiencies of Cornersville in scenting conditions, it lacks neither for galloping country nor for places to leap. Those who bridled their exuberance and saved horses on the first few hills now settled to a swinging gallop behind a long-going red fox.

The fox made a wide circle while that raving chorus flew across valley and hillside, packed and driving. Mooreland and Hillsboro side by side exulted in the thing for which nature made them. The field had been sorted to a hardy few, forward on their horses, "[w]e few, we happy few, we band of brothers."[4] Stirrup to stirrup they galloped and leaped, swinging with hounds and smiling whenever they looked at each other.

The hounds drove the fox through the broad green pastures of a local farmer named John David Hamlett. The now steady rain made the going soft, and cows with new calves splashed puddles as they romped away from that flying squadron. Half across the field a pickup truck appeared. Master Sharp wheeled his horse away from the sirens' song. While the field pursued their sport, he quietly trotted over to speak to a landowner, to offer a horse for his lad, to compliment his cattle, and to thank him for his friendship. Hounds' music faded. Far away and faint they sounded as though they might be turning. Still Sharp lingered,

invited his listener to hunt the next week, and passed pleas-
antries. Then the gods, as if to preamble a glimpse of heaven,
brought back their choir. Down the hills they came, through a little barnyard and back onto that great green sward. The master
mounted, casually waved a friendly good-bye, reiterated his invitation, and, with the blessing of his host, galloped like blazes to
the baccalaureate.

Hounds were not strung out. They were remarkably bunched
as they closed with the red. The fox, which had so jauntily dared
the chase, now sought refuge in a huge pile of brush that had
been pushed up by a bulldozer. The huntsmen were ecstatic.
They cheered each hound, called it by its kennel name, and blew
"gone to earth" as a finale. Some riders dismounted and climbed
on the brush pile while others protected against the rain with a
toast to the sport.

Then a hound yipped and pandemonium struck. Out of the
south end of that tangle exploded a red-sided gray that resented
uninvited company, while simultaneously northward bound, the
hunted red elected to seek the solitude of its cave. Riders and
huntsmen alike set up a mighty cheer as it careened through the
encircling pack. Inches from death it passed them. Their astonishment over quickly, they clamored for its brush. Again a resounding cheer arose from the hunters as, scrambling off the
pile, the huntsmen resumed their flying lead.

Two hours' best pace had boiled down the stew to the stock.
"You're not hunting till you draw blood," shouted Felix as he
flashed through a mock orange grove with its clutching thorns.
Hounds were running to catch. They were on terms with their
quarry, which they sought like the youthful Lothario seeks fur,
feathers, and girls. For another hour, they followed its course in
the pouring rain while tired horses and riders rode a cunning line
to stay on terms with them. Finally, at four o'clock, they were
blown off the line as master Rhett and master Sharp saluted a
worthy adversary. Kennels and stables were far away, perhaps an
hour. The downpour, now unremitting, soaked to the bone. Yet as
I heard the huntsmen start their chant and saw hounds cluster
around them, I did not notice the rain. Instead, I saw foxhunters
giving their steeds a congratulatory pat. I watched hounds start
to "come away home" in the gathering gloom and I touched
Royal Fiske, who had carried me the last half hour without one

of his hind shoes. With my soothing hand on his steaming neck, I whispered, "I tried you hard; I pushed today. I will remember well who carried me this meet."

Yes, Timmy, it was a great day for kite flying. Aren't you glad our friends were there to fly them with us?

## Notes

1. Charles Kingsley, *The Water Babies* (New York: Dutton, 1966), 58.

2. Havilah Babcock, *Jaybirds Go to Hell on Friday and Other Stories* (New York: Holt, Rinehart and Winston, 1964).

3. Peter Beckford, Esq., *Thoughts on Hunting: In a Series of Familiar Letters to a Friend* (London: J. A. Allen, 1993), 125.

4. William Shakespeare, *Henry V*, 4.3.65.

# SEVEN

# THE FRENCH CONNECTION

### The Count de Clavière

In the mid-seventies, a sporting painter named Count Bernard de Clavière d'Hust came to Nashville to attend the Iroquois Steeplechase. He was a friend of Ambassador and Mrs. Guilford Dudley. During his stay, I asked him if he would like to go hunting and, although his English was very limited, he accepted. We had to go at dawn because it was the middle of May. Hounds found and were running in the spring foliage when Bernard informed me, "Henri, zay run zee deer." "No," I said. "Do you hear that 'Auk, Auk!' coming up the valley? That is the three-legged bitch Ladybug—she has the fox. It is a red fox. Look down the path and you will probably see it cross. When it does I will blow and hounds will all fall in behind Ladybug." Bernard looked at me for a moment and then began watching down the path. Shortly, he was rewarded with a view and saw the whole pack hark to Ladybug. "Henri, I paint her for you!" he exclaimed, using virtually all the English he knew. Later, I joked with Bernard that he had never had a sense of humor until he learned to speak English. Whenever he called me on the telephone, he would always say, "Henri, it eez so nice to hear from you."

## The Forests of France

Bernard came to stay at our house. He did paint Ladybug and he invited Alice and me to come hunting with him in France. We accepted. It was a wonderful trip. Bernard had hired an award-winning moviemaker, Bernard Bronk, to travel with us and make a movie of our adventures. The movie he made shows him to be a master of his craft.

We started by going south of Paris to the forest of Tronçais. It was a forest laid out on a three-hundred-year cycle by Colbert, the finance minister to Louis XIV. Colbert succeeded Fouquet after the king threw Fouquet in jail for building the magnificent château Vaux le Vicomte with wealth that the king thought should have been in his coffers. The day before our first hunt, we went to Anay le Vielle, the château of the Colbert family. When we got there it was closed, but there was a nice little lady in a cloth coat in the garden. She told us about a place to get lunch in the village and told us there would be a tour of the château at three in the afternoon. We followed her advice and got back in time to take the tour.

When the tour was over the guide asked us to wait a minute, and when the crowd had gone he pushed back a wall in the library to expose a secret passage to a room where the lady from the garden waited to give us tea. She was the Baroness de Ligne, owner of the château and descendant of Colbert. She and her beautiful daughter gave us tea and a history lesson.

## Pignot and Vigand

The next day we hunted roebuck with Bernard Pignot, master of Rallye L'Amognes, and the day after that we hunted the European stag with Gerard Vigand and his Rallye L'Aumance. Gerard made it very clear to me that he spoke no English. There was a very long run, an exhilarating forty-five miles long, which ended at dusk in the lake. Alice and I were the first to reach the lake. When Gerard got to the lake on his second horse and saw that he was going to account for his stag, he said to me, "Monsieur

Hooker, I remember the English now." We waited with him almost a quarter of an hour for the exhausted field to join us. When we turned and rode back by the stragglers, Gerard pointed to his right eye and said, "I see zat horse." He bought the horse I was riding for himself for the next season.

## Diégo de Bodard

From Tronçais we went on to hunt with Diégo de Bodard, master of Rallye L'Araize and president of the Masters of the Chase. Diégo and his brother, Étienne, were great hound men. When the roebuck was lost, the brothers would ride in opposite directions, each blowing his horn. The pack would separate and divide into two packs, each responding to the appropriate horn. Diégo and Étienne would make a semicircular cast, each taking one half of the circle. In this way, they cut the time to recover substantially, if not in half.

Diégo took us to a forest in Brittany called Foret le Garve where we had a successful roebuck hunt. After it was over, they had a party for us. I heard a great tribute to Diégo. The toaster, a connoisseur of hounds and hunting named Dr. Guillet, said, "Diégo de Bodard has been to the Foret le Garve ten times, and he has killed ten. The Duc de _____ has been ten times also and he has killed none. But if Diégo had come with the Duc de _____'s hounds he would, I am sure, have still killed seven." Fortunately, a very nice lady, very fluent in English, took me on to entertain. When I caught her name, I asked, "Isn't your husband the famous shot?" "Yes," she said looking in my eyes with a steady gaze, "but he speaks no English, and we take our pleasures where we find them." Right then I knew it was time to move on.

## The Duchess of Margenta

From Brittany we went to Normandy to hunt stag with the Duchess of Margenta and her Rallye Malgré Tout in the forest called Beaumont et Roger. Hounds got on a young stag and ran it down a bluff to a river. Alice and I went down the bluff in pursuit with the result that we got to the water fifteen to twenty minutes before the staff and the field. When Anne Marie, then Countess de Clavière d'Hust, got there by car and heard what had happened, she came to me in the field and said, "Henri, you be careful. If you keel yourself, you be dead the rest of your life!" We both laughed. It became a kind of signature line between us. When the huntsman got there, he did not want to go in the river because it was very swift and cold. Bernard then offered to go and did so, but he could not get to the young stag due to the swiftness of the current. When everything was over, Bernard, who was soaked and freezing, asked us to lead his horse back. We started for the kennels. We noticed some vans and trucks pass us going the other way but they did not seem to be interested in us.

When we got back in the forest, it was getting dark and we were soon lost. Then we happened on some young boys sliding down a muddy embankment. I asked them directions in my poor French. To my surprise one of them, who was about ten years old, looked at me and said, "Perhaps it would be better if I told you in English." He then proceeded to give us directions that were not simple but which sufficed for Alice to get us back to the kennels. The Duchess of Margenta by that time had an all points alert out for us. Her daughters were vastly relieved to be able to report to her that we were in hand and being taken back to the Courré, which is the ceremony at which the music that tells the story of the hunt is replayed by the hunters themselves, the visiting dignitaries are awarded a trophy, and the hounds are allowed to eat their part of the game.


The Return Trip


We had so much fun hunting in France that we talked Polly and Joe Murphy into going back there with us the next year. Our friends at Rallye L'Amognes and Rallye L'Aumance were tending to business. Ben Hardaway, Harry Rhett, and Leslie Rhett had been there during the fall. Harry had told me about a big horse he had ridden there named Herc. The brute had no mouth, reported Harry. He just took you wherever he wanted to go.

Now just think of it. I thought I had found this secret place to hunt in the valley of the Cher and what happens but my hunting friends from back home are right there quicker than a fox. Moreover, what should the horse coper bring out of the van for me the first day but Herc, all eighteen hands of him. There was nothing to say except "fine." Of course, he was the same horse. I could feel him tense up when I picked up the reins, so I let them out to the buckle. I swear he practically looked back at me. From those few minutes, we had an understanding. I was going to ride him on the buckle. I would touch his mouth only when necessary and as soon as he responded, the pressure would be gone. Herc floated through the woods and over the fallen trees. When we came to a ditch I would grab Herc's mane, give it a squeeze, and say, "Alléz, alléz." The result was phenomenal. Herc jumped like a stag, never tired, and would stop on a centime when I touched his mouth.

After a shakedown cruise with Bernard Pignot and his roebuck pack, Rallye L'Amognes, I took Herc out with Gerard Vigand the next day. It was another huge run with the stag going to the water at about eight o'clock on a very cold dark night. Of the one hundred who had started, there were eight or nine of us at the finish. Gerard had got-ten off his horse and donned a loden cape. He came along the edge of the lake holding a lantern. When he got to me, he held up the lantern to shine on my face. "Henri, I knew you be here," he said, and then pointed to his eye with a finger. "I see zat horse; I buy zat horse." "Don't you know they just have me over here showing you horses?" I joked, and we both laughed. However, he bought the horse.

Gerard set a bye day for the last day of March, two days away, which was the last day of the season he could legally hunt. He said he wanted me to ride his new horse. When we met, however, the horses had been sent to the wrong place in the forest. No matter. He waited until they were retrieved, having complete confidence in his limier, who had marked the stag's whereabouts in the dawn hours. His confidence was rewarded as hounds struck almost immediately, and we had a great run. Herc was on automatic pilot. He glided through the forest with the grace of a ballet dancer to the music of the trumpets. He flew the downed trees with spirit. He was up with hounds when they closed and backed the stag up against a brush pile. Alice and Polly were right there with me. "Do you want to kill him?" asked Gerard. I looked at the ladies, thinking that Gerard was asking me if I wanted the stag's life spared. However, that is not what he meant. What he meant was, did I *personally* want to take a sword in there and kill the stag.

By the time I had begun to sort this out, the stag broke from its cover and headed for the lake. Polly let out a shriek: "Run little deer! Run little deer, run!" Some of the French looked at her with a look that would have fermented grapes. The stag reached the edge of the lake in a tie with the hounds and the hunt shortly ended, but not by my sword. I still wear on my stock the button of the Rallye L'Aumance Gerard gave me to remind me of the fun I had with this great sportsman and his friends.

## Françoise and François Civireis

On these tours, I got to know François Civireis and his wife Françoise, who were big game hunters. They told me about their adventures, including a very close call in the Yukon when François shot a caribou and the guide accidentally stuck into his own thigh the knife he was using to field dress it. The guide immediately began to lose a lot of blood and went into shock. Françoise dug a tunnel in the snow, helped François to bandage the wound, and put a kind of tourniquet on it. She then took the guide down in the tunnel and cuddled him through the night until they could start back to their base camp in the morning. The guide had to be carried piggyback. Even with the guide able to help with directions, it took them six days to get back from the place that had been a day away. The guide survived.


## Jacques Gontard

While I was hunting in the forest of Tronçais, I met Jacques Gontard. He was a keen hunter and a great wit. He and Bernard immediately crossed swords verbally and the hunters laughed freely at their thrusts. Jacques told me that he was just forming his pack of boarhounds, which he was going to hunt in Tronçais. His Rallye Folie was shortly established with the motto Écoutez au Vent (Listen to the Wind). Jacques came to the United States to visit me. He brought his fiancée, Sylvie, with him. Although she was as glamorous as a movie star, so far as I could tell, the beautiful lady spoke no English.

During his stay with us, I asked Jacques what was his greatest adventure because I knew he had been sailing around the world by himself when his father died. He responded by telling me about going to Africa to the Kalahari Desert. There he encountered a Bushman from a tribe that spoke in clicks. Jacques wanted to meet the Bushman's tribe. The Bushman sat on the top of the cab of Jacques's Land Rover with a long stick and directed Jacques's driver out into the middle of the desert. Then the Bushman jumped off and ran away, leaving Jacques to make camp and wait.

In about a week, the Bushman returned with his tribe. The Bushmen let Jacques live with them and study their customs. They had little bows and arrows. The arrows were tipped with neurotoxic venom made by squashing a certain worm with the tip of the arrow.

The Bushmen would locate a herd of antelope and stalk them with bow and arrow. When they got close enough to one, they would shoot it and chase it in relays until the venom took effect. Then the famished tribe would fall upon the antelope and begin eating it raw. Jacques told me that he had learned to follow this custom. He went on with the story, fascinating me with observations about the tribe's lifestyle in the harsh desert.

Finally, when it was time for Jacques to leave the tribe, he gathered up all his tobacco. The Bushmen were heavy smokers of everything from acacia thorns to antelope dung because they had to endure long periods of hunger due to their getting separated from the herd or because the little arrows were not successful. Therefore, everyone from the smallest children to the oldest wise men smoked to fight the pangs of hunger. Jacques gave them all his tobacco and showed them by gesture that he wanted an antelope with big horns.

The next morning before daylight, one of the oldest men of the tribe came, got Jacques, and took him hunting. The old man began clicking even before Jacques could see the herd, and they finally crawled up on a trophy specimen, which Jacques killed. It turned out to be the third best in Roland Ward's book of big game records. "So that was my greatest adventure," he said. "Wait a minute," I said. "If you learned to stalk those antelope and eat their raw flesh, how long did it take for those tribal women to start looking good to you?" "Ten seconds," interjected Sylvie, holding up ten fingers with a smile before Jacques could answer. Of course, all three of us laughed, but I wondered what else I had said or asked about while around the beautiful Sylvie on the assumption that she did not speak or understand English.

In 1999, Jacques sent me the most beautiful and charming hunting book I have ever seen. It is his carnet du chase of the Rallye Folie, and it is illustrated in color with many amusing pictures drawn by Jacques himself. I was very excited to see that he had awarded me the Bouton de Honneur for the Rallye Folie.

# EIGHT

# MANGING FOR FUN

### Foxhunters of the Future

Perhaps because of the example set for me by Mason Houghland, John Sloan Sr., and Vernon Sharp, or maybe because of my wife, Alice, I have always thought that the very most fun part of fox-hunting is encouraging children to enjoy their hunting experiences. This has caused me to invite many of the young entry to ride with me. We usually talk about the woods and the fields, the trees, and the birds, especially the hawks. We look for signs of wild animals and invariably the conversation turns to scent. Later they tell about their horse's or pony's exploits and about funny things they saw on the hunt. They are delighted when I help them identify at least the few hounds most likely to strike. I celebrated these young fox-hunters in a story in *The Chronicle of the Horse*.

### The New Year's Fox

After a dry autumn in Middle Tennessee, the last days of 1965 were unseasonably warm and wet. Dawn on the first day of 1966 glistened on still soaked ground. The barometer fell throughout the morning; however, temperatures in the middle sixties were not encouraging to the large field that gathered that afternoon at

Hunting Hollow for a New Year's Day adventure. Because rain was again threatening, riders sported a variegation of yellow slickers and scarlet. Many young entry were out for their last hunt before returning to scholarly pursuits. All shared the same New Year's resolution: to find and run a fox.

Hounds handled well but drew Four Fox Hill without enthusiasm. Joint master Vernon Sharp was heard to suggest that the Gregorian calendar might be discarded for one that let New Year's fall on a crisper day. Hounds worked down the Harpeth River bank towards Hicks Bend. Covert after covert was drawn and crossed without so much as a pluck. Before a despairing field, the huntsman worked the huge bend counter clockwise into the wind wafting from the northeast.

Suddenly hounds opened with a crash. Fifteen couple, bunched and driving, unkenneled a muddy red fox. They were near it when it jumped up. Around the river bend in full view, the fox raced them. The fox was excitement dashing over the green. The hounds closed on it with a blood raving clamor. Forty yards, twenty yards, a desperate fox elected to risk its chance for life on the river. Abruptly it turned right-handed into the tide. Hounds swarmed behind it and were soon streaming up the opposite bank. Here the field divided into those for whom hunting is a spectator sport and those for whom it is a life. Into the river followed the livers behind a reverberating chorus as Reynard took a deep cut into the dark woods. No paths were there, no relief from the briars and thorns. Three miles the fox sallied in that thicket but emerged onto Merritt's broad pastures with hounds still packed and driving. Despite the softness of the earth, it had left some carnage in its wake. Although miraculous escapes were frequent, Sidney McAlister had a broken collarbone on the wrong side of Becher's. Still, on drove our fox leading the thrusters down long green declines. The fleetest hounds were clearly showing their rank as Preacher, Bullmoose, Missile, Mystic, Arbor, and Stewardess pursued that fox back to the river. There it crossed at a deep place into Hunting Hollow and turned left-handed through pastures. Bradford Hooker, age eight, who had made the long sortie, now nearly lost his pony in the swirling waters but recovered to swim across, sputter up the other side, and, water sloshing out of his boots, gallop on to hounds. The Burns girls, Lee Anne, age ten, up from her fall, and Betsy, age nine, gamely came across there, too.

Now the much-viewed Reynard crossed Four Fox Hill and raced westward to another river. This time it turned and set its mask for an earth at the point of origin. Although scent was spotty, hounds were running at it. Some of the field that had been earlier thrown out tasted shortly the exhilaration of first flighters. Heroes still abounded. Leslie Colley, age eight, recovered from previous evening festivities to hunt up with the front end. Rodes Hart Jr., age six, took a stone wall on his gray pony to stay in the race. What a run to sort the fit! What a bold going fox! It never tacked, never cut back in its wide sweep. That fox was an hour afoot without a check before it reached the safety of its cave scarcely one hundred yards from the striking ground.

The fox was safe to earth but not forgotten. Many a New Year's wish was extended it and many a smiling young face hoped for a return engagement. To the older ones the fox was an auspicious omen, the harbinger of great leaps and dashes to come. It is hoped that our gallant guest as much enjoyed the hospitality it received that evening as we enjoyed the prospect of entertaining it again.

When these children grew older and as others joined them, I have been known to cook up some card games or backgammon, with the loser having to run laps around the house while the winner gives chase and pops a hunt whip behind. This usually draws a crowd from the party to watch or join in the spectacle and hear the loser call the winner "Exalted Leader." Now I have had to run these laps myself, still in my hunt boots. Furthermore, many of my young competition still like to be called "Exalted Leader." I hope that others will agree with me that a master never stands taller than when he stoops to encourage a child. In addition to my children and grandchildren, I remember my nephews, Orrin and John Ingram; my nieces, Robin Ingram and Patti Hart; the Burke girls, Betsy and Jennifer; Margaret Sharp; Crispin and Melanie Davis; Hannah Menefee and her cousin, Ashley Parkes; and Sophie Gray, who has me call her "Champion" and sometimes goes hunting with me on her pony, Pop Tart. They have all ridden with me and listened to me tell them about how to stay with hounds and when scent is likely to be good.

Sometimes I have heard these chats repeated to others. For example, I remember one day when one of my granddaughters, Eileen Campbell, was being handed her pony on a sunshiny day. "Not much hunt today. Too pretty. Have a good trail ride," said the groom. "Wait a minute. See those little wispy clouds over there?" Eileen responded. "Poppie says sometimes when they are there, we can run like blazes because the ground is melting and the clouds help hold down the scent and keep it from going to heaven faster than foxhunters." "We'll see," said the groom, obviously not impressed and expecting to be vindicated by a blank day. However, being as how it is in this book, you do not expect a resounding silence all afternoon, do you? Well, you will not be disappointed.

Hounds found after about an hour and gave a great account of themselves, as did Eileen and Ali, my granddaughters, sailing along on their white ponies. I noticed when the groom took our mounts in the late afternoon dusk that he was entirely too busy to discuss meteorological matters. "You are getting it, girls," I thought to myself as I put an arm around each of them. "Now, if only you remember, someday if you are field masters, to stay uphill or downwind, you can communicate with the hounds through seeing them or hearing them while they communicate with the earth through their noses." I said nothing. The best knowledge about hunting is acquired by seepage from discussions overheard around the fire. I soon saw the girls warming their hands, as their mother used to do, sipping hot chocolate, and listening intently to the field masters discuss the coyote's clever cut when it got to the edge of the cedar thicket by Cheatham's Valley. Some day long into the future, one of them may ride that same cut and remember hearing about it by that fire.

## The Gamest Fox

The dawn came gray and streaked with red.
Atop the glistening grass it spread
Along the fox's phantom tread,
And towards his lair its silver led.

A chilling breeze blew down the slope
Across his back as home he loped
Unknown to hounds who helpless groped
For cheering huntsman filled with hope.

To valley's homeward path he bent
Where melting frost released the scent,
And there he learned from cry unpent
The way the journey must be spent.

More chilling than the wind up high
Across the valley came the cry
That started Reynard first to try
Commanding him to run or die.

So close were hounds when first they hit
On craft he feared his life to pit
So strove himself to save by grit
With burst enough to sort the fit.

Behind him labored a pack still game
Who stalwart still deserved their fame
And nearer pressed their deadly claim
As up the ridge he tiring came.

Beyond his best he sought a place
To rest and hide without a trace
Until he could resume the race
Recovered from his sapping pace.

But hounds so close upon him ran
That he despaired to see again
The den from whence his trip began
If he did slow an instant's span.

So cutting back he played a trick
And made them stop his way to pick
While up the wall he gave a kick
And ran its length their loss to stick.

The huntsman harked behind the rout
Expecting hounds so fleet and stout
To push him through the fields and out
But found them stopped to cast about.

Among the cedars below the rocks
Above the thicket of big bodocks
They quickly searched while silence mocked
And Reynard slipped among the stock.

Then down the wall an old hound struck
And cheered by huntsman for his pluck
He led a chorus through the muck
And to the pen where stock is trucked.

Though scents arising there were strong
Still driving straight they flew along
Before the horn a charging throng
And through the pen away were gone.

Across the fields he dashing fled
Around a pond where once he fed,
And for his life he homeward sped
A panting fox whose strength was dread.

Below the meadow waited wide
With earth and cubs all safe inside
Remaining there with childish pride
For hunting father to well provide.

Instead he ran his life to save
A sinking fox who sought his cave
But left a scent hounds' nostrils crave
And louder brought their bloody rave.

When field and huntsman hove in sight
Against the green they saw him bright
With closest hounds all running tight
And straining now for furry bite.

A trophy on a tack-room wall
A brush to hang above the stall
A sporting finish, that was all
Til Reynard summoned one last call.

And on his stiffened limbs he reeled
As forward on across the field
He passed the earth where whipper kneeled
And for the river made his wheel.

Unguarded banks awaited there
With rocky ledges his life to spare
And leave pursuers unaware
Of Reynard in his narrow lair.

Beyond the brink his body hurled
Beyond the tide that stoutly swirled
About his mask and brush unfurled
To haven rocks he crept and curled.

He waited where they could not go.
He listened to the hounds below
Emerge downstream from current's flow
To start again their cast to throw.

And heard the huntsman then confide
"It's glad I am he saved his hide,
I cheered him on that final stride,
The gamest fox I ever tried."

—Henry Hooker

## Running a Hunt

When the red fox migrated down into Kentucky after the Civil War, the leading foxhunters of that era, the Maupins, the Walkers, and the Triggs, found that their hounds could not catch a red fox. This caused great consternation until a typey little black hound with tan points was stolen out of a deer race in Tennessee and named Tennessee Lead—because he could. Tennessee Lead's blood was combined with the descendants of Mountain and Muse, obtained from Larry Birdsong of Georgia, and became the foundation of the Walker and Trigg strains. These strains came to dominate field trials and change the course of American foxhunting by being in the pack of Harry Worcester Smith when he won the Hound Match of

1905, and of Joe Thomas when he was the greatest hound-breeder and supplier in America.

Those old Kentuckians were not foxhunting to save the chickens for the preacher at Sunday lunch. They were not doing it to protect lambs or calves. They were not even doing it to astonish others in tailored scarlet coats. They were doing it for the *fun* of it, the pure blime fun of it. And their successors, Colonel Jack Chinn and Sam Wooldridge, were doing it for the fun of it, too.

## Colonel Chinn's Perfect Marriage

Colonel Chinn had a division of labor with Mrs. Chinn. She paid all the bills, planted, tilled, harvested, and sold the crops, educated the children, maintained the farm, and looked after the help. He talked politics, bred and bet on racehorses, and foxhunted. Now, this foxhunting was done out of a buggy that could be boosted over a fence when the horse jumped it or driven upon the hilltops at night. And it was not done on holy water. So Mrs. Chinn had to occasionally try to teach Colonel Chinn the error of his associations, like when she had to go and fetch him after a hard night of drinking and foxhunting and she took him back by the lighted distillery to make him smell that raw whiskey.

"My God, Mrs. Chinn!" he exclaimed. "Why did you bring me this way? It will make me sick."

"To show you that you and Sam Wooldridge can't drink whiskey as fast as they can make it," she replied.

Colonel Chinn roused himself, looked out at the barrels being rolled up the lighted ramps, gagged a little, and said, "Well, we've got them working a night shift, by God!"

Another time, Mrs. Chinn admonished him, saying, "Colonel Chinn, you should give up that carousing foxhunting crowd; there has never been a foxhunter in the United States that amounted to anything."

"Wait a minute, Mrs. Chinn," he righteously replied. "I'll have you know that George Washington, the father of our country, was a foxhunter."

"I should have known he was drunk when he stood up in that rowboat," replied Mrs. Chinn.

As time went on, Colonel Chinn and Sam Wooldridge chanced to go to Louisville and stayed longer than expected. When they returned, Mrs. Chinn asked the Colonel what had taken them so long.

"There's an economic depression in Louisville. Sam and I were studying conditions. It was very interesting. Things are so bad that the ladies of the evening are said to be offering their favors for as little as a ham sandwich."

"Then why in this world did you and Wooldridge come back so soon?"

"To kill hogs, by God!" replied Colonel Chinn.

## Sam Wooldridge: The Colorful Captain

It was no wonder that the colorful Sam Wooldridge should become so famous. He stood six feet six inches tall and weighed maybe two hundred and fifty pounds. He was the great breeder of Big Stride, Buzzard Wings, and other champion field trial hounds. He even advertised for sale "Walker hounds of Wooldridge class." It may have been written, "When you say Sam Wooldridge in Kentucky, the ladies smile and the hound dog wags its tail." Nevertheless, Robert Walker never forgot the implication of that advertisement of Wooldridge class.

One time Wooldridge was riding a borrowed horse back from a field trial when a pretty young woman happened by in a Model-T Ford. "Aren't you Mr. Wooldridge?" she inquired. "Would you like a ride back to the casting ground?" "Sure would," he thanked her, and tied the horse to a tree. Well, as it so happens, they stopped for lunch and the afternoon stretched on until the banquet that night, and Wooldridge and the pretty young woman were having a dance. "Sam Wooldridge, today has been so much fun, I would love to really learn to foxhunt," she purred in a dreamy voice.

"Honey," he whispered. "You're hunting one right now."

She smiled and mused on, "and that was such a beautiful horse you were riding."

"Horse! Horse! My God . . . the horse! I forgot the horse!" They rushed back and, sure enough, the horse was still tied to that same tree, and that is how Marcellus Frost's good steeplechaser came to be named Hitch Out.

The next morning Lowry Watkins and Wooldridge were in a cafe about an hour before dawn having some breakfast before going to the cast when the pretty young woman's mother came in, looked behind the counter, and took out a large butcher knife. She proceeded to their table, brandished the knife, looked Wooldridge in the eye, and said, "Sam Wooldridge, if you ever speak to my daughter again I'm going to take this knife and plunge it through your black heart." At which point she stuck the knife in the table and walked out.

While the knife was still vibrating in the table, Watkins looked at Wooldridge, and said, "Sam, you had better be careful. That woman was serious. She was mad enough to kill you."

"Oh no," said Wooldridge, "her own mother said the same thing."

## For the Fun of It

What does this all have to do with running a hunt? I will tell you again: they were doing it for fun. Focusing on fun is the way to solicit new members to your hunt. Make your hunt so much fun that they solicit you. That way they ask to come hunting and you pick who would be good company. Oh sure, we have the Pony Club hunts and we invite out cubbing some people who horse show, but almost all of our members are people who want to join the hunt because a friend told them about how much fun it is. So we have them hunting a few times to look them over before inviting them to join in the fun.

Conversely, if people are let in who then show themselves to be unsafe or uncivil, we ease them out. After all, we are doing this for fun. So we run the hunt for the pleasure of our members by setting the casts at times when they can come and by encouraging the members to entertain. The masters set an example by hosting the Opening Hunt party. Most of all, we strive to show good sport in a country that is made so that you can fly through or poke around through riding gates, as you prefer.

To supplement annual subscriptions from hunt members, we put on a point-to-point race at the Warner Parks, with terrier races, dog shows, a hunter pace event, and some horse show classes, such as a handy hunter and a pair class. In conjunction with these races, we have the Fox Trot Hunt Ball with a silent auction and we sell ads for the point-to-point program. We also put on the Iroquois Steeplechase for which we are paid a management fee.

One year at our point-to-point race, our announcer could not come so I had the job of calling the races. All went well until about the fourth race when I got on the wrong page of the program and completely miscalled the race. When the race was over, General Harry Payne came surging out of Kay Bullitt's box and accosted me on the track. "Jolly good show, my man," he said, clapping me on the shoulder in his British style. "Perfectly marvelous! Best miscalled race I ever heard. Never got a single horse right, absolutely perfect wire to wire." This candid assessment became a source of amusement between us. So when I subsequently invited him back, he would always gently inquire, "And who will be reading the races, dear fellow?"

In addition, the members, as they wish, contribute to a deferred compensation plan for our huntsman and his wife, our first whipper-in. This plan is designed to form an education fund for their children, so long as Johnny and Karen remain with us.

On the subject of public relations, let me say that the best thing we do, aside from our identification with the Iroquois Steeplechase, the Vanderbilt Children's Hospital, and the Friends of Warner Parks, is to give our adjoining hunt country landowners exclusive hunting permits to hunt deer, squirrels, rabbits, dove, quail, and turkey on our property. This makes them partners with us in the hunt country. We also see them riding on the trails and through the riding gates that we maintain. Those of you who are concerned about the anti-field sports would do well to get the farmers and landowners in your hunt country riding and hunting their game on your lands as you are hunting and riding on their lands so that they associate themselves with you in their minds as fellow hunters and riders. We have a party for them in October and if someone has not gotten his hunting permit, we issue it then. At the end of the season, I go through the country to their houses to thank them for the fun we have had because of their generosity.

When a tornado struck our hunt country, we organized and contributed to the Hillsboro Hounds Tornado Fund, which was administered by the local Lions Club to help our neighbors out. The response was tremendous. It gave our members a chance to show their appreciation, and they did not fail to do so. I am sure that tornado will be long remembered in that area, and so will the foxhunters' response.

## Overcoming a Shaky Start

When the Shakerag Hunt in Atlanta was established, the founders, being very conscious of public relations, decided to invite some eminent foxhunter to the festivities of the opening weekend so as to make a favorable initial impact on Atlanta society. They were told that there was a famous foxhunter in Kentucky by the name of Sam Wooldridge, and, to their elation, he agreed to come be a sort of centerpiece of the parties and the weekend. The hostesses gave a great deal of thought as to how to entertain this important personage. Plans were carefully made.

I cannot report what the ladies must have thought when they first laid eyes on Wooldridge, but he was feted at the cocktail party and there was a lovely dinner with fancy wines and appropriate after-dinner drinks. Then, as the crowning glory of the evening, he was taken to the opening night of the Metropolitan Opera tour, which coincided with the inaugural weekend of the Shakerag Hunt.

Wooldridge was duly and comfortably seated center stage in the third row. The lights were dimmed in the warm room and the performance began. Soon people noticed a strange noise blending in with the music. Yes, it was Sam Wooldridge—snoring! Competing with the overture were the sonorous rhythms of Wooldridge's heavy snores. Members of the audience began to elbow one another and discreetly point to the source of the sound, and there were certainly some titters and chuckles as the singers, with great difficulty, attempted to cope with the competition from the persistent snores.

Just then, the Wagnerian soprano hit a high, piercing note. In a flash Wooldridge was out of his seat. "The bitch has got it and gone!" cheered Wooldridge.

The effect was galvanic, anarchic, and chaotic. The audience, the orchestra, indeed the singers themselves, were seized by uncontrollable laughter which, when it seemed to be dying down, rose again and again in crescendo, after crescendo, after crescendo.

I regret to report that the Metropolitan Opera's performance that evening had to be canceled because order could not be restored, and neither the audience nor the artists could compose themselves.

I am happy to say, however, that the Shakerag survived this shaky start. I think they did so because they did not take it too seriously. But be careful whom you take to the opera and, most importantly, never lose sight of the fact that hunting and all that goes with it is meant to be fun.

## Troubles at the Blessing of the Hounds

One is expected to be on one's best manners at the Opening Hunt with its Blessing of the Hounds ceremony. I do think this is handled pretty well now that the whippers-in know to keep the hounds away from the preacher's cassock, which by a poor-sighted (but well-nosed) hound smells too much like a tree. However, I did have a young Episcopal preacher tell me he had called Bishop Juhan to tell the bishop how excited he was to be invited to bless the hounds.

"What?" Bishop Juhan asked. "You are going down to the country where they are drinking and feasting instead of comforting the bereaved and the infirm? Haven't you been to divinity school and become ordained to do the work of the church?"

"Well," the young cleric interjected, clearing his throat. "I suppose I could ask to be excused, but it is a little late for them to get someone else, don't you think?"

"Absolutely," Bishop Juhan said. "Whenever I have done it, the prayers I have always used are so and so and such and such," he continued with a chuckle. "Have fun and let me know how you liked it."

He must have given Bishop Juhan a favorable report, because we have had other Episcopal preachers bless the hounds in ensuing years.

## Joint Masters

The best thing a master of foxhounds can do is to get himself or herself some good joint masters to make hunting more fun. I am talking about people who do not take themselves too seriously and who are especially nice to subscribers and guests. Once everybody understands that this is for fun, the human relations are greatly improved. One of my jobs as a master has always been to repair the self-image of the foxhunters, who in spite of doing their best, are embarrassed by something that happens involving them in the field. Behavior modification is not usually best accomplished in the presence of third parties. A private conversation suggesting a better way to do it is usually appreciated and yields better results than a loud admonition identifying the miscreant to his or her peers. I have learned that pointing out someone's mistakes in private will often make a friend. Doing so in public usually costs one.

If one is so lucky as to have appreciative subscribers, cheered on by mischievous masters, to present a surprise accolade at the annual hunt dinner dance, I would suggest a letter like the following:

Dear Foxhunter:

The awards given me at the Fox Trot ceremonies were cleverly concealed and completely unexpected. There was no suspicion on my part of foul play. As I said then, I am genuinely surprised and very touched by this undeserved accolade. Moreover, I know it was obviously not in recognition of my dancing, although I am sure my steps will quicken when Alice uses the jumper cables on me. The beautiful silver pitcher with which you honored me will serve as a reminder of all the best of my experiences with the Hillsboro Hounds. Actually, it shows how tolerant some people can be of a master who makes a lot of mistakes and says imperfect things. Perhaps my devotion to hunting and the joy of doing it with friends who love it, too, has caused these flaws, so apparent to me, to be overlooked.

I can assure you, however, that among my multiplicity of faults is not included the failure to appreciate the generosity and thoughtfulness of your gesture and your gifts. I will remember the occasion, the merriment, and the sentiment always; like a true foxhunter always remembers the place he viewed a fox. I have heard of the poet who declared that the best of his pleasures were owed to horse and hounds. I can understand his passion but I have found after many an exhilarating chase and long hack home that it is the friends with whom those adventures are shared that make them the most fun. Thank you for being among those friends, always.

Sincerely,

Henry

I will tell you about the joint masters I have had. They are colorful characters. The older they get, the more so they become. They are united by a love of hunting and the ability to laugh at themselves that mellows the memories of their hard riding and hard falls in pursuit of sport.

## Bill Brown and Ned Bonnie

It was my first joint master, Bill Brown, who taught me that it is good to have a few side lines when you are out hunting, in case the action is a little slow. Like, for example, Bill would ride up to a persimmon tree and pick the fruit off for a succulent-looking bite. He would always smile, say "delicious," and take another bite to get you craving to have a taste. Moreover, he could do this with the sourest persimmon you ever tasted in your life. So if you followed his example, you would ride around puckered for half an hour. Naturally, he would express great compassion. "Was yours a touch sour?" he would say. "Oh, I am sorry. Maybe the sun doesn't hit that side of the tree."

No one has ever had better joint masters than Bill Brown and Ned Bonnie. They were classic sportsmen. I respected them, admired them, and had fun with them to last a lifetime.

## Buck Allison and Bill Carter

I became honorary huntsman and joint master of the Cedar Knob Hounds in 1975 with Buck Allison and Bill Carter. They were old friends who had started a hunt together with their friend Ben McKinnon. Buck was a hound man with whom I had had great adventures field trialing and whipping in at the Hillsboro Hounds. He had assembled a wonderful pack of Fell hounds and was interested in the pack until he died. I was lucky to have the opportunity to pick him up and take him to the cast just a few weeks before his death. We put the Cedar Knob Fells and the Brown-Hooker-Bonnie Triggs together; the bloodlines of some of these crosses are still in the Hillsboro pack. Bill Carter opened a vast and rideable country. In 1980, we merged the Cedar Knob with the Hillsboro, and Bill continued as joint master until 1990. He was a tough man and great sportsman and remains a valued friend.

When Bill Carter retired from hunting due to all the injuries he had sustained, particularly to his back, he sent us his good big horse, Roan Mountain, to use as a spare for the hunt. One day Roan Mountain was standing near the barn, and Karen Gray walked up to catch him. Roan Mountain waited until the last minute and turned between the parked pickup truck and the barn to walk away from her. Johnny Gray, seeing Roan Mountain's escape route, quickly went around the front of the pickup to cut him off. Roan Mountain stopped, looked at Johnny, and then looked back at Karen. Seeing both escape routes blocked, he rolled back on his hocks and jumped the bed and the sides of the pickup truck cleanly, not so much as touching it with a toe. Then he waited for Karen to walk over and catch him.

## Sidney McAlister

I can never forget the day when one of my other joint masters, Sidney McAlister, came to my office and pulled down his pants to show me a huge hematoma that covered his entire posterior. I waited until his britches were down around his ankles before reaching for the phone. "Miss Smith, would you come in here please?" I said into the phone without pushing the intercom button. I can tell you Sidney may have been stove up from his fall but he didn't let any moss grow on him while getting his pants back up. Then he realized that I had not really called anyone and a lively discussion followed. However, it is hard for even a redheaded man to fuss when he cannot stop laughing.

Now maybe I should be contrite about playing that joke on Sidney, but he had a horse named Arthur that you would not give to your worst enemy. Whenever Sidney and I rode together, Arthur would always point his backside at me and take aim as though he were going to kick me into the next county. I will admit that, although I saw Arthur do a lot of bad things, he never actually avenged the pranks I played on Sidney, like getting Sidney to stick his head in a rotten tree stump where vultures were raising their young when I knew that a vulture's defense mechanism is projectile vomiting. Luckily for our long-term relationship, nature's sanitation workers were away that day, and Sidney emerged with his dignity unscathed.

I will never forget the run we were having in Cornersville with Sidney as field master and with me hunting hounds. It was long and fast. Suddenly hounds came to a "Y" in the road. The road went one way up a long hill and the other way over a little concrete bridge across a creek and up a hill going the other way. When we got to the "Y," hounds had thrown up their heads and were looking bewildered. "They've lost it," said Sidney. I quickly surveyed the scene, called to the hounds, and went up the road about fifty yards. Hounds looked at me with a "not here, boss" look. So I gave a toot and rode back to the "Y." I was sure they had lost the scent on that concrete bridge because it would freeze before the road. "Grab mane. Here we go!" I said to Sidney as I passed him. Hounds were quickly roaded about thirty yards beyond the bridge and with a crash they were away for the rest of the afternoon. As we galloped after them, Sidney hollered to me, "Damn, Henry. You've been reading those books again."

Sidney hunted extensively in Ireland and England. He made great friends there, many of whom came to visit, but he never came home displaying the kind of bruises he picked up with us. I can understand that on the basis that anybody who could put up with Arthur could ride anything they gave him.

## Bruce P'Pool Jr., Albert L. Menefee III, Alex Wade, and Stephen K. Heard

Recent years have brought new joint masters to the Hillsboro but still in the tradition left by their predecessors: they hunt for the love of it. Moreover, they respect and encourage those who do likewise. They remind us to have fun ourselves and help others to have fun, too. These congenial joint masters, Bruce P'Pool, Albert Menefee III, and Alex Wade, are never too busy to speak to a child or help someone who has had an accident in the country. Some day their tenure as masters will be the good old days, the glory days, the gut-up-and-go days that are told to the young entry by the fire at hunt teas. Their personalities will be remembered and their sportsmanship respected.

Now I name you another hunting man: bold rider, capable administrator, and passionate sportsman. He will leave his mark like sterling on silver, by coyotes feared and by thrusters revered. Stephen K. Heard has just been made a joint master of the Hillsboro Hounds after a very successful stint as honorary secretary.

John and Karen Gray: So Many Seasons of Fun

Since 1977, I have had the pleasure and the privilege of hunt-ing with Johnny and Karen Gray. They came to the Cedar Knob Hounds that summer during a blistering heat wave, which they sur-vived with the help of an air conditioner furnished by Bill Carter. They took over the Hillsboro Hounds as huntsman and first whip-per-in, respectively, in 1980. They consistently have shown great sport. Both are good riders and good horsemen. In many ways, Johnny is an ideal huntsman. He has excellent rapport with his hounds; he trains them well. Always wanting to show good sport, Johnny is very competitive. He gets the pack fit and stays out there and works at it. Furthermore, he has the best, most vigilant first whipper-in I ever saw: his wife Karen. She is a dedicated hunter with a refreshing sense of humor. Both of them have an invaluable trait in their ability to get along so well with our subscribers; they appreciate the subscribers and the subscribers appreciate them.

Johnny and Karen understand our hound-breeding program. They are even beginning to think I do. In a recent article in *The*

*Chronicle of the Horse* Johnny was quoted as saying how many disparate elements the Hillsboro Hounds started with. However, he went on to say:

> In the last 10 years or more, . . . Mr. Hooker has gone a little more heavily into the line breeding, and we now have a pretty closely bred pack that look similar and all run together, and that's what you want. You want to go out on a day and take them all out and bring them all back, and we've got a type of hound now that can do that—and they're pretty quick too.[1]

After a quarter of a century hunting with Johnny and Karen, I can say, "I have run with the best."

## The Provenance of Hunting:
### From Ancient Greece to Cornersville, Tennessee

The Greeks, Egyptians, and Assyrians all had hounds and hunted for thousands of years before Christ. Later, as the cities grew in size and the countryside around them was cleared for agriculture, the big game was pushed back and hare, wolves, and foxes became the quarry. The Egyptians got horses in 1650 B.C. and the Greeks and Assyrians were horseback hunters. In these cultures, hunting was taken by Alexander the Great, Xenophon, Cyrus, the Pharaohs, and others as a training exercise for war and hardship.

The Romans were hunters. As central Italy was cleared, the hare and the fox became the preferred game. When the Dark Ages settled on Europe, hunting became the preferred sport of royalty. Charlemagne reenacted previous laws that reserved to royalty the stag and the boar.

Sir Walter Scott's *The Lady of the Lake* starts with a stag hunt:

> The stag at eve had drunk his fill,
> Where danced the moon on Monan's rill,
> And deep his midnight lair had made
> In lone Glenartney's hazel shade;
> But, when the sun his beacon red

Had kindled on Benvoirlich's head,
The deep-mouth'd bloodhound's heavy bay
Resounded up the rocky way,
And faint, from farther distance borne,
Were heard the clanging hoof and horn.[2]

When the headmost horseman rides alone, he turns out to be the king hunting his royal game. Without giving away the story, I can tell you that he meets some landowners nearly as fierce as some of the ones I have had to go ask permission to hunt over their land.

There were practical reasons for this policy of reserving the royal right to the stag, which existed prior to Charlemagne. The forests were the source of food for the royal court at the great castles and palaces. The monarch provided court so he could spy on the earls, dukes, and barons to keep them under control. In order to do this, an enormous amount of game had to be harvested and, therefore, the site of court was moved from castle to castle to renew the supply of food. By the time the Renaissance came to France under François Premier, there was not only St. Germain-en-Laye near Paris, but also the châteaux in the valley of the Loire and the valley of the Cher, such as Amboise, Blois, Chenonceau, and others.

The pleasures of hunting so intrigued François Premier that he interrupted his Italian campaign to go back to the forests of France during hunting season. He brought Leonardo da Vinci to France and built Chambord, the great hunting lodge designed in part by the old master and for which da Vinci brought the ultimate housewarming present, *La Giaconda—the Mona Lisa*. This painting was in the bedroom of Louis XIV and was later removed to the Louvre, but the ingenious staircases and the rooftop of Chambord, reminiscent of an Italian village, remain to remind of the great Renaissance artist's presence. Some say that Fontainebleau was named for a hound called "Bleu," which the huntsman found drinking from a spring while it was relieving itself; hence, the fountain with the four hounds doing that same thing in the courtyard of the castle.

At this same time, Henry VIII was building a prodigious number of palaces in England, many from which Elizabeth I hunted throughout her long reign. There, as the centuries progressed, foxhunting became a popular pastime because it provided venery with an inedible quarry and was, therefore, not an offense against the monarchy. You have perhaps heard Oscar Wilde's famous characterization of foxhunting as "the unspeakable in full pursuit of the uneatable."[3] There is cleverness in this description because it goes to the point that one did not have to be in the royal entourage to pursue this sport. Thus, merely wealthy men such as Hugo Meynell and Peter Beckford could study and articulate the sport. Fortunately, both of these men left books on their hunting methods. It is said that a good book can last a foxhunter for a long time, and theirs certainly have proved this over centuries.

Then came the Enclosure Laws. Beginning in 1760 and for the rest of the century, huge areas of England were enclosed, fenced, and came under private ownership with the result that the yeomanry were forced off and the great landed gentry class was formed in England. As these lands were cleared and strongly fenced, a daring hunter named Childe Kinlet taught his horse to stand back and fly these fences at a gallop. Suddenly foxhunting, which had been described by Somerville as "the image of war without its guilt," had added to its description by Surtees "and only five-and-twenty percent of its danger."[4] The officers of Wellington's army were attracted to hunting and Wellington himself was a mad keen hunter, even taking hounds with him during his campaigns.[5] He followed the ancient conquerors in regarding hunting as training for war. These officers were clad in scarlet coats that came to be euphemistically called "pink" after the mythical tailor who supposedly made them.

As the industrial revolution spread across England in the first half of the nineteenth century, it brought railroads that caused congregations of people to be pushed off the land, out of the cottage industries, and into the cities where factories were located. Thus it became paradoxically easier to travel to the remote, sparsely populated countryside. Moreover, the affluence of the British merchant class brought to hunting an enthusiastic following that saw hunting not only as a pleasant pastime, but also as a culture denoting leadership. Hunting was supposedly egalitarian, but it was in fact organized in such a way as to distinguish the wealthy from the rest. The current struggle in England between the field sports and the anti-

fields has at its core this historical exclusion, despite the fact that now people from every walk of life imaginable take part in the enjoyment of hunting. It may be that the United States, with its frontier traditions and its blue-collar sportsmen, will avoid this conflict or perceive it in a different context.

The colonies in America were full of game and it was natural that some of the settlers imported hounds. Colonel Robert Brooke brought hounds to Maryland when he arrived in 1650 and, by 1690, there was wolf hunting in Virginia with hounds. George Washington, who inherited Mt. Vernon as a relative by marriage of William Fairfax, was an avid foxhunter and was given a draft of French staghounds by the Marquis de Lafayette.

Hunting continued throughout the United States in the early nineteenth century. By the time of the Civil War, the red fox migrated into Kentucky and the hunters there began to try to breed hounds to catch this new, longer running quarry.

## A Vision of Valhalla

Mason Houghland dreamed of the day he could find a grass country good for galloping, where wire fences could be overcome and hounds could be seen. He knew after a lifetime of foxhunting that the life of a useful master of foxhounds is not predominantly spent parading in a scarlet coat and riding a gray horse while surrounded by his pack and friends. Instead, it is spent by someone dressed in country clothes visiting the landowners and the kennels, always opening country, and making breeding decisions to enhance the suitability of the hounds that hunt that country. The useful master is someone who quietly determines the quality of the country, the field, and the pack.

In the early sixties, I was a young protégé of Houghland's successors, Vernon Sharp and John Sloan Sr. Sloan frequently invited me to his department store for lunch. One day he told me I would be the master of the Hillsboro Hounds someday, and that there was nearly three thousand dollars in a savings account at First American Bank earning three percent interest. Someday, he said, I would have the say-so over that account. To his surprise, I told him he could either wait until he was dead, and I would take that money and put up jumps in Cornersville, a hilly country about fifty miles south of Nashville, or he could spend that money right then and jump those jumps with me. He immediately called Sharp, and we went to Cornersville that afternoon. This was the beginning of the Cornersville hunt country. It expanded during the years into a country approximately seven miles square where members of the Hillsboro Hounds have bought land and established their hunting boxes. This country is now paneled and gated for equestrian pleasure.

### Dealing with Landowners

In dealing with landowners, I have tried to keep in mind the lesson taught me by Albert Menefee Jr. When Albert first bought land in Cornersville, he was summoned by his new neighbor, Mrs. Ewing. She wanted to talk to him about the chickens she was raising for the state fair. It seems these chickens had run "afowl" of our hounds. "How much were your chickens worth?" Albert asked. "Five dollars," Mrs. Ewing replied. Albert fished in his wallet and came up with Mr. Lincoln's portrait. This seemed to be very satisfactory to Mrs. Ewing until about a week later when she sent word to Albert that she had forgotten something. He dutifully called upon her right away and inquired as to the problem. "I forgot the eggs those chickens would have laid," Mrs. Ewing informed him. Without so much as a wince, he once again fished in his wallet. Not even asking the value of those subjunctive eggs, Albert handed Mrs. Ewing a twenty-dollar bill with a portrait of Tennessee's own Andrew Jackson. "What is this for?" asked Mrs. Ewing, catching her breath. "I am just trying to get ahead of you," said Albert straight-facedly with a twinkle in his eye. Mrs. Ewing carefully put the bill away in her sewing basket and said, "So you have, young man, so you have." So far as I know this was one of the greatest deals since the Louisiana Purchase. We hunted that ground in peaceful coexistence with Mrs. Ewing's chickens until she sold her land to one of our hunt members, who went out of the poultry business altogether.

Henry Hooker and Stephen K. Heard

Eileen Campbell, Alice Hooker and Lisa Campbell

Bradford Hooker on Our Big Girl

Timothy Hooker on Platternash

Diégo de Bodard, President la Societe de Venerie,
awarding honors to Henry Hooker at Rallye L'Araize

(l. to r.) Patricia Hart, Jack Sewell, Rodes Hart, Harry Rhett,
Henry Hooker and Alice Hooker

(l. to r.) Nancy Hooker, Alice Hooker holding Heather Hooker, John Campbell, Lisa Campbell with Eileen Campbell in front, Henry Hooker and Ali Campbell

Evolution of a fisherman; Charlie Hooker at age five on Lake George, N.Y., and at age nine with his catch on the same lake, a 36", 16 1/2-pound lake trout, held by his grandfather, Dick Prant and accompanied by his sister Heather.

Ned Bonnie, Nina Bonnie and Henry Hooker

A. C., Joyce Brown, Bill Brown, Alice Hooker and Parker Poe at Mayhaw Plantation

Henry Hooker, Ray Reid and Jamie Clements

(l. to r.) Alice Hooker, Joyce Brown, Ned Bonnie, Bill Brown
(on Jeep), Roberta Henderson, Nina Bonnie, Henry Hooker,
Steve Beshear and Ian Henderson at Groton Plantation

Henry Hooker, Kate Ireland, Alice Hooker and Ann
Cundle at Foshalee Plantation

Alice Hooker and Henry Hooker

(l. to r.) Eileen Campbell, Palmer Campbell, Heather Hooker, Charlie Hooker, Ali Campbell, Alex Hooker, Henry Hooker II, Alice Hooker and Henry Hooker

Bearing in mind my lessons from my role models, Sharp, Sloan, and Menefee, I undertook to mollify Willard Hyde, one of our landowners who had wired us out of his strategically placed farm. Thinking that it might help my plea, I took along Clayton Fox, a long-time neighbor of this landowner, to bolster my entreaty. When we arrived at Willard Hyde's place, we found Willard in his barnyard feeding pigs. I noticed that he and Clayton did not have much to say to one another, but I launched into my case immediately. Willard seemed very receptive. I thought I was making real progress when Willard said, "Here, help me with these pigs, Sonny." He seemed to approve of the way I was slopping his hogs and even interjected "I could do that" when I told him how helpful it would be for us to be able to cross his land. When all the hogs had been fed and, I thought, Willard's permission obtained, I stuck out my hand and started to thank him. "Yes, I could do that, Sonny," said Willard, not taking my hand, "but I'm not going to. I never liked that guy, Ronnie, that you fired a couple of years ago and I'm not going to let you through here." I noticed that he glanced at Clayton as he delivered the blow. Then he turned back to me and said, "But you come back next year, Sonny, and give me time to think it over. I might change my mind."

In due course I learned that Clayton and another neighbor of Willard's had previously had a fight with Willard about the damage some of Willard's loose pigs had done. So I was reasonably optimistic when I went to see him a year later without any accompaniment. In no time, he had me slopping hogs again and seemed in a much better frame of mind until I asked him to allow us to cross his land in pursuit of the hounds, and then I heard how much he disliked the man I had fired, and so on. Now, I am a slow learner, but he was beginning to get his message across, which was that I was a long way from getting permission to hunt on his land.

Fortunately, sometime later, while out riding around our farm, I saw a deer hunter sitting up on our ridge with his back to a tree and a high-powered rifle in his hands. Naturally, I went up to speak to him and to see if he was from our country. Indeed he was. He was Joe Berry Hyde, the son of Willard Hyde. I told him I was very glad to meet him and where I thought the biggest bucks were hanging out. I never mentioned foxhunting but wished him good luck and invited him back any time. The next night he called me and invited me to put jumps and gates on the Hyde place wherever I needed them. He and his family moved in there, and they have been very hospitable and friendly neighbors ever since. Moreover, he does not keep any pigs.

Another story of landowners involves Mr. and Mrs. Cheatham, who had "his" and "her" farms. We hunted over his farm until he died and his became hers. This was trouble because Mrs. Cheatham leased her land to a cattle farmer from a town called Odd Fellows, and he immediately began tightening up the perimeter fences, locking the gates, wiring up the jumps, and nailing "NO HUNTING" signs on them. Now this gave me the idea that it might be aimed at our foxhunting, so I called the gentleman. As soon as I told him my name, he said he did not like foxhunting and he had no use for foxhunters. I told him I wanted to come see him because I knew the coyotes and hounds would be running across his land, and it would be much better for us to be with them so that we could see that no damage was done, no cattle run, and so forth. "No!" he said. "Don't come to see me. I can tell from just talking to you on the phone that you are just the type of foxhunter I don't like and don't want to see." "Well," I said, "suppose we just hunt through there and be responsible and keep the jumps and fences repaired, and I won't come to see you until you call me." "All right," he said. "But don't make me call you because I can tell right now I don't want to meet you."

That was about twenty-five years ago. I cannot count the number of great runs we have had through that part of the country. But I can tell you that I smiled on every one, thinking of that generous gentleman and being happy that we never met. Thankfully, one of our senior members bought this bit of country some years ago, and I no longer have to keep an ear cocked for a call from Odd Fellows.

## Changes in Habitat

As the years progressed, our Cornersville hunt country went from overgrown with cover to more pastureland, causing red foxes to predominate until the arrival of the coyotes. The coyotes killed or ran off the red foxes. Our response to this change in the game population was to breed faster hounds, more explosive at the find, with more drive. At the same time, we manicured the country with trails, coops, and gates. We still continually reengineer the country trying to make it easier and quicker to cross and safe for riders of different abilities. The state game and fish commission maintains that the more you press coyotes, the quicker you get up on them, and the more you make them think they are going to get caught, then the more they procreate and the more they propagate. We have got a wonderful pack of foxhounds and wonderful people who hunt with them, but, in light of what we have done for coyote lovemaking, the coyotes are bound to have a monument to us in the woods.

Whatever the reason, we are fortunate to have plenty of coyotes and plenty of keen hunters to chase them. Nevertheless, the essential ingredient of foxhunting is the permission to ride over a large tract of land, sometimes composed of many parcels with different owners. The good will of the landowners is the one thing we cannot do without.

Anyway, Cornersville is certainly a big improvement over the country Mason Houghland described in his letter to *The Chronicle of the Horse* under the pseudonym of T. T.:

I had never hunted in America although I have been over here now nine years. But my business can afford a day now and then with the hounds and I have had my eyes open for good hunting countries in my territory.

"Twenty by forty miles, post and rail mostly grass, hunting by invitation only," sounds inviting. But in all those hunting countries that seem to extend throughout the Eastern section of America, I have few acquaintances that hunt. In the Chronicle it said that, "anybody who liked to hunt was welcome" with the Hillsboro Hounds. Now I travel selling leather and make Nashville twice a year, so the other day when I was there I phoned up Mr. Sloan, the secretary, and he loaned me a mount and invited me out to hunt, which was certainly kind of him.

The hounds met at Foxview Farm. There were about twenty riders in the field. A few were on blood horses and were well turned out. Others were on unclipped half-breeds and at least two were on mules. From what I saw, these long-eared animals jumped as well as the horses, although their riders were not quite properly rigged.

My friends always say that frankness is my great strength and Mr. Sloan asked me to describe the hunt just as I saw it, so I will do so for the good of everybody concerned.

Hounds found in a small evergreen covert and went out of it with noise enough to have indicated that a lion was afoot. One gentleman told me that he liked this pandemonium. At home, you would never hear this sort of thing.

The first fence we came to was a wooden one, and by it was a large sign, "No Trespassing of Any Sort." To this no attention was paid by anyone. The second fence was a combination of wire and wooden poles, a sort of a trap. It caught one horse. Just beyond this, hounds checked in a brush-grown enclosure of about forty acres, and their actions here were quite odd, for they quested about with complete independence and without any direction that could be observed. Nevertheless, they rather quickly recovered the line and went away through some less brushy fields at a high pace—too fast throughout in my opinion.

A stone wall of no great size provided the next obstacle and here I took the opportunity to show how we handle walls at home. In doing so, I approached at great speed and distinctly heard shouts of approval. Many afterwards insisted that they shouted to warn me. Frankly, English as we know it is not spoken often in Tennessee. There was a large deep and muddy horse pond on the other side of the wall.

Hounds had now penetrated a maze of wire that would have defeated a Tinner with a blowtorch, but since the others continued, I did likewise.

Ahead of us, the cry grew fainter and fainter, and someone commented that hounds must have crossed the Nolensville Pike. I asked where that led to and a lady replied, "To Nolensville." This knowledge was of little advantage to me for I was now determined to return to the city.

By now, it commenced to rain and we were completely out of touch with hounds and my horse had lost a shoe. It also developed that we were some nine miles from Foxview Farm. At times like this, spirits have their place, but in provincial hunts their value is not always recognized.

To sum up the hunt (and with all appreciation to the secretary) it was a long gallop through a trying country, behind hounds you seldom saw, and ended without even a view—to say nothing of a kill. I mean no disparagement by this, but it was not the way we hunt at home.

T. T.

Thus did Mason Houghland imbue his hunt with the wit and wisdom that characterized his tenure as master. He loved the fun of it, as do his successors in the saddle.

The culture of the Hillsboro Hounds begins with the precept that all its members and supporters share the responsibility to make the landowners feel appreciated and important. We entertain them and reciprocate their generosity by inviting them to hunt our lands. It is such a pleasure to thank a landowner for a great season and hear him say, "Come back."

Hunt Teas

It is apparent to every master of foxhounds that there is a correlation between the size and the enthusiasm of the field and the quality of the hunt tea. I have cast many a promising covert but none so full and fetching as those provided by the hostesses and hosts who have entertained us so regularly and gloriously during my many years of hunting. They have been there with glowing fires, good food, satisfying drink, comfortable surroundings, and charming hospitality. They have overcome hardships and inconveniences to produce unfailingly delicious fare whatever the circumstances. At the risk of unintentionally overlooking some of the many of them, I would like to mention Sarah Sharp, Margaret Sloan, Alice Hooker, Joyce Brown, Poochie Berry, Polly Murphy, Valere Menefee, Sissy McAlister, Shocky P'Pool, Bunny Allison, Linda Dale, Ellen Martin, Claudine McKinney, Miss Pansy Poe, Kate Ireland, and Ann Cundle.

There were many more, but two in particular stand out. They are Jane Carter and her daughter Flo Young, on whom fell the brunt of entertaining in our Fayetteville country. Starting with the Cedar

Knob Hounds and continuing with the Hillsboro Cedar Knob, for over a quarter of a century they gracefully and tastefully put on opening hunts, hunt suppers, and hunt breakfasts. Sometimes the hunt would fail to return until long past dark, but they would always be there with a smiling welcome. Jane finally said to me one day, "You foxhunters are the bane of my existence." Since then, I have called her "Janey Baney" and when she answers the phone, I say, "Jane, it's Bane." She replies with a delightful chuckle, "Hello, Bane, . . . how are you?"

## The Secrets of Scent[6]

Scent deserves better than it gets because it is blamed for virtually every bad day of hunting, not to mention losses, checks, huntsmen's and field masters' mistakes, heel lines, overruns, and changes to fresh game. Indeed, scent is prominent even in the excuses made by guests who are expecting a bad day's sport.

The Hillsboro Hounds had an example some years ago when British Major John Rogers came to visit us from his deployment as an instructor of cavalry tactics to the United States Armored Cavalry at Fort Knox. It was a day in mid-February. I was just in time for the cast. As I was getting on my horse and turning to confer with our huntsman, Johnny Gray, I saw the Major and his wife coming up to speak. "Damn," I thought. "Here is some VIP visitor just when I need to get on with preparations."

As he came forward, making his manners and introducing himself, I saw he was in the blue and the buff, the Duke of Beaufort's hunt colors. As he began his speech, I looked back and saw almost all our field was mounted and the rest in the process. I hurried through the welcoming formalities so as to turn and converse regarding our choice of country and plan of attack with Johnny, who was sitting amongst the hounds, which were smelling houndy, their sterns animated, attentively waiting for him to set off.

Then I heard the Major's predicate for a blank day. "Terribly warm for this time of year, isn't it?"

"Yes, Major, it is a bit warm," I replied as I turned my horse.

"Do you usually have this much wind in February?"

"Not usually."

"Seems to have dried the ground a bit. I suppose you would like a good rain."

"Yes, Major, that would be helpful, I think."

"Well," he continued, "it's a beautiful day for a ride."

I quickly concluded my business with the huntsman and announced the presence of the Major and his wife Pam to our field before turning to my polite and well-meaning guest and addressing him in low tones. "Major, do you see those puffy little clouds in the sky with the flat bottoms and cotton tops?"

"Oh yes," he said.

"Tighten your girth, Major. We run."

Thus began one of the great runs. A coyote was struck at first cast and driven into the wind at best pace, then in a big circle through cattle and back straight away to the west across a large creek, viewed and viewed with hounds driving, five miles out across pastures and more pastures and five miles back down the wind, finally going to ground right in front of the first flighters, with the lead hounds only fifteen feet from its brush.

The horses were cooked. Subscribers were offering to double their subscription, and our ambassador from the Beaufort was ecstatically proclaiming, "Wait until they hear about this! The run of a lifetime! Wait until they hear about this at home!"

Meanwhile, I put my ego back in its scabbard and asked myself: "Merely a lucky guess? What happened? What makes those days with their yinging and yanging and slashing and dashing, with hounds driving and striving like a fast breaking team passing and swarming, penetrating and dominating?"

There are a number of elements in determining scent, which in various combinations can make it bad or good.


## Quarry and Proximity of Quarry

There has been much discussion and debate about the scent of foxes, hares, and coyotes, and from whence it emanates. I think everyone is agreed that there is an anal gland or body scent, and in foxes a caudal scent that comes from a spot on the top of the tail. Some writers also refer to the saliva or breath of the fox because, like a dog, it perspires through its mouth.

Additionally, of course, there is the scent with which the quarry marks his territory by micturition. The so-called body scent is what one smells at times from the saddle. It is thought to be different than the scent from the pads, which is outside the olfactory range of man. Thomas Smith, the great huntsman, established that it is the pad scent that hounds trail and run. Thus, when game has lain up in covert for some time, with its brush over its pads, it is very hard for hounds to find unless the game is stirred or hounds come right on it.

Many huntsmen come quietly to covert in order to surprise their quarry. This may be a fine tactic hunting birds that fly off. However, when a huntsman causes foxes and coyotes to depart on their pads, preferably running instead of creeping, they are likely to leave a more easily detectable trail. Moreover, a cast to drive the quarry upwind is obviously preferred because hounds are thereby given scent to follow blowing down the whole line of the quarry's track and the cheering huntsman is more likely to get hounds away together with the field not far behind.[7]

This is not to say that experienced hounds cannot associate body scent with the quarry. There are, indeed, stories of hounds winding this scent from great distances or from moving vehicles in favorable conditions, and of hounds moving up on their quarry in long grass or herbage, where the body scent has brushed off onto the growth.

The more important means of trailing our game is, however, the pad scent, which is augmented by the scent of bruised or crushed grass or the miniscule disturbance of the molecular skin of the earth. Pad scent seems to abate for periods when the game is startled by an unexpected danger, and either its adrenal glands or a flexing of its pads seems to briefly cut off the secretion of the scent.

The phenomenon of sinking scent of a tiring fox has been much noted and discussed. When I had a pack in Mississippi with Bill Brown and Ned Bonnie, Bill had a hound named Zip Code. This hound would bound up over the sage grass when the fox's scent was sinking. Seeing the grass moving where the fox was running, Zip would move up to deliver the mail. Zip was the dam of Slide Rule, who became the leader of the pack, and Slide Rule was the dam of Sly Eye, who was in her turn the leader of the pack.

One morning at home we were having a flying run on a red fox out of the Hicks Bend for our guest, Frank Richardson, when the fox jumped up on a chicken coop, turned left-handed ninety degrees, and crept down inside the honeysuckle growing on the fence. The pack came on, bunched and driving; Sly Eye was perhaps a head in front. While the pack was clearing the coop on the fly, Sly Eye, in a display of exceptional scenting ability and athleticism, turned her body in mid-air and started down the honeysuckle. Upon her "Auk, Auk," the other hounds turned so fast that many of them rolled over in their desperation to get back on the train leaving the station, which they knew was an express.

Various authors have recorded or opined on how long scent lasts from different quarry. Let us assume that under ideal conditions the trail of our quarry is discernible twenty to thirty minutes after the quarry has passed. Of course, this would be true on some ground but not on other. Now, obviously, on other days the scent would hold for a shorter time. However, even on relatively bad scenting days, it would hold on some places for some time.

The art of the huntsman in our part of the world is to find patches of scent. He should then be quick on the quarry so that hounds find and close and drive it into a run that enhances scent and shortens the time necessary to get the pack up on the line. In other words, when the dance begins, get up and stay close.

If there is no scent I doubt that it is beneficial for the huntsman to try to convince hounds that there is, given the importance of confidence between hounds and their master.

Capacity to Hold Scent

Obviously, different countries have different capacities to hold scent. However, within a country, there also are parts that have different capacities to hold scent. There are the wet parts where the secretion emitted from the scent-producing glands of the foot spreads on the moisture, thus giving a broader area over which the hound can discern the smell of its quarry.

There are bare muddy places or plough where mud tends to cover or carry on the quarry's pad and thereby blocks the deposit of the scent-producing secretions; grassy spaces where the scent is enhanced by the juices of the grass, bruised by the quarry's impact on it; and woodlands where the quarry brushes against leaves and undergrowth. In our country in the autumn, if the leaves on the floor of the forest are snappy, scent is generally bad. However, after repeated hard frosts or rains rot them, when the old-timers say the weather has "knocked down," those leaves are moist and hold scent.

Then there is rocky, hilly country with thin soil that does not seem to hold scent as well as the fertile bottom land, which retains heat better. The point is that, within most countries, there are differences and no one knows these differences better than the fox and the coyote, which make their living hunting by scent. One of the great arts of huntsmanship is, I think, to know where to draw under different conditions and to know how to nudge hounds across a bad patch and on to better scenting without getting their heads up.

We have all read the cautionary pontifications of the old wise men who say that the greatest huntsmen do not ever disturb their hounds unless all else has failed. I have had the good fortune to hunt with some great huntsmen, and those whom I have observed are proactive managers of their packs. They breed, cull, coach, and communicate. They respect their hounds and help them. You can see this in the hounds' reaction to their help.

Back in the time when we hunted three days a week, the Hillsboro Cedar Knob Hounds, as it was then called, was honored by a visit from the Canadian master, Bill Birmingham, then president of the Masters of Foxhounds Association of America, his daughter, and his huntsman, Clive Rose. Sherman Haight, a former president of the Masters of Foxhounds Association of America, Mrs. Haight, and Harry Rhett and his huntsman, Tommy Haney, also accompanied him. This august group was scheduled on a Sunday, which was the day I normally hunted hounds.

It so happened that this particular Sunday was very sunny and a little warmish for a midwinter day. The cast was at two o'clock. We tried the woods across the road from the kennels in a deafening silence. Hounds showed not much ambition. Then we drew the pastures by the lake house. Hounds did not seem to cast very well, and I am sure their progress seemed very deliberate, if not pottery, as they resignedly trudged along. My guests reflected an understanding of this attitude with a demeanor untroubled by hope.

It was well after three o'clock when we came to the edge of a little plateau, where a creek bordered by a steep drop of rocky ledges and cedar trees separated the pastures below. Here in the gloom of constant shade, the ultraviolet light of the sun had not penetrated and the air was perceptibly cooler. Hounds that had been dragging were suddenly more animated and seemed to respond to the note of optimism in their huntsman's voice as they were presented to the narrow covert. They struck and ran lengthwise strongly for a few minutes. I went off the precipice and down the steep banks to the creek, only to find them standing in the pasture on the other side looking bewildered.

As I came out into the sun-splashed pasture below, I looked across a road to some cedary hillsides leading to woodlands. "There's just no scent. Wasn't any yesterday, either," said one of our guests. Then I saw the farmer on his tractor up in the field. I quickly went to him and inquired, "Seen anything?"

"Not a thing," he said.

I looked back across the pasture. I could hear opportunity ticking away in the silence. Then I noticed some cattle running in the far corner of the field near a road separating the pasture from the cedar hillsides. "What's running those cattle?"

"I don't know. Beats me. They were standing still a few minutes ago," the farmer replied.

I signaled to the field as I blew for the hounds and galloped to the far corner of the pasture toward those cedars.

Three hours later, as we were making the long hack back to the kennels in the moonlight, Bill Birmingham discovered that his horse had bowed a tendon on the long run. It was the last call on his fortnight's tour, and he pronounced it the best run by far. The combination of cooler air in the shade, some moisture, and quickness on to the game once put up had let Grit and the rest of the pack do their thing. As they boiled through the woods, the sun faded and that race between darkness and good scent had begun. So one comes to hack home in the moonlight.

## Temperature: Of the Ground and of the Air

Many famous foxhunters who were among those able to write have realized the importance of understanding scent. William Somerville, Peter Beckford, Thomas Smith, and Joseph Thomas all observed certain days and signs when scent would be good. When H. M. R. Budgett came out with his famous book, *Hunting by Scent*,[8] many of the foremost practitioners of the art in America, such as Redmond Stewart and Mason Houghland, thought that all had been made more or less clear.

The answer, according to the colorful Budgett, is in the temperature of the ground (i.e., below the surface) and its relationship to the temperature of the air. If the air is colder than the ground, the earth will be exhaling and hounds will run. Conversely, if the air is warmer than the ground, the earth will inhale and hounds will not have a clue. Budgett's granddaughter Heather is a charming lady, a sporting artist, and master of the Bicester (as was her ancestor). Alice and I have had the good fortune to be her guests at dinner and hear many delightful stories about the inquisitive Mr. Budgett and his bloodhound, Hopeful of Hambrook. This hound performed many experiments to prove Budgett's hypotheses and once entertained some polo spectators by being sent home to fetch his master's glove.

Some of Mr. Budgett's discoveries were truly enlightening, such as the proof that the intuition of his wife was correct—that crushed or bruised grass gives off scent and that this scent enhances the trail of the quarry. Perhaps this is why the quarry scratches the ground after marking its fence line (i.e., the perimeter of its territory) or its intelligence posts to make sure the sign is noticed.

One thing to remember is that the ground changes temperature much more gradually and by fewer degrees than the air does. Thus, the ground might change only five degrees in a day's period, whereas the air might change twenty-five degrees in the same time.

Parts of the ground change at different rates from others and similarly with air, as, for example, between air in the sun and air in the shade. This differential in change is what makes the scent good sometimes and some places, and bad others. If good sport is to be shown, this must be understood by those who make the fixture card and by the huntsman. When cubbing starts the first of September, we cast at dawn. In December and January, we go at one o'clock in the afternoon to be out when the air cools over the warmed ground. In late February and March, we go at two o'clock. Moreover, the huntsman plans his attack with the relationship between ground and air temperature in mind.

It is actual temperature, and not apparent temperature, that is important to scent. The wind chill factor can make riders very cold and then the wind can lay and it seems warmer, but in fact the actual temperature may have dropped and scent may suddenly improve dramatically. Or the sun may come out and warm the ground by radiation while the air is still cold. Guess what? You've got it. Gut up and go.

Humidity: Absolute and Relative

> When the drop is on the thorn
> Huntsman, sheathe thy horn.[9]

This means that when you see that little drop hanging off the tips of leaves or on the little knots on tree limbs, there is not any scent because the relative humidity is at or near dew point and probably ninety-five degrees or above. Dew point, as you probably know, is that temperature that causes the moisture in the air to condense. A good example is your bathroom mirror after you have taken a warm shower. The moisture condenses on the colder surface of the mirror. So scent cannot be diffused. The cobwebs sparkling in bushes, on the grass, or on the trees say the same, even though people will ride up to you and say, "This ought to be great," or "This is just like England." However, when the fog lies in the valleys and along all the creek bottoms, there is no scent there. On days hounds roll on the ground, they will look at you in all your enthusiasm and wonder why you do not understand it. They are cooling themselves by rolling on the cool ground. But when the temperature, which has been near dew point, begins to drop, and it can be just a little, when the fog lifts, or the drops come off the thorn, or the frost is coming up off the ground, the earth can breathe out and hounds begin to draw with ambition.

Sometimes on a drippy day, a little wind will come up, or sometimes the sun will begin to burn off the solid cloud cover and a patch of blue or even a few patches of blue will appear. These are the harbingers of happiness.

> Everything is going right
> and then spring comes with
> those noisy little birds
> and stinking flowers.
> —Sam Wooldridge, MFH

> Hunting season sort of ends itself.
> —Albert Menefee III, MFH

When the sky is totally blue, not a cloud in it, when the humidity is down around fifty-five percent, forget it. When the exhaust from cars disappears and you can hardly smell it, have a hack. Those high old dry days may be beautiful but there is a lot of riding around. The scent is going to heaven faster than any foxhunter. On such a day, wait for the sun to set and the breeze to lay. Draw the edges of creek banks or look in the gloom of a grove of shade trees next to a pond. In those shadowy sanctuaries may lurk excitement ready to depart on swift feet. Better yet, come back at dawn when there is a touch of moisture in the ground and the nightlines of game on the way back from its nocturnal hunt still lie near the ground. It may last only an hour but it can be spectacular.

The fact is that temperature is the controlling factor in relative humidity. This revelation, by H. B. C. Pollard, was the predicate for his book, *The Mystery of Scent*,[10] and his instruments that took the Budgett theory to its conclusion. Absolute humidity is the amount of moisture a cubic foot of air can carry at its temperature. Relative humidity is the amount it carries as a percentage of the amount it could carry at that temperature before reaching dew point. Hot air can carry more moisture than cold, so as the temperature drops the relative humidity rises. Conversely, when the air warms, the relative humidity falls. Now as quarry scent is borne or diffused by the evaporation of moisture into the air, rising relative humidity until one approaches dew point is desirable for good scent. Pollard's work contradicted some of Budgett's conclusions. As Pollard diplomatically said, "I find myself at variance with many of the conclusions he has drawn from the facts he has assembled."[11]

However, it cannot be doubted that Pollard used the findings of Budgett as a platform from which to attain a higher understanding of the subject of scent. Pollard himself has been the catalyst for further investigation. P. C. Spink has produced a number of papers in furtherance of Pollard's and Budgett's theories. The best of Spink's papers appeared in *Hounds* magazine.[12] It gives a table of relationships between temperature and relative humidity, which shows that as the temperature falls and the relative humidity rises, scent becomes good over grass and plough. Spink further notes the importance of the bruising of grass or herbage or disturbing the skin of the soil in producing the line.

Barometric Pressure

Actually, the barometer is of limited use when trying to fathom scent and produce a good hunt because relative humidity has extremely localized variances. One can go hunting with the barometer rising, expecting a great day's sport, only to find things starting to cloud over and a storm brewing. Although you would bet that the barometric pressure is now falling, you are unfortunately miles away from the barometer itself. Therefore, the barometer is not useful for determining immediate conditions.

There is likely to be no scent as the storm clouds form up. Then it starts to rain and suddenly the oppressive atmosphere begins to lighten and hounds oblivious to rain begin to be more investigative. Before you know it, hounds start to run and you sail off like a larker at large. Just when the proceedings are most pleasurable, it suddenly rains harder and the scent seems to wash away. Thoroughly soaked, you see to your horse, cast the last promising covert of the day for which you thank your hostess, and go home to look at the barometer to try to determine what tomorrow might be like.

The Wind

There are horizontal winds and vertical winds. You can see the latter on a hot day when heat is dancing above the asphalt road.

These winds cause ground turbulence and are bad for scent. The horizontal wind, if from the right quarter, can bring the coolness or the moisture needed for good scent. In our country, a wind from the west or the north is usually all right. A wind from the south or the southeast (which is rare) is usually not desirable since it brings warmer, moister air and rain to wash away the scent.

On a still, humid day when the air is near dew point, wind can cause enough evaporation or stirring to allow scent to diffuse. In other words, it can save the day.

Wind can dry the ground, as one observes in March. However, hounds can run in the wind, sometimes quite downwind from the actual trail of the fox. There is one disadvantage to a high or gusty wind that does not relate to scent but which does affect sport. That is its tendency to scatter hounds and cause difficulties in following cry.

A breeze of five to ten miles an hour is thought to improve scent, as it disperses the scent over the ground like a patch of smoke, whereas a perfectly still day would allow the smoke to rise in a small column straight to the sky.

Sky: Sun and Clouds

> All things by immortal power,
> Near or far,
> Hiddenly
> To each other linked are,
> That thou canst not stir a flower
> Without troubling of a star.
> —Francis Thompson,
> "The Mistress of Vision"[13]

The sun has an effect on scent that is different at different times of day or of the year. The sun can help when the air is approaching dew point or it can hurt by heating the air until it is warmer than the ground, or it can heat the ground by radiation and cause turbulent vertical winds or layers of evaporation that can ruin scent. It is also understood that scent deteriorates in the ultraviolet light rays of the sun. As the sun gets higher in late February and March in our part of the country, its direct rays are more potent than in December and January.

Clouds also can have a tremendous effect on scent. Although it muffles cry, an overcast warm day with high humidity can produce good hunting, as Peter Beckford noted.[14] A cloudless sunny day is unlikely to be productive. After all, clouds are just the air reaching dew point up in the sky. So a few clouds around are telling you that there are caps on those columns of evaporation over certain parts of the countryside. These caps are holding the evaporation down; thereby they are containing the humidity. On such a day, we can go sailing on the grass.

Snow on warm ground seems to preserve scent and running can be quite good when the snow is melting. However, if the snow falls on already frozen ground or a hard frost, scent will not diffuse until the ground thaws. Although scent can be quite good before a frost or dew, it is spoiled when these are down. Scent is not good when the frost is melting or coming off of the ground, or when drops of heavy dew moisture hang on the grass or are coming up. However, when this process is finished, the ground can again become warmer than the air and diffusion of scent returns. The explanation is that this evaporation is cooling the ground. If there is a heavy frost on the ground, the bruising of grass does not leave scent.

## Foils

Certain scents overpower or mask the scent of the quarry and certain substances block scent. Nobody knows this better than the quarry, which makes its living hunting primarily by scent. The quarry, when pushed, will resort to those stratagems such as re-tracing its own track, running through a patch of mint or onions, or a freshly fertilized field, or a pig pen, or a herd of goats, or a pasture full of cows, or in deer tracks, or down a paved road where cars have passed, or where hounds and foxhunters on their horses have foiled the ground. The list is endless. However, sometimes scent just remains a mystery. Thank goodness.

Where we were hunting in Mississippi, an old man would come out on his gray mule using a gunnysack for a saddle. He rode sidesaddle style with his leg hooked over the withers. Gallop and dash as I would, he would beat me to the checks. Finally, when we lost, he would say: "The fox licked his feet. He ain't thar no mo'."

## Picking the Right Casting Ground

Another time we were hunting wolves in some piney woods in Texas at Jack and Claudine McKinney's New Camp. It was great. The timber companies would clear-cut a few hundred acres and push the scraps up into windrows. Then the truck farmers would plant a one-time crop of watermelons in the devastated tract. When the harvest came, many watermelons were left to swell up and burst. When one arrived there at dawn, it was like a dream of Africa. The mice, the rabbits, the deer, the bird life, the coons, the possums, and the wolves were all there with more watermelons than a Sunday school picnic.

The wolf would run for hours and hours. If it came within ten feet of a certain cottonwood tree, it would pass that exact place on its next round. If it crossed a burned spot, an hour later it would cross it in the same place. The wolf knew where stinking dead chickens had been thrown out by the poultry farmers, and it would take you back through there and dodge around until you were almost sick from the stench of it.

Furthermore, the wolf knew those chert roads better than the mailman, and it thought nothing of a mile or so of roadwork down through the country. On one such occasion, I could see its track down the road when, to my dismay, the whole pack threw up their heads. Finally, one hound, Quiver, at my urging went down the road, opening on every track. She had a romantic spring.

## Hardaway Appeals to Higher Authority

I was once hunting with Ben Hardaway on one of his regular Sunday fixtures. He had a big field out to enjoy the sunny afternoon. Ben drew and drew, covert after covert, blank. Through the long afternoon, the blank translated into blankety-blank. Ben was cussing the scent, the sun, the game—everything. Then he began talking to his hounds in a sort of low mumble. Naturally, I wanted to hear what the great huntsman was saying so I sidled up close, being careful not to step on a hound. When I got within hearing range, I was surprised to learn that Ben was not talking to hounds at all—he was appealing to higher authority. His supplication went something like this: "Lord, you know I am a backslider and you know I ain't been to church like I should have. So it ain't nothing I deserve, Lord, but for the sake of Sarah and those sweet little girls you let me have, please, Lord, just send me a little gray fox before Hooker leaves. You know how irascible I can get, Lord, and those sweet pills don't always work, so please, Lord, just a little something to run while Hooker is here, for the sake of Sarah and the children."

Finally, near dark, we got on a red fox. After a long run, the fox went through a field full of cows and crawled under a collapsed chicken house. Ben and I crawled under there, too. It was dark and the scent brought tears to my eyes. Ben had a little flashlight and as he would shine each hound, he would congratulate it. By this time, I was so covered with chicken compost and my eyes were so watery that I could barely see that it was me I was smelling.

Ben found Wade, his favorite hound, with the fox. "Wade, I knew you'd be here, Wade," said Ben, giving Wade a congratulatory pat. "Nobody better offer to trade with me for you or for somebody else because somebody else will be gone, Wade, she'll be gone if they do." I do not know whether it was the smell or my quotation of Ben's assurances to Wade that made "somebody else" give me so much room at the party.


Hounds: Nose vs. Intelligence

Without getting too technical, it is possible to observe that some hounds have better noses than others. By that, I mean that they are better able to discern the scent of the quarry under certain conditions. Some hounds have what is called a cold nose, which means they have an ability to discern the scent in conditions when others cannot. This is true. Ned Bonnie had a hound named Show Girl who sounded like a pig sniffing truffles. However, it is also true that certain other hounds may be faster when the quarry has been put up and is running.

Many writers have advised concerning the characteristics one should stress in a breeding program. Joe Thomas argued that nose is the most important attribute. Another great American hound man who made his mark in England and Ireland, Isaac Bell, put intelligence and biddability ahead of nose. I have observed over some forty years many exceptional hounds, that is, hounds that could strike a very high percentage of the game run by a pack. We had a hound named Pastor who would just stick his nose in a briar patch and announce whether it housed the desired occupant. Bill Brown had an exceptional strike hound that had been renamed Yellowstone because Bill had switched to the bourbon by that name.

When Ben Hardaway brought his hounds to Mississippi to hunt with us, a man named John Carruth, a longtime friend of Bill's, also came to hunt. That morning Carruth poured himself a glass of gin with a splash of the soft drink Wink to fortify himself for the rigors of the chase. Unfortunately, this predawn cocktail loosened Carruth's tongue, and he had a bit too much to say about Ben's rough-coated hound Sparkle. Finally, Ben said, "Listen here, Fats. You can say whatever you want about my family, but if you say anything else bad about these hounds we are going to fight or dance, and you had better learn to dance because I'm a mean fighter." I told Carruth to shut his mouth, get behind me, and pray for lockjaw.

Of course, Bill's Triggs had the home-court advantage because they knew the coverts, the soil, and so forth. Therefore, it was not surprising that Yellowstone trailed up the red fox and got it running by daylight. Then Sparkle adjusted her nozzle to that fox's scent and started to laugh at it. "Haha, Haha, Haha." Always in the tremendous roar, you could hear Sparkle, "Haha, Haha, Haha."

When Sparkle's cry began to dominate, a recurring theme in the roaring music, Ben looked at Carruth and said, "How do you like that, Fats?" Luckily, Carruth was too busy hanging on to more than grunt acknowledgment. Then the fox jinked and hounds overran. In a flash, Ben was off his horse helping their cast. Hounds were snuffing under every pine needle, with Ben encouraging them. Then Yellowstone came through and took the line. Ben looked around at his hounds disgustedly and said, "Hark to Yellowstone, can't you see she's got it?" Off they went and soon the laughing lead had resumed: "Haha, Haha, Haha." It went on like this through a few more checks, with Yellowstone always arriving to work it out. On about the fourth check Ben looked at his hounds and said, "Wait a minute. Yellowstone will be along to show you the way." I am afraid Carruth had not endured long enough to enjoy this moment, however, as he had hit his knee on a tree and had gone in after Ben had asked, "What's the matter, Fats? All the gin run out?"

The point is that there is more than one kind of great hound for a pack. Great packs contain individual hounds with different qualities that contribute to the team. One thing that we have done sometimes is to lay back our fastest hounds or our strike hounds and take the pack hunting without them. This develops depth and brings to the fore new stars, forges new relationships, and makes the huntsman and the master plenty nervous, especially if they have done it on an iffy scenting day when a large field has shown up to hunt.

During stag hunts in France, the whipper-in will drop his thong and stop the whole pack so that one hound can be sent forward to confirm the line of the hunted stag. The huntsman casts: "Écoutez, Écoutez Aggressor," and then waves his cap and cheers on the pack when the line is confirmed. "Ah ha ha, mon petit valet, ah ha ha."

Or as the English huntsman said in his poem, "But the casting vote on a doubtful note is left to the old Blue Pye."[15]

I have found that intelligent hounds find the ways to escape a kennel, learn to get the most biscuits at walk, and make a higher percentage of successful casts at a loss.

## How To Tell Scenting Conditions

Pollard pointed out that members of the field accurately prognosticate scenting conditions only twenty percent of the time, and that aged farmers, soothsayers, and warlocks only get the correct percentage up to something below thirty percent. However, Pollard claimed eighty percent accuracy for his instrument, the scentometer, which took into account temperature, relative humidity, percentage of visible cloud, wind force, direction of the wind, and correction for extreme cases such as heavy rain, mist, or frost.

Now, obviously, out hunting, it would be inconvenient to lug around a scentometer, so I suggest instead an understanding of these principles, observation of the patches of country, the sky, the sun, the relative humidity, and so on, and, most of all, keen attention to the attitude and activity of hounds, especially the strike hounds and their usual hunting companions. The result should be accuracy that rivals the scentometer but which is a lot less cumbersome to carry.

> But as he trotted up to cover
> Robin was watching to discover
> What chance there was, and many a token
> Told him that though no hound had spoken,
> Most of them stirred to something there.
> The old hounds' muzzles searched the air,
> Thin ghosts of scents were in their teeth
> From foxes which had crossed the Heath
> Not very many hours before.
> "We'll find," he said, "I'll bet, a score."

> —John Masefield, "Reynard the Fox"[16]

It had been a long, cold winter afternoon. Hounds had drawn and drawn with never a touch. The field looked blue cold and aching, with fingers and toes hurting in the cold wind. Finally, with an hour of daylight left, I relented and suggested to Johnny that he turn back to the trailers and the party. "Then I'll just cross the road and draw Doolin's Ridge since it is on the way," suggested Johnny, who never quits trying, always keen to show sport.

"Fine," I said, and appointed someone else to take the field so that I might trot up the road and wait north of the cast. Johnny took them to the steep wooded face of the hill on the north side. There Gatwick stuck his nose in the briars, announced the coyote, and proceeded to run around the patch to where the coyote had come out before ecstatically reconfirming.

The pack honored with a crash and went down through the creek and north across the road where I was sitting quietly on my horse. First, the coyote came out and took a coop into Hyde's field. Then the pack came in full cry and tight formation maybe forty yards behind.

The coyote ran into cattle, which formed a kind of skirmish line and stomped at the coyote. This turned the coyote back westward, and it ran under the pasture fence and circled back to the north. When hounds got near the cows, the herd turned and attacked, scattering hounds in all directions. Some turned all the way around and headed back toward the coop they had just come over.

I immediately galloped past the cows and blew for hounds. As hounds went into the woods I saw Johnny, a real thruster, come flying by on Hyde Road, going north off to my right. I heard Johnny cheer them from on Hyde's hillside. Hounds swung east along the ridge straight for the woods in Charlie Martin's. Karen Gray, who was as usual well in front on a good vantage point, saw Swimmer carrying the line, leave it, and gallop back toward the pack, which was running the line behind him. Swimmer went to a prominence where he could be seen and heard, stopped, and gave tongue, causing the other hounds to throw their heads up and scramble like blazes to get to him. I do not know exactly how to duplicate Swimmer's cry in English, but to that pack it must have sounded something like "All aboard!" Swimmer then went back to the line he had left and led the pack deep into the woods and the night.

## Blowing for Home

Foxhunting is a culture that becomes of great significance in the lifestyle of many who pursue it and who, therefore, want to recognize, at their death, its meaning to them. During my career as a foxhunter, I have had occasion to arrange to have "Gone Away" blown for many foxhunters gone on. It makes a very touching moment at a funeral, recalling as it does the values and friendships of a sportsman whose presence lingers long after the notes of the horn have faded to silence. Some realize hunting to be so much a part of their lives that they elect to be buried in their hunting attire. Harvey Pride was one of these. He died young, and a mutual friend, Herbert Fox, called Alice to borrow a stock to put on Harvey. Alice thought a moment and then said to Herbert, "Borrow it? Why don't I just give it to you?" Nobody would have laughed more heartily than Harvey.

## Notes

1. Nicole Lever, "Huntsman John Gray has an Impeccable Reputation," *The Chronicle of the Horse*, vol. 50, no. 38 (Friday, September 22, 2000): 28.

2. Sir Walter Scott, "The Lady of the Lake: A Poem in Six Cantos." *The Poetical Works of Sir Walter Scott: Including Introduction and Notes* (New York: T. Y. Crowell) Canto First, The Chase, I, 110.

3. Oscar Wilde, "A Woman of no Importance." *Collected Works of Oscar Wilde, including The Poems, Novels, Plays, Essays and Fairy Tales* (New York: Greystone Press), First Act, 314.

4. Jane Ridley, *Fox Hunting* (London: Collins, 1990), 104.

5. *Ibid.*, 101–03.

6. In addition to the references cited in the text of this section, the author also referenced the following works:

    a. Isaac Bell, MFH, *Foxiana* (London: Country Life Ltd., 1929).

    b. Isaac Bell, *A Huntsman's Log Book* (London: Eyre and Spottiswoode, 1947).

    c. W. Lovell Hewitt, *Hare Hunting* (London: Seeley, Service & Co., 1975).

    d. Alexander Mackay-Smith, *Foxhunting in North America* (Millwood, Va.: The American Foxhound Club, 1985).

    e. Thomas Smith, *Extracts from the Diary of a Huntsman* (London: Edward Arnold & Co., 1921).

7. Thomas, *Hounds and Hunting through the Ages*, 13.

8. H. M. R. Budgett, *Hunting by Scent* (New York: Scribner's, 1933).

9. This adage was taught to me by Ben Hardaway, who told me that it was from William Somerville's *The Chase*. However, I have been unable to find this quotation in Somerville's works or in any other source.

10. H. B. C. Pollard, *The Mystery of Scent* (London: Eyre and Spottiswoode, 1937).

11. *Ibid.*, 30.

12. P. C. Spink, "Thoughts on Scent." *Hounds*, vol. 9 no. 3, January/February, 1993: 26.

13. Francis Thompson, "The Mistress of Vision." *Francis Thompson, Poems and Essays* (Freeport, N. Y.: Books for Libraries Press, reprinted 1969), vol. 2, page 9, verse 22.

14. Peter Beckford, *Thoughts on Hunting*, 85.

15. *The Old Blue Pye.*

16. John Masefield, *Reynard the Fox: or The Ghost Heath Run* (London: William Heinemann, 1921), 52.

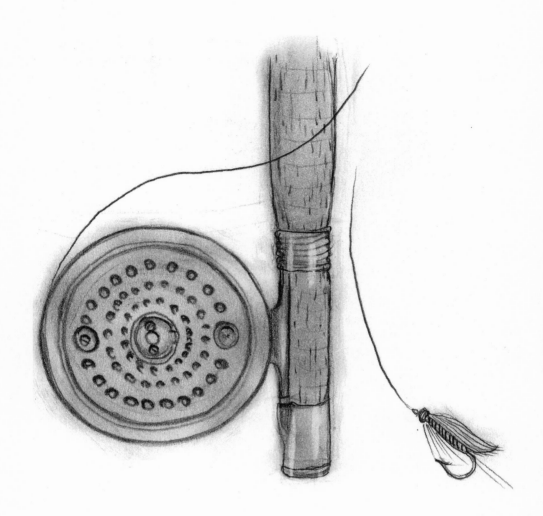

FIN

NINE

# THE FANCY OF FISHING

### The Honeymoon Fish

Alice and I went to Acapulco, Mexico, for our honeymoon. We stayed in a suite with a balcony that overlooked cliffs above the ocean. Cliff divers made spectacular dives off our balcony into waves breaking onto the rocks below. There we were, just arrived. Alice said she would take a bath before lunch. I offered to get a bottle of wine to celebrate our arrival. So Alice got into the tub and I left, supposedly, to find the wine steward. However, after a short wait, I doubled back to our suite, pounded on the door, and shouted in my imitation Mexican accent, "Abrio la puerta, abrio la puerta! Da te prisa!" which was close enough to "Open the door, open the door, quickly!"

Alice answered from the tub in a shy voice, "My husband isn't here. Could you wait a minute?" At that, I made the mistake of repeating my performance. This time Alice recognized my voice. Her identification was confirmed by the giggling of the maids who had stopped to enjoy the joke. "Wait until I get my hands on you," Alice advised. "Just wait." That was how I happened to hurry downstairs to the concierge before Alice opened the door.

The well-tipped concierge had just the ticket for young honeymooners. It was sailfishing. So the next day Alice and I went sailfishing. It was a beautiful scene. No wonder I had heard of an old lady who looked at the Pacific Ocean for the first time and said, "By cracky, that's the only thing I ever liked that there was enough of." The day was warm and sunny. The sea was shining for us. We were young, in love, and off on an adventure. It was natural to hold hands, think of the future, and smile.

Then a big sailfish struck and pandemonium broke loose. The crew was everywhere, getting Alice seated to fight the fish and coaching her. The sail was walking on the water, cavorting, spinning, running, leaping, and twisting in an acrobatic display of fish agility. It was so fascinating that I almost forgot to get my just-purchased honeymoon movie camera to film Alice land the big one. However, the captain was skillful, the tackle was tourist test, and my bride was successful, much to my delight.

When we returned to port, the captain informed us with pride that the fish was nine feet six inches long and weighed one hundred and fifteen pounds. The captain told us that we must, of course, have such a magnificent specimen mounted. Furthermore, he emphatically stated that only a taxidermist in Miami, Florida, was worthy of such a fish. The sail was not the only fish to take bait that day.

In due course, when the fish was delivered to us magnificently mounted, Alice and I got a bottle of champagne and toasted it. Then we started figuring where the fish could be displayed. Her father's recreation room won the process of elimination, and the sail lived there before going to my office and ultimately to an attic. It does not make any difference to me that my memory has temporarily misplaced that fish because the sunny day, the blue sea, the sailfish, the captain and crew, and my magnificent sporting bride are very fresh in my memory. Alice started my enduring interest in fishing with a whopper.

## The Pond Fish

While we were field trialing around and going down to Bill and Joyce Brown's Fox Camp in Mississippi, Alice and I enjoyed the company of the Browns' great friends, Jim and Louise Burke. Bill made sure the Burkes were well mounted. With his characteristic generosity,

he even gave Louise his famous horse Frosty, which had retired the trophy in the High Jump Class at the National Field Trial for Fox-hounds. The Burkes were great fun so it did not surprise us much when Jim presented Bill with a nine-foot-nine-inch mounted sail-fish, which weighed one hundred and eighteen pounds when caught.

Now I do not think Joyce thought she needed that fish domi-nating a room in her camp any more than Louise had fancied it in her elegant house. As usual, Bill came up with the perfect answer. He thanked the Burkes profusely for their wonderfully thoughtful gift and proceeded to hang it on the outside wall of the camp where it was plainly visible to anybody passing in front of the camp on the dirt road. It did not take long for the success of this strategy to be confirmed. The next morning, while we were grooming horses to go hunting, a pickup truck speeding up the road passed the front gate, slammed on the brakes (throwing dust everywhere), backed up, came in the gate up the driveway, and stopped to inspect the display.

"Mr. Brown," the driver inquired, "what kind of fish be that there?"

"Where?" Bill innocently responded.

"There on that there wall," pressed the awestruck driver, pointing at the sailfish in all its splendor.

"Oh, that fish," Bill answered. "That's a pond fish."

"Pond fish? Where do it come from?"

"Don't you have any ponds over where you live?" asked Bill, now back to brushing his horse.

"Yes, suh, sho' do, but I ain't never seen nare fish like that there in any of them ponds over there."

"Well," said Bill, finishing tacking up and glancing towards the kennel gate, "why don't you come over here fishing some time?"

"Yes, suh, sho' 'nuff! We sho' thank you, sho' 'nuff."

We got on our horses, opened the kennel gate, called the hounds, and went hunting. About four hours later we came in to find about thirty people arrayed around the pond with various poles and rods, intensely tending to the business of fishing.

"How does it go?" hailed Bill.

"It's sho' good, Mr. Brown," came the reply. "We done caught a whole mess of crappie."

"Good, good, I'm glad," said Bill, walking on and then adding like an afterthought, "How about pond fish? Have you caught any?"

"No, suh, we ain't got nare one, but Roscoe and Horace saw one."

One of the pleasures of camp thereafter was getting to know these ardent sportsmen who tirelessly hunted the pond fish while we hunted the fox. The Loch Ness monster itself could not have stirred up a more faithful following than those who greeted us with tales of sightings of pond fish.

That happened some years ago, but it would not surprise me to find out that some ambitious angler is sitting with a pole by that pond this very afternoon, as stories of sightings have periodically resurfaced in that country.

## The Bear Fish

One of the things I have learned about fishing is that you do not always catch what you expect. This lesson was brought home to me in a quite dramatic fashion when we went to Montana to stay at Tommy Sloan's, who is my good friend and honorary whipper-in. Since Alice and I had never seen Glacier National Park, I suggested we go early and drive up to Logan's Pass on the Going to the Sun Highway. This plan seemed to work well. We rented a car and made a leisurely swing through beautiful Montana. We stopped at the Charles M. Russell Museum and other points of interest, finally arriving at St. Mary's, the southeastern gate to the park. Here we stopped at the trading store to look around.

As soon as we walked in the door, it was obvious what their most impressive display was. There at the main doors, in the most prominent place, was a glass rectangle around a full grown, stuffed grizzly bear. Moreover, the glass case was only inches away from the bear so you could put your head down and study it in the minutest detail. The big round black eyes, the dish face, the hump back, the caramel coat turning to silver gray, and the huge paws were distinctive features that made a great impression in those close quarters. The plaque explained why this ferocious rogue had had to be hunted down and killed for the sake of the countryside, which it had been terrorizing. Alice and I took the opportunity to study the bear a long time since we had never had a chance to see one at such proximity.

After a while, we left St. Mary's and took a drive through the magnificent park. Then Alice decided to take a nap, and I dropped her off at our motel in the park to sleep while I continued looking around. I soon found myself on the Going to the Sun Highway, heading to Logan's Pass. The scenery was spectacular even in the fading light of early evening and, frankly, I did not notice that the traffic had increased until I got on the western slope of the Continental Divide. Then it occurred to me that Alice might awaken and be ready to go to dinner. I turned around and got in the line of traffic going back the way I came. It was a bit slow, but I was enjoying the scenery and I did not have very far to go, maybe twenty-five or thirty minutes.

Then, to my consternation, I saw that one of those sport utility vehicles coming towards me had stopped in the middle of the two-lane road. "What in the hell?" I thought, and started to put down the window to motion him over so I could pass. Just then, I saw it. It was a grizzly cub, a yearling I would guess, walking by the stopped sport utility vehicle and heading directly toward me. I made sure my doors were locked and took a good look at the cub. However, the look was short lived because just then another cub appeared in the road a few feet behind the first one. I gently brushed the accelerator to be sure my motor was running. "There must be a momma bear there somewhere," I thought, and indeed there was. All at once, she came around into the middle of the road and came straight by her cubs, right towards me. I wondered if my hunting friends would say that it was a good death.

By now the big grizzly bear (maybe eight hundred pounds, judging from the one on display at St. Mary's) was up to my headlights. I could see all the features I had studied at the trading post—the black eyes, the dish face, the hump, the caramel colored fur turning to silver gray at its tips, and those huge deadly paws. However, there was one difference. This time I was in the glass cage and the grizzly was coming at me from the outside of it. Up to the driver's side mirror she came. That powerful head was not more than eighteen inches away from me with only a window she could smash with one swing of her paw between us. The big black eyes were coming towards me as I sat stock-still and gazed into those depths as dark as death. This was no benign Teddy to tuck into bed to sweeten a child's dreams. This was a big menacing mauler and maimer, capable of inflicting destruction and death with devastating quickness and power. "URSUS HORRIBILUS" the sign on the cage at St. Mary's had said. Ursus means bear, I knew. Horribilus I found out about when I looked into that dish face. Just then, she swung her head toward the cliff on the up-mountain side of the pass. One of the cubs had begun climbing that cliff about twelve feet to my left. The bear turned and started up the cliff, climbing easily.

When the bear got about twenty-five feet above the road, all stretched and splayed out, I thought she was the biggest thing I ever saw, big enough to scare the stuffing out of me. However, just then, the cub dropped off the cliff and went by me headed for the down-mountain side of the road to join its littermate. I looked back at the agile mother as she turned and came down from the cliff in a graceful drop onto the highway. She was cat quick, softly landing on the highway then dropping off on the downhill side in pursuit of the cubs. Suddenly, I saw a bunch of crazy people getting out of their cars and running to the downhill side with their cameras at the ready. "Damn fools!" I thought. "Henry, you had better squeeze by that sport utility vehicle because the fool killer might be coming and you might not get a rain check."

I got through with inches to spare and went back to Alice, who was ready for dinner. Guess where we went? Exactly. I wanted to show her the features that had made such an impression on me. After a couple more days exploring the park, we went on to Tommy's, joined our adventuresome friends, John Alden and Elizabeth Rodgers, and caught a lot of trout out of the Yellowstone River. It was a great trip. Dale Sexton, a friend of Tommy's, guided Alice and me. He made it a special occasion, full of learning, laughter, and fun. But you know what? Every time I try to think about those trout, I think of that big-eyed bear. I guess those Yellowstone trout we caught will always remain in my memory as the bear fish.

## The Movie Fish

While I was working in New York, a grouse-shooting friend, Gene Woodfin, suggested that I might like to meet a friend of his. I said that would be fine and Gene had us to dinner at the Running Footman. The friend was presented and sat by me. I, of course, started searching for a topic of conversation. My ineptness, combined with his unpretentiousness, made for slow going. I covered art, adventure, travel, and business without getting much of a rise. I was struggling. He seemed to have nothing he needed to say. Finally I got to shooting, figuring that connection may have been what prompted Woodfin's suggestion that I meet this friend of his. It was with a great sense of relief that I found he had an enjoyable shoot at some ducks circling off the side of Mount Kilimanjaro.

Encouraged by his description of this sporty pass shooting, I asked if he had ever done much fishing.

"Not much," he replied. We sat in silence for a few minutes while I searched my mind for another subject when he added, "But I had a theory."

"What kind of theory?" I asked, thankful for the opening.

"Well, I had this theory that the biggest fish eat the biggest little fish."

"That's interesting," I said.

"And the biggest little fish, according to my theory, eat the most nutritious plankton."

"Well," I inquired, "what did you do about your theory?" thinking to myself that this burst was as near to talkativeness as I had gotten him all evening.

"I had a boat built," he said.

"Oh, really, why?"

"So as to have an especially low transom in the back."

"A low transom?" I was beginning the question when he volunteered the answer.

"So that a really big fish could be brought on board."

"Oh," I said, at a loss for any scrap of conversational inspiration.

"I sent it down off the coast of Peru," he continued.

"Why there?" I asked.

"Because I thought the two ocean currents that came together there scoured up the most nutritious plankton for the little fish to eat and that, therefore, the little fish there would be bigger than the little fish off the coast of New Zealand, where the biggest big fish had been caught."

Now I was in the current myself, scoured up off the conversational bottom and sucked toward some conclusion that yet escaped me.

Then he said, "After a week the boat captain telexed me. He had weighed and measured the little fish where the currents came together and they were bigger, he thought, than the ones off of New Zealand. So I went down there to see my new boat and try to prove my theory."

"And what then?" I eagerly asked, sensing that he had some adventure coming.

"Well, the first day we just took a shakedown cruise, but the next day they took me out to their ranges where the currents came together and scoured up the plankton. So," he said, "I went fishing."

"And how did you do?" I encouraged him.

"I caught the third biggest black marlin in the world and the biggest black marlin in the world."

"The biggest in the world?!" I gasped. "What a thrill!"

"It was 1,560 pounds caught on a 130-pound test line and it still holds that record."

"Wow!" I exclaimed. "How long did you stay?"

"Oh," he said, "I went right home."

"You went home? Why?"

"Well," he looked at me, "I had proved my theory. Of course, there must have been others there at Cabo Blanco, but there will always be others if you hunt long enough in the right places."

"And what did you do then?"

"I sold my boat."

"You sold it? Why?"

"Because I had proved my theory and so I didn't need it."

I tried to understand, but it was so strange to me, so foreign. I tried to grasp it so I could ask some intelligent question. Here was this soft-spoken unassuming man who had had such a great sporting adventure and who had set a world record destined to endure for decades, yet who showed no emotion.

We sat in silence. I was speechless. Then he looked at me and I confessed my perplexity.

"We are from different tribes," I said. "I would have had to stay a few more days to savor the victory."

He merely looked at me blankly until after a few minutes he broke the silence. "Have you ever seen a movie called *The Old Man and the Sea*?" he asked.

"Yes," I said, "that was the movie they made with Spencer Tracy based on the Hemingway novel."

"That's the one," he said. Then, after a pause and a sip of wine, "Did you see that fish?" he asked.

"You mean the fish in the movie?"

"Yes," he said, "that one in the movie."

"Yes, I saw it."

"Then you have seen it," he answered.

"Yes, I saw that one in the movie," I repeated, wondering why he had asked. There was a pause.

"That's my fish," he said. "You have seen it then."

"What do you mean?" I showed my confusion.

He explained, "I took a photographer to Peru with me. That's my fish. The movies bought the film from me. They used it in *The Old Man and the Sea.*"

I stared at him in complete admiration and consternation. "Now I *know* we are from different tribes," I said. "I never would have come home so soon after catching the world record, and I wouldn't have immediately sold the boat—but most of all I would never have had the presence of mind to take along a photographer. I congratulate you." I extended my hand. "I congratulate you, Alfred Glassell."

"Junior," he said. "Alfred Glassell Junior."

I shook his hand and said, "It has been a great pleasure to meet you. Tell me, what did your father do?"

"He created the El Paso Gas Company," he replied with a smile that I can remember even without a photographer.


## The Porch Fish

It was a great boondoggle—a business trip with enough investment bankers and customers for us to put on the dog for a week in Iceland. What's more, I got to take Alice and our son Timmy to round out the group. Once we were ensconced, the routine was more intense than I had followed in Canadian North Atlantic salmon fishing. In Iceland, we got up at about five in the morning, had a quick cup of tea and a piece of fruit or toast, and hit the river. We fished from six until about ten thirty and came in to breakfast. Then we went back and fished until three in the afternoon when we took lunch and about an hour's nap. Then we went back and fished until dinner at about ten at night, after which we fell into bed until the five o'clock call to start it all over again the next morning.

As we were wading most of the time, the cold river and its current made sure that sleep was sound. The company was good and spirits were high as we walked out on the front porch of the lodge and surveyed the river below us winding like a silver ribbon across the Icelandic tundra. To enhance our expectations, a small trophy was put up for the most salmon caught in the week and another was put up for the biggest salmon caught in the week. Certainly neither of these was a concern of mine as there were in our group some expert salmon fishermen. However, I was somewhat dismayed when I was assigned the youngest guide in the party. John was his name in English but something a bit different in Danish. He was a conscientious guide, but he must have been disappointed when he realized what a neophyte he was coaching and guiding. Nevertheless, he took me to the best pools on the beat I was assigned, and he made sure I understood where to cast before he repaired to some ditch or swale where he could lie out of the wind while I beat the water with my clumsy casts. Several days went by and John got a lot of rest in the swales and ditches along the riverbank during which my board chairman, Derald Ruttenberg, caught a mess of salmon out of the slack water from which his guide had said they would not take. I was so intent on catching a salmon where he had taken so many that I passed up the invitation to go with Alice to see a whale processed. As a result, she had a wonderful side adventure seeing that fascinating process while I came up blank again.

However, perhaps seeing my frustration, John asked the next day after lunch, "Do you want to catch a big fish?"

"Of course I do," I said. "What do you think I have been trying to do all week?"

"Well," he said, "come with me. I think I know where there is one."

Alice and I set off following him, which was not easy as he had a ground-covering gait in his hip boots and I was considerably less agile in my waders and hat and carrying my salmon rod. It was quite a long walk, but we finally arrived at an improved pasture where the river seemed to meander through the grasses and wildflowers on which grazed a few Icelandic ponies. John pressed on and we came to a huge boulder about twelve feet high at the edge of the pasture. Here the river separated into two streams, which made a ten or twelve-foot drop into a pool behind the boulder. There was a little ledge in the shadow of the big boulder and John, Alice, and I squeezed onto it to survey the river.

What a scene it was! The river went from that boulder down to the sea in a series of ten waterfalls and pools. Gouging out the granite, the river shone in the gloom of the canyon like a string of pearls leading to the gleaming sea, sparkling in the sunlight at the end of the shadowy canyon. As I looked carefully around, I saw that the little ledge on which we were crowded followed the river down to the sea in a torturous pathway of drops from pool to pool. However, John, who pressed his finger to his lips in a sign to be quiet, interrupted me from my surveillance. I watched him intently. He dropped the Polaroid lenses down over his glasses to take away the glare of the first pool into which he peered. Immediately he turned to Alice and me and signaled silence again. Then he leaned towards us and in a low whisper put my heart rate out the roof.

"Big fish," he said pointing just behind a rock in the center of the pool. "Why is he signaling silence," I thought, "when that fish is bound to hear my heart thumping?" John was busy selecting a fly from my box and tying it on. When it was ready, John showed me exactly where to cast over the protruding rock behind which lay the fish. Nothing! Although my shaking hand had managed to deliver the fly more or less where I was told—nothing. John again pressed his fingers to his lips and proceeded to select another fly, which he used to replace the first. Again, he pointed to the desired spot. Again, I cast it more or less there. Again, nothing was the result. There we were huddled up on that cramped little ledge with me throwing blanks at a fish I could barely see. The seconds seemed to crawl by with excruciating slowness while John selected yet a third fly and attached it to the tippet. Once more he signaled silence, once more he directed the cast.

This time the big salmon surged up and struck it. Suddenly John was shouting, "Tip up, tip up, big fish, big fish!" as before my eyes it came up shaking and flashed over the pool. Then in a surreal moment, it started circling around that rock in the center. Still shouting encouragement and instructions, John suddenly launched himself off that narrow ledge down to the pool, tipping the line over the rock to prevent the fish from breaking off on it. "Big fish! Big fish! Tip up! Tip up!" he repeated from his landing on that slippery rock some eight feet below me. Then, to my astonishment, the fish swam straight up the waterfall on the opposite side of the boulder and started out across the pastures. "He's gone," I thought, as my line sang out and laid against the boulder. However, just then, John gathered himself and leaped up onto the side of the boulder, clinging and crawling up it and tipping the line over it. "Tip up, tip up!" he cried as he scuttled up the boulder to watch the fish run upriver. "Tip up, tip up!" he admonished. "Run! Run!" Run I did towards the disappearing fish as I looked down at my reel and saw that I was nearly out of line. The fish's burst had taken nearly all of it. I thought that it was going to beat me as I clumsily lumbered along in my bulky waders, but just then, it turned. It inexplicably turned and came at me. "Reel! Reel!" cried John. "Reel, reel!" he repeated as the fish came back to the boulder and leapt over the little ten foot waterfall on the off side with John gently slipping the line over the boulder. Again, the fish tried to wrap that center rock sticking out of the pool, but John leapt down off the boulder and tipped the line again. Was this to be it? Was I finally going to get it in my clutches? Just as the hope sprang in me, it was dashed as that silver streak turned towards the sea, jumping from pool to pool and looking for rocks to wrap. "Run! Run!" cried John as he went down the middle of the river leaping from rock to rock and tipping the line like a great basketball player.

If running in the pasture had been hard, running down that narrow ledge with its drops and squeezes against the granite canyon was almost impossible. I was slipping, scraping, and clinging to that narrow ledge in its precarious and precipitous plunge down the canyon to the river. Moreover, Alice was instructing me to "Throw away the rod. You're going to be killed!" So there we were, my leaping and tipping ghillie screaming, "Run! Run!"; my wife screaming, "Throw away the rod. You're going to be killed!"; and me tripping and slipping and scraping down the canyon ledge expecting any second to fall off into the canyon or see my big fish disappear into the sun-bright foam where the river came out of the shadows into the sea. But just as I somehow got to the bottom, John dove off the last rock into the white water, wrapped his arms around the big fish, rolled with it up onto the bank where I was bent over panting, and said, "Hit it with a rock." I did and John rolled off of it as the salmon gave a last great shudder.

Alice looked at the scene as she carefully climbed down to us and immediately saw that the hook had gone through the salmon and was buried to the eye in the heel of John's hand. "We must get you to the infirmary," she said, taking his hand to inspect it. "No," he said, looking at the fish and then at the sun. "There is light left and you are beginning to catch on to this," he said as he looked at me. We fished a while longer but got back to the lodge in time to show the fish in the white light. The party and the guides, the cooks and the staff, all came to see it. It was put down on that porch overlooking the river and a burning piece of wood was brought out. The outline of the fish was burned on the porch with my initials and the date and the weight of the fish, which I think was twenty-five pounds. They gave me that little trophy that has long since been misplaced—except in my memory where it remains a souvenir of a Danish lad with great athleticism and drive and of that gallant porch fish.

## It Hunts by Scent

Alice and I had gone to southeast Alaska with Joe and Polly Murphy to see the icebergs, visit the great Tongass rain forest, and cruise the inner passage in the domain of eagles, humpback whales, and coastal grizzly bears. We were on a converted mine sweeper, the *Liseron*, with nineteen passengers and a crew of nine. Many of the passengers were experienced fishermen, so I naturally made a damned fool out of myself by telling them the story of the "porch fish" Atlantic salmon I was lucky enough to catch in Iceland some years ago.

The activities offered by the *Liseron* were varied and enjoyable until the next to last day when we went halibut fishing in a small skiff in a cold rain. We were told to lower our lure, which was baited with a herring, to the bottom at one hundred and five feet or so, give it a couple of cranks up, and then sit. This is a good way to get hypothermia and become bored all at the same time.

After several hours we were taken back to the ship for a welcome warm shower and a tumbler of whiskey, having had what I supposed would be our first and, thankfully, final experience with halibut fishing. But not quite. That night we anchored at Mole Harbor next to the island the Indians call Koozoonoohoo (Land of the Bears). The next day I was talking to the captain, Steve Riehemann, about the halibut and he related that it lurks camouflaged on the bottom waiting for its prey, which it hunts by scent. Suddenly there were those words that have characterized so much of my sporting life, whether it is after coyotes, quail, or Chanel No. 5 luring me to the dance floor. "Hunts by scent?" said I as I reminisced about the great runs, the covey rises, and . . . well, you get the point.

"I'll go halibut fishing today," I immediately volunteered and went to rig up in rain suit, rubber boots, fishing hat, life preserver, and polarized glasses. "Hunts by scent; hunts by scent," kept going through my mind as I tried to visualize a great fish chiseled and changed from prehistoric times into the efficient predator of the cold darkness and depth of those glacially fed waters. A dark fish lying on its white bottom with one of its eyes moved by evolution into a socket protruding from the topside of its head to watch out above in that kill-and-be-killed, eat-and-be-eaten environment of wondrous beauty and deadly struggle.

"Hunts by scent; hunts by scent," I thought. "So I will catch it by scent in honor of all the hounds and bird dogs and foxes at the dance who have taught me so much of the mystery and magic of the chase."

The captain took our skiff to his spot, marked in his mind by ranges of things on the far-off shores, and we put our bait and sinkers to the bottom at about one hundred and five feet. A couple of cranks up and I was ready to begin the long sitting vigil to see what luck there might be. However, today there was a difference. "It hunts by scent," I said to myself as I began systematically to jig my rod up and down to make my herring move a few inches up and down in the water with each jig. It was still a sedentary pursuit for me, but I cherished a new hope because I had heard the secret: "It hunts by scent." The captain's mother, Jane, and Joe Murphy were in the skiff with me and soon Jane caught a twenty-five or so pound halibut much to the glee of all of us. It was good to know for sure that they were down there.

The jigging went on as I asked the captain, "What is the best time to catch them?" "When the tides change," he said, and I figured that made sense if it hunts by scent because the reversal of the tide would scour up prey from the bottom and produce currents to carry the scent and change the temperature to make the scent more easily detected by my quarry waiting in the deep. While I was working on this theory for encouragement, I felt a twinge on my rod. Was it the change in the tide or had some passing forager in the kelp had a snack on my herring? Very deliberately, so as not to jerk the hook, I raised the tip of my rod to see if I needed to reel in and inspect my bait. As I raised the tip, I felt a wonderfully encouraging tug and then a mighty pull. My rod bent into an inverted "U." I was holding my rod up but the tip was pointing straight down at the ocean floor. "Have I hooked the planet earth or is it a big halibut?" I wondered. Then it took the line out and there was no stopping its powerful run. It was either a homesick devil or a big fish.

Immediately the captain began to coach. "Don't pull against it. Take only what it gives you. Let it tire. Crank when you lower and then let it take some back. Do you need a fighting belt?" I tried a belt. "This belt isn't working." (Which was bad news considering where I had the back end of the handle of the rod; it was not only the fish among things in danger). Nevertheless, I held on and fought on. "It must be big," said the captain, "real big." For forty minutes or so, I fought. "Hold on, hold on." I followed instructions, and I held on despite a mind wandering to endangered precious parts. Then, little by little, I worked it closer, ever closer, to the boat. The captain readied the harpoon. "Don't get its head out of the water. Don't let it see you or the boat. It will go crazy when it does." I could feel its presence. Then I saw its dark hulk as it glided past the skiff.

I had the sense that this would be the crux, that we must set the harpoon before something busted loose. "Get ready!" I croaked, as I worked it back by and the captain struck with the harpoon just as the huge dark halibut saw us and went crackers. Suddenly I saw the white bottom as it bucked and rolled. In halibut language, "Hell No!" is expressed by furious thrashing, roiled water everywhere, and power strokes to take it back to the bottom. However, the cat-quick captain secured the rope from the harpoon. It was just in time. During that ocean rodeo, the halibut had bitten the leader in two and would have been gone, irretrievably gone, back to its lair were it not for the harpoon and rope. Quickly, but with an unhurried economy of motion, the captain skillfully placed another harpoon in the hell-raising fish and surveyed it approvingly. "We'll have to lash it to the side," he said. "It's too big and too strong and too full of fight to put in here with us." "Suits me," I said, thinking how good and free it felt to have the butt of that rod out of the threatening position it had been in during the fight.

So just like *The Old Man and the Sea*, we lashed it to the skiff and started back to the ship. Frankly, I was in a kind of euphoria. I had a very positive attitude adjustment when that great dark monster was finally secured at our side. I knew the captain was radioing ahead and that crew and passengers would be there to take pictures and congratulate us, but I supposed the captain said nice things about every halibut caught by one of his passengers. I sat there assuming it was no big deal and enjoyed the ride, musing over other hunts and other rides that somehow led to this place and were part of this adventure. After all, "It hunts by scent."

Then as we rode along I noticed the captain stepping up to have a look over the side. It seemed every few minutes he would step up, look again, and then say, "*That* is a really *big* fish!"

As we neared the ship I could hear the other passengers and the crew cheering, and I knew they were taking pictures. Yet I sat quietly facing the stern. Then, just before coming alongside, I stood up, turned, and threw my arms into the air. It was very testing for the photographers and competitive fishermen, who were tempted to throw their cameras in the water but restrained themselves and instead began to chant: "Big fish, big fish, tip up, tip up," cajoling me with the words from the Icelandic salmon-fishing story I had told them earlier in the voyage.

Then the haul chain was put over the side. It was attached to the fish very carefully to ensure it did not slip off and return to the bottom in an agonizing last minute loss.

The scales, usually hooked up in series with the chain and the fish, could not be used because they only went to two hundred pounds and would be broken if my halibut were put on them. It was beginning to dawn on me what the captain meant when he said, "*That* is a really *big* fish!"

The fish was secured, lifted onto the ship, hung, and measured. It was six feet six inches long from its nose to the middle of its tail. According to the charts, that made it two hundred and fifty-five pounds and forty-one years old, exactly the number of years I had been foxhunting. By strange coincidence or twist of fate, that fish had been waiting for our decisive rendezvous the whole time I had been learning to hunt by scent. The mystic connection between the hunter and the hunted swept over me. The foe fought well. Now I would honor it by telling its story.

This was the largest halibut caught from the *Liseron*, and perhaps the largest by the boat company. When the fish was cut open, we found a pink salmon, my herring, and three large Dungeness crabs inside it. It could not have done better dining at the Savoy at a table by the window.

Dinner that evening was very festive with the other passengers giving sporting toasts and warm congratulations. One lady made up a funny story about Lord and Lady Hooker having a "Habilot" party, always mispronouncing the fish to rhyme with "Camelot." Alice, true to form, gave everybody all the halibut they wanted. The remaining eighty pounds of halibut steaks were vacuum packed, blast frozen, and FedExed to Nashville where they arrived before ten o'clock the next morning, some eight days before we made it home.

It was great fun, but it was luck. It was just luck, the kind of luck I love. And as long as you are going to have great luck, it is fun to have some theory that at least you had something to do with it. Like, you can say, "It hunts by scent . . . so do I."


## The Seven-Fly Salmon

Since my first invitation from Ned and Nina Bonnie to Groton Plantation in South Carolina, I was fascinated by the lifestyles of Nina's father, Robert Winthrop, and her uncle, Fred Winthrop. Their annual cycle of duck shooting, quail shooting, trout fishing, salmon fishing, grouse shooting, partridge shooting, and back to quail shooting seemed idyllic to me. I avidly listened to them recount their adventures. Their prowess with rod and gun and their appreciation of the far lands and waters where they took their sport stirred my imagination and gave me a standard that stuck in my mind. Descriptions of the moors and the marshes, the bicolor strips, and the olive tree groves danced in my fancy. And, of course, great rivers ran in the accounts of their adventures.

The most fascinating of these rivers was the Moisie, where Bob Winthrop fished for Atlantic salmon all of his adult life and where he caught some whoppers. The magnificent Moisie and its scenic passages remained in my mind, prompted by pictures painted by Ogden Pleissner that I have seen and admired in plantations and houses visited on my wanderings in search of fox, fin, and feather. The great landscape and sporting artist caught the beauty and the tranquility of that place. Although I might see it only in pictures and experience it only in the stories of friends, I was an enthralled listener to tales of this enchanting river.

Then Ned Bonnie invited me to stay in the Winthrop cabin and fish the Moisie River near Sept Illes, in eastern Quebec, north of the St. Lawrence River. Ned and his son Shelby had leased Jonathan Winthrop's and Robbie Winthrop II's rods for a week at the height of the season in June. Jonathan and Robbie are Robert Winthrop's nephews and members of the Moisie River Salmon Club, consisting of only twelve rods and in existence for over fifty years. Business commitments made Shelby cancel his fishing plans at the last minute. This meant that Ned and I could fish two rods (Jonathan's and Robbie's) instead of one rod for an entire week. Anticipation permeated my bones. So what if I might shoot a blank? I could not wait. Skunked or not, I would get a turn in such a place as dreams are made of and maybe there would be a susceptible salmon.

Ned and I met in Montreal and flew on to Sept Iles. We arrived in time for dinner. It happened that Charlie Godchaux and Judge Jack Weiner were there. I knew the first from college and the second from law school. Fred and Jane Hamilton, shooting friends of Kate Ireland, and my nephew, John Ingram, came later in the week. There were others, ladies and gentlemen who had come from far away places to rendezvous with the salmon season. They were good company and there was a certain focus, a singularity of purpose, as they described their ruminations and ramblings around the world in search of fun in pursuit of fin. Their conversation did nothing to hasten sleep, nor did Robbie and Jonathan Winthrop, who regaled me with river reminiscences and who rigged me with Robbie's Bogden reel and a ten-foot Sage rod before leaving the next day.

The next morning was bright with blue skies. The river was dark but clear, swiftly cutting through the stunted spruce forest. The motor launch and the canoes were at the dock with the gaffers and the anchormen at the ready.

After breakfast, we got in the boats and went to our appointed pools. Now and then, a salmon jumped, working its way upstream. The gaffers and anchormen knew the river, pool-by-pool, rock-by-rock. They knew how they wanted the boat to hang and drift as the gaffer instructed me how and where to cast. Their surveillance of the water was intense. They hunted the salmon. They searched for its sign. Then a salmon rolled at a fly, and they commanded the two-minute drill. That meant I had to wait two minutes before throwing a fly at it again. I do not know who discovered this tactic, but it was very effective. Somehow, those two minutes were very motivational for the salmon. The selection of the flies was very important, with the Monroe Killer, the Blue Charm, and the Mickey Finn being particularly popular. However, if the fish rolled again and did not take, then it was time to "changéz la mouche"—change the fly.

My gaffer and anchorman were cousins, Ludwig Beaudin and Roland Beaudin. They were skilled canoeists and avid salmon hunters, observing every ripple and movement. Ludwig could cast a fly about fifty percent farther than I, a fact that he demonstrated with regularity and obvious satisfaction. Ned and I for the most part fished from the same canoe, and I got good fly-casting and fishing lessons from him. I invented a game of casting at bubbles as they went by. This improved my casting and made the unproductive time go faster. Occasionally a tiger swallow tail butterfly flitted over the sunlit water out beyond the shadows. Things went well.

We were both catching fish and enjoying company and country until it rained the third night. The next morning the water was muddy and, although we had one of the best pools, it was nothing doing until Ned picked the biggest fly in his box and got a salmon to take just before lunch. That was, I think, one of only two salmon caught in the river that day. Anyway, even though I used a fly like Ned's that afternoon, my scorecard showed up blank for my sojourn in the muddy pools. This redoubled my determination, and Ludwig sensed it. The next day Ludwig kept changing flies to find one that might work in the still muddy but slightly clearing water. Finally, he put on a small Monroe Killer, and I caught a good-sized salmon. He immediately took that fly and put it on Ned's tippet. Within ten minutes, Ned had one on, which he eventually landed. I thought we were off to the Camptown Races, but that was it for the day. Fishing is as fickle as a filly on the dance floor.

Then came the final morning of our expedition. We had drawn a pool called Jordan. It is in some ways the hardest pool to fish at the club because the current there is very strong making the canoe very tippy, and if a powerboat comes by, the wake is treacherous. Moreover, Jordan is in the ominous shadows of a rock cliff. I noticed Ludwig and Roland put on their life jackets whenever we fished there. The last morning was no exception. The current was strong and choppy, and the wind was blowing upriver right in my face. I had to cast hard and be careful at the same time so as not to throw myself out of the boat. Ludwig was, I am sure, dying to get his hands on my rod, but he restrained himself. Then when I was about three quarters of the way out to the farthest I could throw it in that wind, a salmon rolled. "You see da fish?" asked Ludwig. "Oui," said Roland before I could answer. "Deux minutes," said Ludwig, with two fingers in the air, holding my rod away from the side of the boat where the fish had rolled. We waited two minutes with the boat rocking and my heart pounding. "Please beautiful salmon, don't leave us," I thought, as I stared at my watch.

Then it was time. Ludwig pointed to the left side of the boat where the fish had rolled. I cast and mended the line so the fly would swing straight in front of the silver salmon. It rolled again. Ludwig grabbed the rod and held it back over to the right. "Changéz le mouche, no like da fly," he said and started his work with clippers and knots. After carefully testing the knot, he dropped the new fly in the water and gestured with his hand where to throw it. Again, I gave it my best effort and waited with pounding heart only to see the fish roll again. "Gudt. Changéz la mouche. No like da fly," said Ludwig as he caught my line and started the procedure and the two-minute drill all over again.

So it went, with me riding that bucking canoe in the gale, Ludwig changing the flies, and six straight two-minute drills before Ludwig reached back to my reel and pulled out about three-and-a-half more inches of line. "A leetle bit," he explained, smiling mysteriously. Then he gestured with his hand to the left indicating where he wanted me to cast. I followed his instructions. "Gudt," he grunted, as I mended the line. Just then, the fish struck. Suddenly it was on. I held the tip of the rod up as the powerful salmon ran to the middle of the river and leapt out of the water into the sunlight. It was a silver streak, bright from the sea. It must have been three feet in the air shaking and shining. "Beau pêche!" exclaimed Roland. "Don't lose this fish, Henry," I told myself. "This is your last fish of the week. Be careful."

Ned began coaching and encouraging me as we drifted and the Beaudins paddled. That feisty salmon was sideways in the center current, taking the line out at a high-pitched whine. It is a sound that produces the same reaction as "Point!" and "Tallyho!" It was the culmination of a wonderful week, a great sporting experience. I looked back at the scene of the river and the woods and the other canoes anchored at their pools. The sight painted a Pleissner in my mind of the Seven-Fly Salmon. The music of the reel and the line, the rush of the river, the splash of the salmon, and Ned's encouragement whispering in the wind were all part of the poetry of that place.

When the beautiful salmon was taken, we went ashore and said our good-byes and thank-yous. Ludwig and Roland seemed pleased to be called "bon pêcheurs." As for Ned, who has had so many sporting adventures with me, it was a pleasure to thank him and his sons, Shelby and Robert, for an unforgettable thrill.

Thanks, men. The Pleissner is in place—in my mind and on these pages.

FEATHER

## TEN

# SHOOTING STARS

### Ames Plantation

When I was thirteen years old my father, John Jay Hooker Sr., and my uncle, Seth Walker, took me big game hunting in Montana and Wyoming. It was an exciting experience. We packed into the mountains with cowboy guides and a cook named Jack, who was always prospecting for gold. At night after dinner, Jack would tell me about Cooter Brown, a drunken brawler who made his mark in Alaska during the Gold Rush. I learned the meaning of the expression, "drunker than Cooter Brown," which has stuck in my vocabulary ever since.

When I graduated from college and was getting ready to go off to basic training camp courtesy of the U. S. Army draft, my father took me bird shooting at the Ames Plantation in Grand Junction, Tennessee, where the National Field Trial for Bird Dogs is held annually. Alan Pruitt, the chief justice of the Supreme Court of Tennessee, and Associate Justice Swepston were there. The night before the big shoot, Rube Scott, the head of the whole operation, had us up to the big house for dinner.

It was quite an evening. My father and these members of the judiciary evidently believed that the truth is in the bottom of the glass, and they set about to find it. The next day when we met the dog wagon and the horses, I was the only one designated to shoot. There was plenty of game and I got my share even though Chief Justice Pruitt insisted that I shoot his gun. It was an old double-barreled Parker with a broken stock patched with friction tape. It would, however, fill up a croaker sack if you pointed it at the birds.

As the end of the day neared, Justice Swepston, who had had cancer of the larynx and spoke in a strange loud whisper, offered to shoot the last covey with me. He got down off his horse and we advanced to the dogs. When the birds flushed, they all seemed to go to Justice Swepston's right, directly in front of me. I shot a couple and turned to him. "Great shot, Judge!" I said, putting my hand on his shoulder. He did not quibble about the allocation of the bag. He looked me in the face and said, "Thank you, young man," as the birds were collected and the dogs were put back in the wagon. The next morning we made our good-byes, and I went on to the army and then to law school.

About four years later, I made my first argument before the Supreme Court of Tennessee. Mr. Justice Swepston was on the bench. He seemed to be studiously reading the record, which caused me some concern until he looked me in the eye as I was leaving and whispered loudly, "Great shot, young man!"

My Friend Gus and the Duck Shoot

One of my first legal jobs was to guide a company pension plan through qualification and enrollment. This caused me to meet an actuary named Bob who was a great cribbage player, maybe the best I ever played. I was very excited when Bob invited me up to northern Minnesota for a duck hunt. His recitation of adventures in the wild rice wetlands had my head dancing with anticipation. At last, the appointed weekend came, and I flew to the Twin Cities. Bob and his two duck-hunting pals met me at the airport in their station wagons with skiffs in tow. Inside the wagons were mountains of gear and guns. Amidst the decoys, the coats, the waders, and so forth, the dogs sat, proudly surveying their domain. Bob introduced me to his German shorthair, Gus, a fine looking dog with very sympathetic eyes. Next Bob even showed me a picture of his pretty wife and five fine children. He had not been to the hospital for the birth of any of them, he said, because they had all been born during duck season, so he and Gus had been "gone hunting." When I found out that he had made his own boat and loaded his own shells, I should have known I was overmatched.

Away we went on a wintry night headed straight north. After several hours of driving, we arrived at their lodge for a late dinner and bedtime. However, there was no sleep for me because I was so excited and so conscious of the need to sleep fast because we would be getting up before dawn. When the wake-up call came, I was all ready to go. I tried to help pack up and launch the boats with the dogs on board, but the three experts moved so swiftly and quietly and with such an economy of motion that my proffered help was more of a hindrance than a help to their smooth routine. We were soon afloat in the marsh gliding over the gooney grass in the darkness. The hunters knew their places and slid into little tufts of vegetation to await the dawn flights. I could hear the wild wings making a whistling noise over my head and regretted that it was too dark to shoot. Just then, Bob leaned forward, quietly lifted his shotgun, and fired. "Bam, bam! Splash, splash!" went the sequence, sending Gus out of the boat in a high arching leap to retrieve. However, at the apex of his launch, he was suddenly stopped and slapped down into the water by his collar and chain. "Oh no!" said Bob in a whisper. "I forgot to unhook him."

The dog swam around in the freezing cold water while Bob unhooked his collar and situated him to take signals for the retrieve.

Gus gave us a baleful look and asked Bob some searching questions in dog language, but finally went after the ducks and brought them back to the boat where he was hoisted aboard to shiver. That dog was a champion shiverer. Moreover, he could shiver and think about ducks at the same time. Bob would watch Gus as he looked rearward over Bob's shoulder, and whenever there was a chance I was going to let any ducks get close enough to get a shot, Bob would see Gus's eyes following the flight, would seize his gun, whirl, and take two out of my range.

By the time he was on his second fifty ducks, I figured it out that I had to go somewhere else if I was going to get even one duck. Bob produced a plank, maybe two feet long and a-foot-and-a-half wide, for me to stand on so the swamp would not suck me down. He stationed me aboard the plank in my waders off in the gooney grass. I was happy beyond belief when I got some mallards working to my call. To my satisfaction, they came right in close, and I triumphantly dispatched them into the wetlands. What a mistake! I immediately realized that the recoil from my shot had driven me down in the gooney like a nail, and I went from being hip deep to being barely able to hold my nose out of the water. Adding insult to injury, Bob, in his haste to keep me from drowning or at least salvage my shotgun (which I was holding above my head), forgot Gus was unchained. So Gus got to me and went after my ducks. This caused a bit of confusion because when he finally arrived, Bob seemed more interested in getting Gus back than in getting me back.

Well, with much help and whispered instructions, I did manage to get myself back in the skiff. However, I was completely unprepared for my host's next statement. He looked me in the eye and said, "You are in danger. The temperature is dropping. It will get well below freezing and we still have several hours of shooting left. Unless you do something you will be in terrible trouble." "What should I do?" I asked in my miserable wet condition. "Shiver," he said. "Shiver yourself warm. Let your teeth chatter. Shake all over until you begin to dry out." "Well, hell," I thought, "if these guys think I am going to beg them to take me in, I am going to show them these Southern boys don't wilt so easily."

Some fancy shooting by Bob and his friends and great retrieving by Gus and his friends—and some serious shivering by me—took up the rest of the afternoon. When it got dark, we started in and, believe it or not, I felt pretty good. Then they explained to me the need for quiet. "Listen," they said, "these are the meanest game wardens in North America. They are hooked up with Immigration, the Canadian police, and the Highway Patrol. They have these very effective noise detectors. Whatever you do, no flashlights. They will be on us in no time." "Got it," I whispered, wondering how things were back home.

Bob's friends beached their boat very quietly. Then they turned to help Bob with our boat as he glided the bow up onto the bank. Delighted to be going back to the lodge, a splash of whiskey, and a good fire, I stood up and walked forward to disembark. Just then, the hunters grasped the bow of the boat and gave it a vigorous jerk to put it well up on the bank. They all later assured me that it was a perfect back flip. All I know is that my feet ended up in the air and my face and shotgun barrels were stuck in the mud. It came closer to killing them than me because they couldn't laugh or make a sound. They were all doubled over, first holding their sides, then covering their mouths.

Finally, they hauled me out. This time the admonition was more severe. "Look. You will freeze up and get sick quick if you don't do something, so while we hide the ducks, you take off all of your clothes, get in the station wagon with the dogs, and put over you whatever coats and blankets and things you can find, and stay under them so the heat from the dogs warms you up." "Oh, well," I thought, "at least it's not so far to the lodge, a drink of whiskey, and that good fire." I did as I was told while watching them hide ducks in the spare tire, in the hubcaps, under the hood, and other bizarre places.

Soon we were on our way and I was mighty happy when I heard the wheels get off the wilderness road and onto a highway. Then the wagons turned and stopped and my friends piled out. I rose up and peered out to see if we were back at the lodge. To my horror, I discovered we were in a Red Owl shopping center, right in front of a Red Owl store. You could have read a newspaper by the light in that parking lot. Then I looked at the car sitting next to me. It was a

Highway Patrol car with two troopers drinking coffee. "My God," I thought, "they could get me for indecent exposure, a quadzillion ducks, *and* unnatural friendships with dogs!"

I am happy to say that about that time my hosts came out of the Red Owl where they had purchased the ingredients for a delicious dinner, which they prepared and I ate sitting by the fire with Gus and friends.

I learned from that night of anguish that I can never be happy hunting without a license when one is required and I can never be comfortable when my host shoots over the limit or expects me to. It is not just the law of which I am afraid and respectful, it is mindfulness of all the creatures that would be here now if all hunters were sportsmen aware of sustainable use of renewable resources.

## Bob Winthrop and Aunt Meg

Alice and I were invited by Ned and Nina Bonnie to go with them to Groton Plantation at Estill Springs, South Carolina, which was owned by Nina's father and uncles. It was twenty-three thousand acres, part swamp and part magnificent quail shooting. Sometimes it seemed to go on forever. Once I even heard the spotter say to the dog handler, "I ain't ever been in this part of the world before."

Nina's father, Bob Winthrop, was famous for his prowess as a wing shot and a fly fisherman. His wonderful wife, called Aunt Meg by Nina and us, enjoyed sport with him. She was a superb hostess. On one of our visits I put my bag down on the luggage rack, which collapsed like fiddle sticks. She bolstered me up and then at dinner she looked at me and said, "I heard you were a Democrat; the first we've ever had on the plantation." I told her that a great Tennessee sportsman, Rogers Caldwell, told me to stay away from a woman's hips and vote a straight Democratic ticket, but that I had not adhered to that political advice.

## Poochie and Charles Berry

Bill and Joyce Brown had some great friends in Columbus, Mississippi, named Poochie and Charles Berry. Well, her real name is

Lounora, which is kind of between a rock and a hard place with Poochie. They were great sports and the Browns got them to include Alice and me in their fun. They had a big farm and swamp called Hogeye, full of game. Moreover, Poochie is a superb chef with a staff at her direction. Charles is a great shot, as are many of his friends, but all he wants to do is see that his guests are having fun. We had wonderful sport with them. Poochie is a very good rider. She had a little horse we called Bouncing Bunny that she rode over whatever came in front of her and lent it to Nina Bonnie to do the same when she was not there.

Charles had a big dove shoot for his friends, their boys, and their boys' friends. It was very festive. I played the card game crazy eights with the boys for laps around the outside of the house and we supplemented the winnings or losses by throwing rocks at a stop sign, or betting on the dove bag, or playing tennis. It was a relaxing and tiring day but if you were the first one to sleep, you might wake up as I did with Erno Lazlo's seaweed gunk on your face, put there by Poochie and Joyce and the other ladies to keep me from looking old.

Alice and I puzzled over what to take the Berrys for a gift since we had so much fun as their guests. Then Poochie mentioned that she liked good wines, but that they were hard to get in Columbus. With that as the clue, I got a case of Latour, a case of Margaux, and a case of Haut Brion to take her the next time we went there. She was ecstatic and we thought we had hit the jackpot.

The Berrys had a very good friend named Dr. John Murphy. He was a prominent ear, nose, and throat doctor; however, his favorite pastime was hunting. On the day the wine arrived, Poochie was in the kitchen supervising the lunch for fifty she was serving to the hunters as they came up out of the field. The wine had been put down on the corner of one of the tables when it was delivered. Johnny Murphy eased over to the three cases and began opening the bottles. "Here, try this one," he urged a friend. Charles was probably down in the field riding around to see if his guests had everything they needed. Well, you would not think fifty or sixty hunters could drink thirty-six bottles of Bordeaux with their barbecue lunch. But they can. I know because I saw them do it at Hogeye, and I saw Poochie and Charles laugh it off like perfect sports. I knew Charles really wanted to sic Mighty Dog, his Jack Russell terrier that slept in the bed with him and Poochie, on Johnny Murphy, but he didn't.

When Poochie told me stories of her childhood, I was fascinated and I understood her resilient approach to life. Charles and I always had some good-natured banter. He was redheaded and rose beautifully to the fly. He regarded me as a tenderfoot. When we were going on a walk-up quail shoot, he told me to just stop when I got too tired. He said he was used to walking in his factories, and he realized I led a more sedentary life. I took a wrong turn to get a little lost and wound up getting us really lost. We did not get in for lunch until about three o'clock in the afternoon. The ladies were worried about us, but Bill Brown just figured we were lost. So he knew where we were—lost. Charles immediately started telling on me—how I had gotten him lost and had not stopped to rest since nine o'clock that morning. He probably would have told more if he had not fallen asleep with his head on the lunch table before he even ate lunch. You might think he would not go bird shooting with me anymore after that, but he is a good-natured sport.

It was not but a few years later that he took Bill and me on a little walking shoot where he knew the way. Everything seemed to be going fine, and he was telling a story when I happened to see a skunk lining up on him and checking windage. Charles was busy talking and headed right for the target area when I said, "Excuse me, Charles." But, he went on with his story, so I said again, more loudly, "Excuse me, Charles."

"What in the hell do you want, Hooker? Can't you tell this is a timing joke? Don't you know that your interruptions are throwing my timing off?"

"Well, Charles," I said, "I am sorry to stop you, but if you take two more steps that skunk by the oak tree is going to spray you good."

"Oh my God, Hooker. You have saved me. If that skunk sprayed me, they would have washed me with tomato juice and Poochie wouldn't sleep with me for a week."

"It's worse than that, Charles. I don't even believe Mighty Dog would sleep with you," I responded.

"That's right, Hooker. You are good for something after all," he said, carefully reversing his path. We never did hear the end of his joke.

Some years later Charles and Poochie and their friends, Ray and Dai Waters and Dr. John Murphy, went grouse shooting in Scotland with us. The Scottish keepers and the beaters were very impressed with their shooting. Those Mississippi boys were quick and deadly. Later when we went on to Ireland, they got all fired up because some horse trainer was feeling Alice's ankle. "He's just showing her how to feel if a horse has bowed," I explained to them. They greeted my explanation with some grumbling. Based on their shooting and their attitude, I don't think checking ladies' ankles is very safe in Mississippi.

## Miss Pansy

I found a good looking mare and set about to get her bred by Mr. Fiske, the sire of my good horse, Mr. Fox and his half brother, Mr. Frost. The task was not easy because the stud belonged to Mrs. Parker Poe, a soft-voiced lady who had the reputation for meaning it when she said no. After a long conversation, Mrs. Poe asked me to call her Pansy, but settled for Miss Pansy. She gave me permission to breed to her great hunter stallion, Mr. Fiske, and then invited Alice and me to stop on our way to Florida and visit her at her lunch house, Quail Roost, on Mayhaw Plantation in Thomasville, Georgia. Ogden Pleissner and Josh, Miss Pansy's great dog handler, were there. Miss Pansy held up the shooting party so we could meet them. It never occurred to me that day that I would never see either Ogden or Josh again.

In the fall of 1967, Alice and I went to the Chagrin Valley Hunter Show in Cleveland, Ohio, with Ned and Nina Bonnie. It was great fun, chiefly because Miss Pansy was there. Miss Pansy and I were a Mutt and Jeff combination because she was only five feet tall in a high wind. She had twinkling dark eyes and the habit of summoning me with a crook of her finger when she wanted to tell me something. When thus summoned, I would fold up my six-foot-five-inch frame and put my ear next to her mouth to hear her whisper.

She arranged for her niece, Louise Humphrey, to invite us out with the Woodfield Beagles, of which Louise was master. We met early. Miss Pansy drove a jeep, and Alice and I were on foot. We had a great morning dashing around after Louise's hounds. When the hunt was over, Miss Pansy suggested that I might like to see the kennels. When we got there, the huntsman, Doug Little, showed me about forty couple of beagles. First he drew the bitches, then the dogs. Then he drew them by litter and sire and dam. I was standing there minding my own business when the question came. "Which four do you think we ought to take to Bryn Mawr for the pack class?" Wow! There were eighty beagles wriggling around in there, and I was supposed to draw four of them for a national championship quality pack class? Reluctantly, and filled with trepidation, I began to choose. "I don't believe it," Doug said to Miss Pansy and Louise. "Three of those four are the ones I was going to take and the fourth is the sire."

When the visit was over, we made our manners and were taking our leave when Doug slid by me and told me that the Chagrin Valley huntsman would like me to visit his kennel as well. That afternoon I went to the Chagrin Valley Foxhounds kennels. They showed me their hounds and I asked about a handsome English dog hound.

"Oh, that's Beaufort Standard," they said. "The Duke of Beaufort sent that hound to Mrs. Humphrey when he met her at the Royal Winter Fair."

"Well, he didn't send a beautiful lady any ugly hound," I observed. "How does he do in the field?"

"Great," the huntsman enthusiastically replied.

"Are you breeding him?" I asked.

"No," came the chorus. "Mrs. Humphrey's joint master always wants to breed to a certain hound he knows and can recognize out hunting."

The plot was then plain to me. They wanted to breed to Beaufort Standard but were frustrated. "Put a leash on him," I said, "and let me borrow him for a while." I then walked with him down to Miss Pansy's box at the horse show. She immediately picked up on it. "What have you got there?" she asked, eyes twinkling at me. "The future greatest sire of the Chagrin Valley," I responded. After a discussion of his conformation, Miss Pansy smiled in a way that made me know Standard would get his chance. Then she began to talk about Alice and me coming shooting. It was a great opportunity for Standard but an even greater one for us.

## The Howard Stovalls

Miss Pansy started inviting us shooting that year although her husband, Parker, made himself scarce until he found out that we were not too "horsey" to suit him. The Howard Stovalls were with us the first time. Thankfully, Eleanor Stovall caught me on the way to breakfast the first morning and suggested I might be more comfortable in a tie at breakfast. She was right—Pebble Hill was a very formal place. Colonel Howard Stovall was a great warrior, sportsman, and raconteur in the last years of a hard-charging life. I marveled at him, clung to his every word, and admired his character. I watched with respect when he hung his two walking canes on his left forearm and took two out of every covey rise. When he told me to let Miss Pansy's Appaloosa shooting pony go on the buckle, we gave him a bucking exhibition followed by a run off and attempted tree climbing show that greatly amused him.

Although I had heard many stories about Howard Stovall, I never really got to know him until that first year we went to shoot at Miss Pansy's. I was eager to hear stories from this famous World War I ace and member of the Lafayette Escadrille. He explained that when the synchronized machine gun was invented to allow the fighter pilot to fire through his propeller, a whole new kind of warfare ensued. Stovall, who had grown up in Mississippi shooting and hunting, applied his talents to accounting for his German adversaries. He came home a hero and settled into the life of plantation owner, outdoorsman, and raconteur. Stovall and Houghland loved to play practical jokes upon one another. For example, Stovall found out that Mrs. Houghland and her bridge-playing friends had taken up consulting the Ouija board. The Ouija board was supposedly moved by supernatural powers to spell out answers to questions put to it in a séance atmosphere. Soon after he learned about Mrs.

Houghland's new pastime, Stovall arrived at the Houghlands' Green Pastures on a day Houghland was away on business. Of course Mrs. Houghland entertained Stovall and insisted that he stay over until the next day when Houghland was due to return.

The next day when Houghland returned home, Stovall was hurriedly packing to leave. He did, however, consent to stay for a cup of coffee. In his usual courtly manner, Stovall thanked Mrs. Houghland profusely for her hospitality and went on to say that he had waked up in the middle of the night and gone to the kitchen for a glass of milk. Then he innocently extolled Mrs. Houghland for her staff, saying her one-eyed cook had been there to offer him a cookie. Now, it so happened that the one-eyed cook in question was deceased. Mrs. Houghland was enraptured by the intelligence that Stovall confirmed the deceased cook's presence and went immediately to the telephone to gather her Ouija board friends to make further contact. Of course, as soon as she was out of earshot, Houghland told Stovall that he was a rascal and that a posse would meet him if he ever came to Tennessee again. They parted laughing at another skirmish in a continuing war.

Bill Brown was invited to hunt with Stovall at his hunting camp. When he arrived, Bill found that the porch floor had been taken up and used as dividers for stalls. Stovall's mare was out on picket line and Bill put his horse in a stall. The two men then sat in the main room of the house talking across the table. After a short while, Stovall instructed Bill to open the icebox and get out their dinner. However, when Bill looked in the icebox, all that was there was a quart of bourbon and two glasses. They made liquid dinner and when it was finished, Stovall went out, got his horse, and put it in a stall off the house. He then pointed Bill to a bed on the stall side of the house and went to bed himself on the other side. Bill, helped by the generous allotment of bourbon, was just going off to sleep when, "WHAM! WHAM!" came a terrible clatter. It shook the wall so hard that Bill thought the siding was coming into the bed with him. Bill jumped out of bed clear onto the table, whereupon Stovall lit a lantern and asked Bill what he was doing up. "I think one of those horses must have kicked the house," said Bill. "It scared the life out of me."

Just then, it came again, "WHAM! WHAM!" and Bill could hear the planks in the side of the house buckle under the force of a two-footed kick.

"All right," said Stovall, "I'll put my mare back on picket if that will help you get some sleep and stop waking me up." So, having had his fun, the host rearranged his horse and the hunters got some sleep before awakening to cast before daylight.

Stovall had numbers painted on his hounds like at a field trial so that his guest could identify any hound he saw do something exceptional. This greatly facilitated conversation about the day's sport. Bill, for his part, never mentioned the kicking mare to Stovall but was invited back many times.

Stovall never lost his sense of humor. When we were together at Miss Pansy's in Thomasville (where the beagles wintered), we were asked out with Louise's beagles again. Stovall told Miss Pansy he had to have his own Jeep because he was the best Jeep driver in the air force. Miss Pansy also had a Jeep, and Alice and I were happy to witness, as pedestrians, their competitive Jeep-driving contest.

After the Stovalls taught us how to act that first year at Pebble Hill, Miss Pansy started her practice of asking me whom to invite or at least checking with Alice and me on the other guests. Ben and Sarah Hardaway, Ned and Nina Bonnie, Harry Rhett, Alex and Marilyn Mackay-Smith, Wick Johnston, editor of the *Thoroughbred Record*, and Bill and Joyce Brown all became guests. What a lineup of knowledgeable hunters and horsemen she invited. It was there that I really got to know Alex Mackay-Smith, whose books I had supported.

The relationship forged at Miss Pansy's was what ultimately gave me the opportunity to purchase Alex Mackay-Smith's library on hunting, a resource I have cherished ever since. It is made infinitely more useful and entertaining by the notations he put in the books, his correspondence, and the references he made as he prepared for his monumental work, *The American Foxhound, 1747–1967*.

Another couple that we got to know through Miss Pansy, Parker Poe, and Miss Pansy's niece, Kate Ireland, was Daphne and Marty Wood. Daphne and Marty were destined to make their mark on American foxhunting by both of them being president of the Masters of Foxhounds Association of America. They have had Alice and me to dinner and to visit the kennels and talk hounds at their lovely home in Monticello, Florida. The evolution of their hound-breeding program has been very educational for me.

Miss Pansy did not allow you to tip her staff. Nevertheless, of course, Colonel Stovall did tip them and told on himself at a dinner party. I remember him opening his wallet on the wagon and counting out one after another crisp twenty dollar bills as the wagon driver A. C.'s eyes got bigger and bigger. Gradually, the spotter and the dog handler drew near to see what was going on. Finally, when Stovall had put out a good stack of twenties and flattened his wallet in the process, he said, "A. C., I want you and Rose and German to have a good summer and be a help to Mr. Parker, which I know you will. Then next year after the season starts, when he doesn't have so much on his mind, just ask him, 'Mr. Parker, is that Captain Snowball coming again this year?'"

Of course, the entire dinner party group laughed heartily and Miss Pansy smiled at her old friend and said, "You don't mind very well anymore, do you?"

"Yes, ma'am, I do," Stovall replied, "but this time I was having so much fun."

Miss Pansy's Secrets

Visiting Miss Pansy and Parker was a wonderful experience. Not only did they invite other guests to entertain and educate us, but they also had a system that was designed to feed us our favorite foods on our favorite china, using our favorite crystal. For example, if they served prune soufflé and we indicated we really liked it, the next year, the first night, they served prune soufflé on the same plates we admired the previous year. I was baffled by this uncanny accuracy. However, I learned the secret. There was a little book just inside the kitchen pantry door. Thelma, the serving maid, cut her eyes around very expressively in sync with the dinner table conversation until Miss Pansy sent her back to the kitchen to recompose herself and straighten her face. However, as soon as Thelma got in the pantry, she would write in a little book what we had said we liked. If you go to Pebble Hill Plantation, which is now open to the public, and take the tour, that little book is there right inside that door turned to the pages when Bill and Joyce were there with Alice and me. You will see what an effective organization produced the caring hospitality there. You will also see an array of delicious dishes and beautiful china listed in Thelma's handwriting.

While on the subject of Miss Pansy's secrets, let me tell you that she confided to me one of her shopping techniques. She liked to wait until closing time and slip into the store just as it was emptying. Then she would get the clerk to take her to the back and around the store so she could examine the paintings and sculptures or whatever at her leisure and in privacy. One time she slipped into a store only to encounter a new clerk that she had never before met. "Do you know who I am?" Miss Pansy inquired. "Well, if you are who I think you are," the clerk replied, "this is my lucky day." Miss Pansy chuckled and proceeded to help him fulfill that prophecy.

It was not long after our first visit to Miss Pansy's that she invited us to visit her at Shawnee Farm in Harrodsburg for the Kentucky State Field Trial. Of course, we wanted her to meet Bill and Joyce Brown and we arranged that meeting the night of the bench show. Bill had his camper, and he set up a well-stocked bar in honor of Miss Pansy. "Miss Pansy," he said proudly, "what can I get you? I have practically everything—scotch, bourbon, gin, vodka, beer, and wine. You name it and I'll fix it."

Miss Pansy said, "Don't you know I am the original Carry Nation? I despise alcohol."

"Whoa," said Bill as he began dismantling the bar and fixing her a lemonade.

Well, despite this start, there was soon a strong friendship forged between the Browns and Miss Pansy. Alice and I were delighted to see these friends we enjoyed so much get to share their mutual interests. After that, Miss Pansy invited the Browns shooting when we were there and she did serve us cocktails before dinner, but it was not the place for hard drinking. One time one of Miss Pansy's guests said something mean at dinner about someone and

Miss Pansy asked, "My goodness, do martinis do that to you?" The woman in question never touched another drop during the visit.

At Shawnee Farm Miss Pansy put us up in Colonel Chinn's house and she entertained us for our meals at the big house. I made the mistake of refusing dessert at dinner and Miss Pansy told me she did not like for her guests to make her feel fat. "Thelma," I called to the kitchen. "May I have some of that pudding?" It was the beginning of a long line of delicious desserts that I devoured to the last crumb.

After dinner, I walked into the hall where there was a life-size carved wooden horse. I bumped my head on it. Maybe that made me cuckoo because, as we were leaving to go back to Colonel Chinn's house, I asked Miss Pansy if I knew her well enough to ask her a personal question. I intended to ask her if it was true that she had buried one of her old cars in her front yard when some parts for it were no longer being manufactured. However, before I could form my question, she put a hand on my arm and said, "Right over there under that oak tree." "The car," I confirmed. "An old friend. Right over there under that oak tree," she repeated. I went on to bed to dream about hounds running and me trying to follow on a wooden horse and passing a bulldozer digging a hole for an old car under a big oak tree.

The next morning, Miss Pansy let me drive to the cast. It was a real breakthrough because she was so small she had to look under the steering wheel when she drove down the middle of the road. Thank goodness, she let me drive henceforth whenever we were together. The other drivers on the road must have been much relieved when I began driving because they were accustomed to diving for the ditches whenever they saw Miss Pansy coming.

Miss Pansy always had a few excursions up her sleeve in case of inclement weather. For example, she would organize going to lunch at Shakertown. On one such occasion, she took us to a remote farm where she ran her hounds at night and raised some kind of fancy cattle with a white stripe around them. The bottoms of the interior fences were off the ground so the foxes and hounds could squeeze under them. She showed me where they had found a lost hound that had fallen into an abandoned well. Miss Pansy was, of course, willing to move heaven and earth to get that hound back to safety. She found a slender lad and arranged to have him fitted with a harness and ropes. He was then lowered down into the well to the hound and then pulled out. Then she had the well filled in so that neither man nor beast would ever fall down there again.

We wound up at Shakertown, a historic restoration, which she had supported substantially. We had a tour and then went to lunch. I arranged to get the check. When it came time to leave Miss Pansy looked at me and said, "Boy, give me that check." Her eyes were like one of her posted signs that said, "SLOW DOWN—I MEAN IT." I pretty nearly broke the sound barrier giving her that check.

Alice and I wanted to entertain Miss Pansy in return because she made us have so much fun. We did succeed in getting her and Parker to come stay with us for the Iroquois Steeplechase. She liked stories with animals in them best; therefore, I wrote her a letter about an adventure at camp.

## A Letter to Miss Pansy

Dear Miss Pansy:

Since our wonderful week with you, Alice and I have had good hunting. The day that most made me wish you were with us occurred in Mississippi. Alice and I had planned a trip before she broke her thumb, so she insisted we go for a late March hunt. We took a Nashville couple, Scott and Ruth Harris, to hunting camp for the weekend. Scott's father was Gene Harris, who did quite a bit of field trialing with Mason Houghland and Howard Stovall. The son is a real nailer across country, eager to be with hounds and very fit. I thought it would widen his horizons to see some of those Mississippi ditches from right behind Bill Brown, which is kind of like learning to wing walk on a plane flown by an astronaut. Then, when we all arrived, I got the vapors about whether hounds would run. Our pack, with its eighteen couple of predominantly Trigg foxhounds, has three sidekicks, a St. Bernard named Kimbo, a long-haired terrier named Funny, and a small white poodle named Charles. They are Joyce Brown's pets, which at our hunting camp is close to divinity.

After a big breakfast to fortify the initiates, we cast early in the morning. I was so glad when hounds struck that I didn't even mind stopping to fix the barbed-wire fence Bill jumped and Scott galloped through. Seeing it to be a major repair job involving some new posts, I clattered after them, took a good turn, and fell right in with the pack in full cry across some open pastures. Hounds put that red-sided gray up a tree or caught it (I am not sure which), although I was right with them in the woods when they shut off. I looked around for the fox but could not find it, so I gathered up the pack and set off in search of the barbed-wire boys and their wives. I soon found them with Kimbo, Funny, and Charles and had the pleasure of telling them the story, ending with "you should have been with me."

Bill Brown would jump a church without letting down the steeple, so you can imagine how he rode our next race, which developed very shortly. This ended with another red-sided gray in a hole. We had a third chase with a fox going to ground in a briar thicket before lunchtime. Knowing about Joyce's cooking, I suggested we hunt back toward that fence for a little repair work. That was one fast job, because hounds struck their fourth fox and took off before we were half through. We might never have known for sure what happened to this one except for Kimbo, the pack's bodyguard. Kimbo got that fox out of the creek where it had been caught and laid it by my horse, Blackthorn, which I had tied up while we were looking for the fox. Then, when I came back to untie old Blackthorn, Kimbo growled, just to be sure I saw what he had done. You can imagine how warm I felt towards that big furry brute when I realized he had fished that fox out of the water for me to give my friends as a trophy. Those monks over there in Switzerland didn't know they were starting a breed of fox retrievers, but Kimbo couldn't have looked prouder with a keg of cognac around his neck.

It was close to two o'clock in the afternoon by the time we rode into camp with most of the hounds. Alice and Joyce were there to hear our story. While horses were being untacked, I began putting hounds in the kennel. Some had turned off into the woods down by the lake so I had to blow for them. I might as well have saved my breath. Another run was tuning up. It sounded hot like a rabbit. But soon they began to move the line. I knew then it was no rabbit and called to everyone to watch with me. Sure enough, a red-sided gray immediately burst out of the woods and went all the way around the lake in full view. Hounds were not far behind, although somewhat strung out. Bill said, "They're running to catch, don't turn my horse loose." Scott quickly saddled his again, while I took the ladies in the car to get a crossing at the dirt road. The fox did not cross. Instead, it made a series of loops in a briar thicket. Hounds were raving. We were on one side of the thicket and Bill was on the other with Scott. I heard Bill whoop. He was at the edge of the briars by a deep ditch. "It's gone up; let's get a picture," I said. We bumped and splashed over the tractor trail around toward the other side of the creek. I left the car on high ground, and we walked down to the tangle.

The fox had gone up a little oak tree about as thick as the barrels of a twenty gauge. There it was, sitting in a fork, waiting for hounds to leave. Scott had never seen a fox up a tree, so we suggested he climb up and have his picture taken. Of course, we neglected to tell him that foxes develop a very weak bladder when they see a man climbing a tree towards them. Once it happened, we argued very persuasively that since it had already occurred, Scott might as well stay up there for the photograph. Besides, we said we certainly didn't want him with us for a while. Well, that fox let Scott get closer to it than most foxes would. Perhaps it was because Scott was standing on a limb about as thick as a pencil, which bent and swayed with the slightest shift of his weight. From where Scott was perched, it was about thirty-five feet straight down to the muddy bottom of the creek over which the tree leaned. Bill was very reassuring, however, saying oak nearly never breaks and the creek would wash off some of Scott's newly acquired aroma if it did.

Then Bill got the great idea of having Scott catch the fox. He told him just how to do it. Just lean way out over the ditch and reach around behind the fox, which was watching his every move, then slowly bring his hand up over the fox's back and grab its neck right behind the ears. I will say in Bill's defense that he told Scott he would only get one grab. He didn't mention the rabies shots he would have to take if the fox bit him and got away, but there is no sense in cluttering up a young fellow's mind when he is concentrating on something important. Several times Scott reached his hand around the tree and over the fox. Each time the thin branch waved precariously. Each time Bill reminded him that there would be only one grab. I encouraged him to hurry, as the fox looked fidgety. Finally, Scott slowly brought his hand above the neck and with a lightning snatch plucked the fox right out of that tree. Amidst much picture taking and general congratulations, he climbed down with his prize. We decided to take the fox back to camp in the car to release it in its home woods, away from the hounds.

None of the ladies noticed as I whispered to Scott to wait until we were all in the car, with the windows up and the air conditioning turned on, before slapping his free hand on the seat and shouting, "Oh, it got away!" Well, you never saw doors opened so fast in your life. I had to slow down because it looked like Joyce and Alice might bail out. Then, for some reason, Alice looked at me when she saw the fox was not actually loose and said, "What makes you do things like that?" I told her it was a warm-up for April Fools', which explanation did not seem to be completely satisfactory.

Later that night I was cooking steaks over an open fire. We were thinking back over the five foxes of the day and especially the last one now back in its own woods. I pretended I did not hear him the first time he asked, but Scott persisted, "How many times have you and Bill done that?" he inquired. "Done what?" I said, glancing at Bill. "Caught a fox out of a tree like that." I thoughtfully turned the steak and looked at Bill, who seemed just then to have had his attention diverted by some stars. Scott asked again so, finally, Bill looked at him and said, "Well, it did seem a logical way to get one out of a tree, didn't it? Remarkable you didn't get bitten. I'll tell you," he said, his eyes twinkling brighter than the stars, "if I ever have to explain to anyone else how to do it, I am going to describe your method because you did it just about perfectly."

Best Wishes,

Henry

When Ogden Pleissner got sick, Parker Poe followed his condition very closely. Parker decided that a letter from me might perk Ogden up and make him feel better. Of course, I did as Parker asked although I thought Mr. Pleissner might just think I was crazy. In due course, Parker told me how much his friend had enjoyed my letter. Based on Parker's rendition, I think the conversation between Ogden and Parker went something like this: "That friend of yours named Hooker wrote me a good letter, which cheered me up—even if he is crazy."

Back at Pebble Hill in Thomasville, Georgia, that winter, Miss Pansy arranged a rainy day excursion to Honey Lake just over the Florida line toward Lake City and Jacksonville. She had a retired colonel feeding the hundreds of geese and ducks using the lake. Miss Pansy had a cottage with a huge glass window for viewing the wildlife that came to her submerged platforms that were laden with corn. The china at her cottage was magnificent, decorated with fish and wild fowl. There were appropriately matched pairs of different species of miniature ducks in the finger bowls and so on. After lunch, she took me to see Noah's Ark (a boat-shaped building used as a bathhouse) in her side yard. She fished a key out of a long purse and took me inside. A mural featuring pairs of animals eating their favorite foods covered the whole interior. I asked her how long it had taken the artist to do it. "Which time?" she asked, smiling at me. "What do you mean?" I replied. "Well, when he finished the first time I took a look and the animals didn't have anything to eat so I had him do it over and put in each animal's favorite thing to eat. I don't like to see any animal go hungry." I may have been speechless, but I was able to put my arm around her for a hug.

## The Dropper

Miss Pansy hired a dog handler and trainer named Bill Daves to come to Thomasville when we were there. He was some kin by marriage to a man named Bolton who had won a lot of the big field trials for bird dogs. One year, Bolton rode on the wagon with us. I could not resist asking him about his field trial successes. He did not mind at all. So with the predicate laid, I asked him which was his favorite dog of all that he had owned. To my surprise, he asked me if I had ever heard of a dropper. When I hesitated, he went on to explain that a dropper is the result of an accidental cross between a pointer and a setter.

"What do you do with them?" I asked.

"You put them down." he replied. "They are a mistake."

"Well," I thought. "You were going to tell me about your favorite dog," I said.

"That's what I'm doing," he went on. "My favorite was a dropper produced by a kennel accident. For some reason, I kept one of them. Every time I went to the kennels, that rough-coated pup looked at me like, 'what did I do?' and I was ashamed to have it. Finally, when it was about a year old, I gave it to a friend. It was home in three days, having escaped my friend's pen. So I gave it to another friend. This time it took a week, but that dang dog came home again. I started to shoot him right then, but it was Sunday and I was going hunting with my son. I chained him up in the kennel and went on out hunting. After we had been out about forty-five minutes, I looked back and there was that damn dropper following about one hundred and fifty yards behind the Jeep. 'Turn around,' I said to my son, 'and let me get that vexatious dog before he ruins these good dogs.' He turned and we went back to where we had last seen the dropper. When we got there, he was lying in the field near the edge of some milo. Then as I got out of the Jeep, he saw me and began to creep forward until he suddenly froze, feathery flag in the air. 'This dog is trying to act like he has birds,' I yelled at my son as I reached for the dropper's collar. Just then, whoosh went one of the biggest coveys I have ever seen. 'You know,' I said to my son, 'I believe that dog might have found those birds and then backed off and laid down so as not to flush them until we came. Maybe we ought to leave him out for a few more minutes.' And that was the beginning of the meat-providingest dog I ever owned or hunted. When you didn't see him you could just tap your horn 'beep' and he would answer, 'Auk!' That auk meant, 'there are birds here and I've got them.' No telling how many birds I killed over that auking dog."

"What a story!" I exclaimed. "How long did you have him?"

"Until he was ten," he answered. "That dog had only one fault. He would figure out how to get out of any kennel and go hunting. He was hit by a car out hunting by himself when he was ten."

"Too bad," I consoled.

"Yeah," he said, "but I miss him and sometimes during bird season when I hear a far away horn honk, I listen for that 'auk' that I'll never forget."

## The World Combined Training Championship

Dr. Jim Holloway called me to ask if Miss Pansy would be the patron of the World Combined Training Championship in Lexington, Kentucky. I broke my own rule against soliciting her and called her to see if she had any interest. She took it up and asked Alice and me to come and go to it with her; the Browns and the Berrys went, too. There was an enormous crowd there walking around, and Miss Pansy had most of the golf carts that were allowed spectators. I was designated as her chauffeur. She did not like off-color stories so I told her every polite story I could think of about a fox, a rabbit, a frog, a snake, or anything else in nature. Three solid days of driving her and entertaining her was joyous fun, but my inventory of stories only just lasted. Miss Pansy, as always, gave as good as she got. She told me the story about the many times she went out at night with the Walkers, Mose Hill, and Sam Wooldridge to hear hounds run. The hunters would sit by the fire and identify the hounds' voices in the race. Later in the evening, as more fortification against the night air had been taken on, the taunting would begin. "I don't think I have heard your hound for a while," one hunter would say to another. "Well, if that hound comes in before the race is over, I'll hang it to this big oak tree and leave it for the vultures," would come the harsh reply. Then another hunter might say, "Well, if my bitch quits I'll shoot her in the head when dawn comes before we leave here." Miss Pansy was silent. She just sat and listened, her eyes as big as saucers. She did not move at all because she knew that she had two hounds sleeping under her big skirt and that they would be there until sunrise when the other hounds started drifting in.

She also told me the story about Princess Hohenlohe, who came to visit her plantation at Thomasville, Georgia. Miss Pansy's mother gave her strict instructions to take good care of the princess and not let her get frightened or hurt. Miss Pansy soon found that the princess was a lot of fun, and she took her riding, wildcat hunting, and sightseeing in the swamps, much to the princess's delight. Then one night Miss Pansy arranged an alligator hunt. All went well and Miss Pansy's swamp guide soon had an alligator all trussed up, mouth wired shut, and stowed in the bottom of the boat. Miss Pansy and the princess were sitting amidships, shining the flashlight at likely spots to see things, including, they hoped, another gator, when the princess looked at Miss Pansy and said, "Ja. You pinch me." Now Miss Pansy knew she had not pinched the lady, so she casually flicked the beam of the light on the princess's backside. There she saw the trussed up gator with his snout right up against the princess. The wiring around its mouth had somehow loosened and the gator was straining for a little nip. At Miss Pansy's request, the princess never mentioned this to Miss Pansy's mother.

Miss Pansy died a few months after I chauffeured her around the World Combined Training Championship. After the funeral, Louise Humphrey came running out into the parking lot and intercepted me. "Because of you she had one last great run in her life," she said, referring to my time with Miss Pansy at the Championship. I will never forget her saying that to me.

## Parker Poe

After Miss Pansy died, Parker insisted that Alice and I come visit that year as planned. Parker entertained us many years after Miss Pansy's death until Miss Pansy's niece, Kate Ireland, began having us while Parker kept having the Browns. Parker had a wonderful sense of humor, and he was willing to include himself as the target. For example, he told the story of walking his Jack Russell terrier on a Sunday afternoon. When he chanced to pass one of the tenant houses, a hen came running around the house cackling bloody murder, closely pursued by the Jack Russell, which was also closely pursued by the inhabitant of the house armed with a rake. Upon seeing Parker, the last in the chain of pursuit slowed to a walk and asked respectfully, "Mr. Poe, is my chickens bothering your little dog?"

There was an often repeated story that when Josh, Miss Pansy's dog handler, was told that Miss Pansy had gotten married to Parker up at the big house, he asked about the groom. "He is that air force man, name of Parker Poe," Josh was told. "Well, he ain't po' no mo'," Josh opined. I cannot verify this account because Josh died before I started shooting at Miss Pansy's, and I never asked Parker about it.

## Kate Ireland

Parker was unsparing with his humor on those he liked. He really liked his niece Kate Ireland. For example, he had made a date for John Hanes to meet us to show Alice, Kate's other guests, and me around Pebble Hill after it had been turned into a plantation museum. Because we kept John Hanes waiting ten minutes, Parker turned Kate's picture to the wall. Then he invited us to lunch and took us in the library at Mayhaw so that Kate would see her chastisement. Kate was unabashed. She had taken me off Parker's hands when I made him nervous by talking on the telephone too much, so she figured he owed her one. Besides, she knew Parker loved her, and she would have her chance to tease him back.

John Hanes's wife, Hopie Hanes, was Katharine Hepburn's roommate in college. It was thirty-five years before Parker found it out. He said, "Hook, if she had been your roommate I would have found out in thirty-five minutes, maybe even thirty-five seconds." Hopie was Lundsford Yandell's daughter; he was a great foxhunting friend of Mason Houghland's. Kate Ireland invited Hopie to come over, ride the wagon with me, and train her young lab to pick up birds. Hopie started out saying she had heard about my shooting, and then began bragging about it on the first few coveys until she kind of mesmerized me as the day went on. I had nine straight doubles but missed the second bird on the tenth covey. It was an unbelievably good half day for me, and it was entirely due to Kate's beautiful quail plantation operation and Hopie's hypnotism.

Parker Poe was very quick-witted as I can attest since I was his frequent target. However, sometimes his quick wit got him in trouble, as when a very handsome local lady came into the dining room of the country club and the gentlemen eating with Parker said, "Look at that," and Parker snapped, "Oh, she was made when Chinese labor was cheap." That night the lady-in-question's husband called Parker and asked what he meant by what he said. Parker said it was not supposed to mean anything—it was just supposed to be funny. Parker's defense is stored in my repertoire for use when explaining enigmatic remarks about striking women.

Parker did not lavish his respect indiscriminately. Therefore, when I found out someone for whom he had high esteem, I usually questioned him rather closely on the basis for his opinion. This worked very well. I learned things about his heroes that I would not have otherwise known. When I asked him about Bill and Joyce Brown, for whom he had obvious great respect, he just said, "Why, it's because they put up with you."

One of the people he liked very much was Ogden Pleissner. He not only admired his art, but he also liked him as a man and a sportsman. This respect and fondness was obviously reciprocated by Pleissner, who commented on Parker's wit and the great times at Pebble Hill in the book, *The Art of Ogden M. Pleissner*.[1] As Miss Pansy's Appaloosa mules, Knothole and Keyhole, became whiter with age, Pleissner produced a stencil of a covey rise that could be put on each mule's backside to sort of replace the spots that had faded to white. When the stencil was wiped over with shoe polish and removed, there would be the quail in all their glory. Naturally, this caused a sensation at the plantation owners' Georgia-Florida Field Trial. The only problem was that when the mules sweated, the quail "flushed."

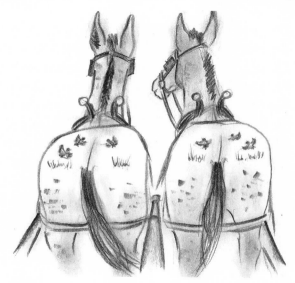

Alice gave me a grouse-shooting Pleissner for our fortieth wedding anniversary. What pleasant memories are triggered whenever I look at it. Parker left a lot of Pleissners to the Thomasville Cultural Center, and Alice and I try to slip by there and have a look at them whenever we get a chance.

## A. C. and Mayhaw Preserves

After Josh was gone, the wagon driver at Miss Pansy's was A. C. He would never tell you how many of anything there were because Miss Pansy had told him not to. He had learned that she wanted him to do just exactly what she told him to. I quickly figured out that that was a pretty good lesson for me, too. If you asked A. C., "What do those mules over there do?" he would respond, "Theys eats." Or he might say, "Not as much as last year." Then one day I asked him how to make the Mayhaw preserves we were being served at breakfast.

"Theys calls you from the big house and tells you theys goin' to make 'em," he said, "and you gets Knothole or Keyhole, it don't make no difference which one, and you get up on his back, don't make no difference which one, and you kick sides down to the swamp. When you gets there, you tie Knothole or Keyhole, don't make no difference which one, and you tip in that grass so you won't disturb any of those rattlin' snakes, and you swim across the little lagoon and don't wake up none of them crockergators, and when you get to that little island where that mayhaw bush is, you be careful none of those moccasin type snakes is sunnin' hisself, and you snatch a little clump of those bushes with the berries on them, and you be real careful swimmin' back across that little lagoon because you don't want to disturb no allidiles, and you get back to the grass and you tip back and don't disturb those bell tail snakes, and you shimmy up on Knothole or Keyhole, don't make no difference which one, and you kick sides up to the big house and you give the cook that clump of berries and she takes that and a fifty-pound sack of sugar. And that's how she makes Mayhaw preserves."

A. C. certainly understood one of the prime ingredients of Pebble Hill cooking. Miss Pansy herself told me that soon after she hired a cook during World War II, she patriotically explained to the woman that it would be important for her to conserve butter and sugar. "Now look here, Miz Poe," the cook replied, "I ain't never cooked for no poor people before."

I am sure that cook prospect thought that she was telling Miss Pansy not what Miss Pansy wanted to hear but what she needed to know. Alice and I were in the same predicament when we discovered that Miss Pansy's chauffeur and car mechanic were dangerously drunk on their runs taking us to the airport.

What do you do when your hostess's driver is so drunk you have to banish him back to the luggage compartment in the station wagon? You hope to save some other person from the harrowing experience of a ride like the Charge of the Light Brigade. Guests and friends who help conceal the fact that a friend's employee is a closet alcoholic do their friend a terrible disservice.

When Parker got sick with cancer, we called him one day from Callaway Gardens and told him that since we were going to be in the neighborhood we would like to take him to lunch. Of course, he knew very well that Callaway was quite a drive from Mayhaw, but he accepted and we took him to a restaurant he knew in an old mansion in Thomasville. He really enjoyed teasing me about saying "Since we were going to be in the neighborhood."

Parker invited us to lunch when we were visiting Kate. Parker continued to impress on me the aphorisms by which he wanted me to live life. "Take the tarts when they are passed, Hook," he would say to me. "Take the tarts when they are passed." Then Parker got so bad that he could not come to the table, but we still had lunch there and went in to visit with him afterwards. On the final visit, we stayed there talking with him through most of the afternoon until he said, "Oh, you have missed most of your shooting," and we replied that it did not matter because we were enjoying visiting with him so much.

It was not until years later that Kate told us that, before he died, Parker asked her to keep an eye on us. When he died we, of course, went to the funeral and Kate had saved us a place by the family. As we sat down in a photo finish with the beginning of the service, Kate looked at me and tapped her watch crystal. If anyone appreciates a photo finish, it is Kate.

Kate's operation has to be one of the best shooting establishments in the world because she is a gifted manager with an indefatigable attention to detail. One of the most pleasurable parts of our long relationship with Kate and her family is the extent to which they let us see the inner workings of their program that produces so much good shooting. This is a fascinating process: management, labor, and capital intensive. Kate is a friend for all seasons. We have visited her, cruised with her in Maine, and been to Spain with her in pursuit of the red-legged partridge. As life trustees, she and Alice are hatching up St. Timothy School initiatives faster than the boys would have put snipe in the grocery bag. Here is one of the thank-you letters I wrote her that I hope shows the affection and respect that I have for her.

Dear Kate,

Maybe it is being around hounds and bird dogs so long that makes me so like an old dog.

Old dogs love the repetition. They love to check a covert where they found before. I suppose they lay in their kennels dreaming of that strike and remembering the fun that followed.

So it is with me. I relish the anticipation of visiting you. Then I enjoy the fulfillment of all those delicious expectations that your invitation conjures in my mind. Long after I am back, the memories of our adventures mix with the recollections of previous occasions to enrich the reverie that remains with me back in my kennel.

This year's visit was another confirmation that the best friends are old friends, and the best fun is the fun with old friends. This is a premise with which my canine cohorts concur.

Thank you for having us to Foshalee again and for all the wonderful memories of our visits with you through the years, which trigger in turn thoughts of Miss Pansy and Parker and our years of friendship with you and members of your family. So rich and pleasurable is the recall of these relationships that it makes up for the occasional aches and pains that an old dog gets.

Sincerely,

Henry

## The Mountcastles

Another great friend of my family, Mr. Paul Mountcastle, whose wife Catherine was my mother's best friend, had us shoot with him at Blue Springs Plantation on the outskirts of Albany, Georgia. This fourteen-thousand-acre paradise was full of birds. The first year I went there, Mr. Mountcastle had broken his arm and was recuperating. He did, however, ride with us and offer encouragement. The quail population was at the top of its cycle. We only shot coveys, no singles. I went back to Blue Springs many times since then with Mr. Mountcastle and then as the guest of his granddaughter, Catherine, a marvelous hostess. She did me the honor of making me the god-father of her son, Hunter. She invited me to bring my friend, Ray Reid, shooting, and she entertained him royally.

## Ray Reid

In the late seventies, Ray Reid began to invite me to south Texas to shoot. He is a magnificent host and a wonderful shooting partner, always making sure his guests have fun. We have shot at the Kenedy Ranch, the Mariposa, the Mansion de Sarita, and at the King Ranch. We began being guided by Rick Smith, son of the renowned Delmer Smith. Delmer was not only a great bird dog trainer and seminar teacher, but he was also an acute observer of nature. Delmer had been invited to foxhunt with the Rolling Rock Hunt when at the last minute his hostess asked him if he needed someone to take him through the gates. "When is the last time you rode?" she asked him. "About ten years ago," he guessed. "And what were you doing?" "I was jumping a Chevrolet convertible, Roman Riding." (Roman Riding is standing up on and riding two horses with one foot on each of them.) Having heard this account, I immediately invited Ray Reid and Rick to come to Tennessee and foxhunt with me. They did and successfully jumped all the jumps on a long run. Unfortunately, I have never been able to get them to come back. Furthermore, when I hear Ray's description of that run, a return visit does not seem imminent.

Ray has been taking me shooting for twenty years, listening to the same stories but, unlike me, he has been getting to be a better shot year by year. He has gone to smaller gauges while I have been slugging away with my twelves, named AT&T and MCI, trying to be slow but far knocking. It is a humbling thing when you bring one of those big old Holland brothers and a guy with something as light as a fly rod wipes your eye all day. Then he let me shoot a course with Jamie Clements, who missed one or two he called a wake-up call and then never missed for the rest of the day.

I did have a lucky covey rise last year. It was at the start of a thick mesquite patch. Al Grumbles, Ray's wonderful dog handler, was warning me that the birds would escape through the thicket when they got up. I shot one straight up overhead from the hip and the other one dodging through the mesquite. As Al was picking up with the dog, I could see a quizzical look on his face. Finally, he said, "Do you mind if I ask you something?"

"Of course not," I responded.

"Did you mean to do that?"

"Let's put it this way. They were in a hurry and so was I." Al did not reply with any of the earthy Texas idioms that no doubt came to mind.

Now it is inevitable when you are invited around shooting that you get some tough days. Sometimes those little drops of water cling to the ends of thorns and there is no evaporation and, therefore, no scent, or the fog closes in and you are just stuck until it lifts. Sometimes there is a high old blue sky without a cloud in it and very low humidity. These dusty old hot days take away every scrap of scent and punish the dogs by running them down fast in the hot sun and the scorching wind. You came a thousand miles to get there and your host has spent a fortune to show you a good time, so what do you do? You relax, enjoy the countryside, and encourage the dog handler by telling him his dogs are beautiful movers and so on. It was a day like that when Rick Smith asked Ray Reid if he would mind if Rick brought along his friend Rodney Davis, alias Rod.

"Not at all," said Ray, always the gracious host, as he looked at the tall thin lad standing out of earshot with a bony old dog. "Do you want to take his dog, too?" asked Ray, appraising with a glance the baleful canine lying in the dusty road at his master's heel.

"If it's all right with you," answered Rick, and soon we were all loaded and on our way.

The forecast of hot, dry and dusty, low humidity, and no scent was accurate and we were treated to a morning of watching Rick hunt hard with dog after dog to no avail.

Finally, just before lunch, Rick asked Ray if he would mind if Rod ran his dog a little. "That's fine," said Ray and we watched Rod gently extract his dog Rocky from his cage on the wagon. Rocky celebrated his freedom by ambling about twenty-five yards in front of the wagon and sitting down on his haunches. Then he stuck his nose in the air and, slowly turning his head, he walked the hot wind three hundred and sixty degrees, all the way around. Rod started up the road. Rocky began his run—if you could call it that. It was sort of a slow lope interrupted by check backs on anything that interested him. In about ten minutes, he circled downwind of a brush pile and stealthily approached it with his tail slowly waving.

"Let's have a look," said Rod as we piled off the wagon for the first time that morning. Well, Rocky may have been a touch past his prime, a little arthritic, and a little deaf. His tail was a little tentative, perhaps, but he did not lie about coveys in brush piles. When we were finished shooting the rise, he pointed us some of the singles and, after that deafeningly quiet morning, it sounded like Chinese New Year. Then Ray eased over by me as we were walking back to the wagon, all smiles and conversation. "Don't brag too much on that dog," he instructed in a whisper. "You will hurt Rick's feelings."

When we got back to the wagon, Rick asked if Rod and Rocky could try for one more covey before lunch. Everyone knew we were dying for them to, but Ray looked at his watch and then at Rick. "If you want to," he said.

All the pent-up hopes of a frustrating morning went with Rocky as he went through his routine and located another covey right in the middle of the day. After we had enjoyed a good lunch the hunt resumed and, yes, Rod and Rocky went with us on the wagon. It was a blank afternoon, but Rocky was never mentioned until about five o'clock when Rick asked Ray, "Do you mind if Rod puts Rocky down for a little while?" Of course, you know the answer and the result. As we were picking up the singles, Rod walked by me out of earshot of Rick and the spotter. "That's a really useful dog you have there," I said under my breath.

"Thank you," he answered, glancing fondly at Rocky.

"How old is he?"

"Ten," Rod said, matching my whisper.

"Nice dog," I said.

"He's won a lot of field trials for me," replied Rod, holding a hand down for the old dog to walk under as he brushed his master's leg.

## Snakes

One year, at a place with preserve status, a group from Tulsa, Oklahoma, came in while we were there. The group consisted of the chairman of the board of the hospital, the administrator of the hospital, and a neurosurgeon with a little ponytail, who used the hospital extensively. You could tell right away that this neurosurgeon fellow was right important to himself and to the hospital, also. They kind of cleared out for him like he was a big dog coming out of high grass. Well, we got to drinking and teasing around and I noticed that the neurosurgeon kept looking at a big rattlesnake on the mantel of the fireplace mounted in a striking position with its fangs being the center of attention. We went on drinking and teasing around until he started wanting to bet on the next day's shoot. He wanted to bet ten dollars a bird on the difference in the bag between them and us. Of course, I told him I had been taught it was impolite to bet on shooting, but he just kept on insisting until finally, for the sake of a congenial dinner, I accepted. As soon as we sat down to dinner, I changed the subject to something that obviously interested him—snakes.

I began telling him about asking Bill Daves what he did when there was just no scent. "We have a jar of gasoline on the wagon and about five feet of hose pipe. We put the hose pipe in one of these snake holes, pour a little gasoline down it, and give it a good blow," Daves told me.

"What happens then?" I asked Daves.

"You put the hose to your ear. If he's there, he'll ring you back. Then you pull the hose out of the hole and he's coming out."

"Is there anything else I need to know?" I asked him.

"Yep. Be sure to remember that some of the holes have more than one entrance."

"Don't worry," I replied, "that is one thing I sure won't forget."

"You remember last year when you met us at the twin gates," he asked, "and the dogs were already pointing and you had that double?"

"I sure do. Why?"

"Because I had just killed one of the biggest snakes I have ever seen when you drove up a few minutes later."

"Well, I never knew that," I said. "You didn't show it to us."

"Nope," he said, "I wanted you to have nothing but quail hunting on your mind."

When the hospital group seemed to enjoy that story, I decided to tell some more. "I knew a fellow in south Texas named Gene Mills. Gene had a nine-shot revolver and he explained to me that when you pointed it at a rattling type snake, the snake would line up right on the end of the barrel and all you had to do was squeeze the trigger and it would take the snake's head right off.

"I never knew that. That's good to know," I told Gene.

"Well, you see that bank of compressors over there?" he asked as we pulled the truck up near them.

"Yes."

"Well, I was switching out those compressors one day last year, and I just happened to look in the shadow of one of them and there was a big old rattlesnake all coiled up and ready for business. I must have walked right by that thing seven or eight times already when I saw it."

"What did you do?"

"I went and got that nine-shot revolver."

"Did you clip its head right off?"

"No, I missed it nine times."

"Wait a minute; I thought it was supposed to line up on the barrel."

"It was, but if you are shaking so hard that you can't hold the barrel steady, the snake has a hard time lining up on it."

"Well, what did you do?"

"I went up on top of the cab of the truck and sat there until I got hold of myself. It was a good little while, but I finally got down and killed that snake."

I had known there were a lot of snakes there because a fellow from there had sent me a picture of his pretty wife, who was five feet four inches tall, holding up a bell tail snake over her head and about eighteen inches of it was still on the ground. I noticed that even in that boiling hot climate, she was wearing gloves.

"Of course you've met the man here that they call Señor Hector?" I asked the neurosurgeon.

"Who's he?"

"He's the older man who carries a five iron in the cab of the truck with him when he is the driver and spotter."

"I didn't know there was any golf around here."

"There isn't. But they say Señor Hector can send a rattlesnake's head flying like a good iron shot. That is why they call him Señor. I told him that when he uses a putter he will be mucho hombre."

This subject matter seemed to hold the doctor's interest, so I told him about Miss Pansy, who had some quail plantations. After World War II, Miss Pansy decided to cut down on the snakes by giving a one-dollar bonus to her employees for every snake they killed. When bonus time came, each of her employees came to her and told what and where they had killed. Miss Pansy would then write a check and thank them. However, Josh, her dog handler, came in and told her he had killed one hundred thirty-eight snakes. "My goodness!" she said as she was handing him the check. "I had no idea we had such a problem. Where did you kill them?" "Just where they were raising," answered Josh. "I just waited for the little ones to hatch out and then I killed them." "Give me back that check, Josh," Miss Pansy said, reaching out her hand. "I am paying you to kill them, not breed them."

Now after these few warm-up stories, I told the hospital group about Bill Brown's experience when he took some foxhound puppies out on the prairie at Columbus, Mississippi. The puppies were running around investigating everything as puppies do, and Bill had a springy stick like a willow branch in his hand that he was tapping along a path near the river as he watched the puppies. Suddenly, he heard it. He knew immediately what it was, but he saw no sign of it. Therefore he did not know which way to jump. Finally, he saw its rattles moving in the grass. He jumped just as the snake struck. Bill's reflex action with the little springy stick caught the snake and brushed it off to a near miss. Bill looked around for a weapon but could find none on the prairie. So as the snake coiled back up, Bill reached in with his stick and taunted the snake to strike. When it struck, Bill beat it with the stick to kill it. It was a slow process because the snake would slowly and more slowly coil again and strike, but Bill, afraid for his puppies, continued the process until the snake was done. Bill dragged it back to the panel delivery truck he was driving, threw it up on the side of the cab, and set off for town.

It was the biggest rattlesnake he had ever seen, at least seven feet long and heavy. Bill thought that he really should take it to his funeral home to have it embalmed so he could display it in his Goodyear store. Bill had counted fourteen rattles on it. However, his thoughts were short-lived because as he was driving down the dirt road, there was a rattle right beside him. It was the loudest rattle he had ever heard. Bill never hesitated. He merely hit the handle of the door and stepped out of the truck, which continued to run down the road until it went off into a ditch. Luckily, the cargo area of the panel truck was not open to the cab area. So when Bill got up to it, he was able to get the tire iron out of it. Bill made sure the snake was good and dead with that tire iron before he took it to the funeral parlor. Bill's embalmer, who did not quit until the next day, dutifully fixed the snake for display. Bill took the snake to the Goodyear store and put it on the counter by the cash register to show his customers.

Now, it so happened that a longtime customer named Cliff Troupe came in that day looking for some screw eyes. When he came to the cash register to pay for them, Bill casually said to him, "Did you see that?" Cliff looked around and saw the snake on the counter scarcely a foot away. "Fo' God!" he screamed and ran through the double glass doors with arms outstretched in front of him. There was a terrible crash. Glass went everywhere, but Cliff kept going and Bill did not see him again for a month. The remarkable thing is that Bill never lost Cliff's business, although he never got him in the store again. Cliff would come as far as the front door and ask for whatever he wanted, but when Bill invited him in, Cliff would say, "Naw, suh. I just stay on out here."

That story ended the evening on a light note. We all turned in to get ready for the following day. The next morning at breakfast, it came out that I was going to be leaving after lunch. The neurosurgeon did not want to lose his pigeon, so he arranged for all of us to have a late lunch. That way the bet could be figured on the morning's bag only. Now, you would have thought I was taking money out of his savings account by leaving early, but he finally agreed.

## Prorating

As we were getting ready to board the shooting wagons, I thought I had better check one more thing, so I said to the neurosurgeon, "Now we will have to prorate since there are three of you and only two of us."

"Prorate?" he scoffed. "You know, I thought you were kind of silly when I met you last night. We aren't going to prorate diddly. It's your wagon against our wagon, cash at lunchtime."

Now, I knew Rick was going to take us to the best place, but I smiled wanly and said, "If that's the way you understood it."

"Hell yes, that's the way we understood it and I have witnesses!"

"All right, all right," I said. "There is just one more thing I forgot to tell you about what you asked me last night."

"About what?"

"About snakes down here."

"What about them?"

"Well, on a warm overcast day like today, they sometimes get up on top of the sachawitza to sun. So they are right at your belly button. The reason I tell you this is that if your singles go down in that salt grass they call sachawitza and you are wading through there watching for the wild hogs called javelina, you need to keep an eye out on top of the grass as well. Just thought I'd mention it. Good luck," I said.

However, he had already turned to talk to his shooting partners. As I recall, we did not get in to lunch until about two o'clock. They were pulling up at the same time. They were laughing and obviously in a good mood.

"Well, how did you do?" I asked.

"Didn't see a one," the neurosurgeon replied.

"You didn't see a single bird?" I asked incredulously.

"Snake, dummy, snake. We didn't see a single snake."

"What about javelina?" I asked, savoring the power of suggestion.

"We saw a few," he said, "but they were moving through."

"Good. How many birds did you get?"

"Nineteen," he said proudly.

"Apiece?" I asked.

"Hell no, not apiece, smart aleck. Our wagon brought in nineteen birds. What about your wagon?"

Just then the dog handler came around the wagon and he must have thought the question was addressed to him, as he immediately answered, "Eighty-nine, but we have a spotter out in the field picking up a few more."

"What?! Oh my God, we have been taken!" bellowed the good doctor.

However, before he could go into his war dance, I quickly announced, "Let's see. That's seventy net by ten dollars by three. That's seven hundred apiece, gentlemen. It has been a real pleasure meeting you." And then I couldn't help saying, "I am glad you didn't want to prorate."

They paid up and every single cuss word just added sweetness to the pot.

I tried to savor the expression on the neurosurgeon's face all the way home, but for some reason I kept remembering a day at Fox Camp when I took my son Timmy and Johnny Ingram bird hunting with their single-shot shotguns. We had Rock Dog, a beautiful Llewelyn, stylish on point and off. Suddenly, he froze in a picture point. The boys and I hurried up to him, across a little drainage ditch. However, I saw a water moccasin and shot it as it disappeared into its hole. "Come on, boys. Rock Dog is still locked up," I said, pushing up the ditch bank. Just then a single flushed, and I waited for the boys to shoot. When they didn't shoot, I took a far-knocking fling at it and luckily added to the pot.

"What's the matter with you guys? Don't you know we're supposed to be bird hunting?" I asked them.

"Sure we do," they replied, "but we were busy looking at our feet."

I supposed that I knew some fellows from Oklahoma who had been doing the same thing.

Note

1. Peter Bergh, *The Art of Ogden Pleissner* (Boston: David R. Godine, Publisher, Inc., 1984).

ELEVEN

# SHOOTING DRIVEN GROUSE AND PARTRIDGE ABROAD

## Lord Weir

William Weir, now Lord Weir, invited me to Scotland to shoot driven grouse at his shoot on a moor belonging to the Earl of Skye. I had great fun shooting there with William, Jan Collins, George Joyce, Sir Archibald Edmonson, Gene Phipps, and Dru Montague. This was an exceptionally good line of guns. George Joyce astounded everyone by consistently taking doubles with a mismatched pair of guns. Then one of his shooting partners retired and gave him a matched pair of Purdeys. The dexterity with which George, then in his seventies, and his loader for forty years wielded those guns was the source of much amazement amongst even the best shots of Britain.

## George Joyce

William told me the story that he had chanced to see George Joyce miss a grouse one day on a drive. William could not resist going by George on the way down the hill after the birds were picked. "How was the shooting?" asked William.

"All right," replied George, turning his head slightly to have a look at his questioner.

"How many did you take?" William pressed on.

"Fifteen brace," answered George, this time looking right at the perpetrator of this unusual interrogation.

"And how many cartridges did you let off?" struck William.

"Fifteen brace," responded George, with the slightest hint of a smile beginning around his mouth.

"But I thought I saw you miss a wide bird early in the drive," said William, who could contain himself no longer.

"Of course you did," said George, "but after that I happened to see a brace flying close together."

I don't think this colloquy was a well-kept privacy, as William told it to me the night before I drew a butt (i.e., a blind) between George and Sir Archibald Edmonson, a celebrated shot who looked as if he were skewering the grouse with the end of his barrel thrust at them. As the drive proceeded, I realized that they were sort of dividing the field of fire for my butt between them, and they were laying down a carpet of grouse around my butt front and back. To use an American expression, I was the turkey in the grouse drive.

Shortly after that, George Joyce invited Alice to take a drive in his butt to watch him. She was thrilled, of course. However, her description of the experience made me realize just how far beyond my ken was his artistry. Alice said, "It's like he had a compass with a long string and he drew a circle around the butt, equidistant all the way around, exactly so and so many yards from the butt. Then when the birds came, he dropped them all, right on that circle. And he says, 'Meet them at the door, my dear. Delighted to see you, bam!' and so on. The whole thing is a ballet. The gun is practically pointed at the grouse when he gets it, and with amazing economy of motion he slightly adjusts it and touches it off."

That night George came to William's for dinner. He and Alice were chatting like old friends. Quite an accomplishment for Alice, considering George's reputation for terseness. "I know you have made so many memorable shots and taken so many spectacular drives that it would take a long time to tell them," she said, "but is there any double that stands out in your mind?" "Yes, my dear," he answered quietly. "It was a jungle hen and a Japanese sergeant during the war. I was out shooting something for dinner in Burma and the Japanese sergeant stood up in the jungle nearby. I gave him the other barrel. Frightful exigencies, war."


## Sir Archibald Edmonson

Some years after that, Sir Archibald Edmonson invited me to his castle for dinner. The first thing he asked me was how did I like the castle. I assured him that it looked fine to me. He said that he was pleased to hear that because he had torn down two-thirds of it and proceeded to show me some pictures of previous models of it. Since he had set off on rather personal family history, I asked him at dinner with his beautiful wife and daughter, "Archie, what is it that you actually do?"

"Well," he said, "I begin shooting driven grouse on the glorious twelfth of August, and I go up with the Earl of Skye to his island to shoot wild fowl, and then I go over to Sir Rupert Buchanan-Jardine's to get a leg over a saddle behind hounds about sixty days a year. In the spring, I have some good beats on the Tweed where the trout fishing is excellent. In the summer I see that the boys get the hay up and I kill salmon." Then he looked at me and delivered the summation. "And the rest of the year I devote to sport."

I glanced at the wife and daughter. They were smiling quite passively. "Sounds like fun," I said. Then the conversation drifted on to family history and Edward VII and the clump of trees on the other side of the lake from the dining room where the train slowed for its royal passenger to step off for a visit. I love these little dinners where you can get sport, architecture, and history before the brandy.

The next year Archie brought his wonderful old black lab to pick up birds. King was the dog's name, and he was treated like one on the moors. A veteran of many great drives and exceptional bags by his master, King laid down beside the butt and waited for his part in the ritual he knew so well. Although I was impressed that everyone who came over to speak to Archie made sure to speak to King as well, King was not. He merely lay there not acknowledging the homage paid him except with an occasional thump of his tail. Then the drive started and with it the wonderful excitement for all except

King, who seemed to sleep through the prologue to his role. Only this time, at the end of the drive, some whippets were turned loose to chase hares through the butts in a kind of helter-skelter comedy of hares turning, dogs rolling over, and mirth among the shooters and the keepers. Then a hare ran by King about four inches from his nose and the temptation was too great. King stretched his neck and encircled the hare with his mouth. Those great liquid eyes immediately sought Archie as King began to display remorse at his breach of etiquette. Then Archie descended on him. "King," he said, "whoever told you to catch little hares?"

By now King's tail was frozen in mid-thump as he meekly offered the hare to his master. However, there was no reprieve. Archie tapped King's nose three times with his finger and pronounced the terrible sentence: "Bad dog." King spit the hare out like a hot pepper and put his head down on his paws in abject contrition. I could have sworn he was going to cry. Luckily for King, this was not the last drive of the day and he redeemed himself by picking all the many grouse Archie shot and by carefully ignoring the most tantalizing hares run right by his nose. King was an inspiration to me.

## The Keeper's Joke

One year I went to shoot with William Weir, only to find out he had to go down to London for a meeting of the board of the Bank of England, of which he was the youngest member. I was very flattered when he told me that he had arranged for me to go on and shoot that day, and that his son and dog would go with me. This all seemed to work perfectly except the last drive was up a steep path to a higher ridge, and I had the butt at the top. We made the climb, had a good drive, and picked up our birds. I was longing to get in the Land Rover and get back to the fire and the Famous Grouse that comes already bottled. As the caravan of shooters walked off the hill, I checked to see that I had both boy and dog cavorting in front of me. The climb down was slick and taxing, though not as bad as the climb up had been.

When we got to the bottom there was a lot going on with the keepers sorting out the bag and the Land Rovers being loaded with guns and cartridges. Just then I looked around and suddenly I could not find either of them—William's son or his dog. I rushed around looking for them and found the boy with one of the keepers. However, he had not seen the dog. Ascertaining that the keeper would be responsible for keeping an eye on the lad, I started to search for the dog somewhat more frantically. I knew the shoot would be moving soon, and I did not want to be the American who lost William's favorite spaniel. I concluded that I must have left the dog on the hill, so I took off at the run and climbed back to my butt in the last drive. It was a very strenuous effort and yielded no sign of the dog.

Very discouraged, I looked down the hill to see the Land Rovers starting up and the shooters starting to load in them. I came down the climb at a run, slipping and scrambling all the way. When I got to the bottom, the head keeper was sitting at a table finishing the tabulation for the day. "Looking for Daniel the spaniel, are you?" he quizzed me.

"That I am. Have you seen him?"

"No, but I saw you go looking for him when he was under my table."

I dropped down on one knee and there was William's dog sleeping peacefully through all the closing activities of the day's shoot. I never asked the keeper why he had not sent someone to stop my climb. I think he enjoyed seeing the American learn lessons for himself. Anyway, I was grateful to have that boy and that dog beside me on the Land Rover ride back to William's house. I had to smile when I thought of the keeper's joke.


George Sloan Dances to the Piper

In the late seventies, we began to shoot on Lord Dalhousie's moors, Milden and Invermark. George Sloan, Charles and Poochie Berry, Rupert Agnew, Jim Steward, Ray and Dai Waters, Dr. John Murphy, Derald Ruttenberg, Gene Woodfin, and Les Welsh were the guns. My friend Lord Charles Churchill helped with suggestions and had Simon Parker-Bowles lay in the drink. The two of them, Charles and Simon, had me to lunch for some last minute coaching, and I innocently asked about entertainment at dinner. The only thing is a piper to pipe you in for dinner they assured me, so I immediately obtained their help to lay on a proper piper's engagement.

George Sloan had apparently gotten into the scotch and was very enthusiastically in support of the program. So much so that when we were all seated at Milden Manor house at the table, which held sixteen and fairly groaned with silver and crystal and flowers, George decided to do a Scottish dance. Despite Alice's discouragement, George took off his evening slippers and stepped from his chair onto the table. My heart sank. I knew this would be my last year at Lord Dalhousie's because the table, the settings, the wine, and everything else were going to collapse into a heap of rubble. Meanwhile, the piper piped furiously and the staff began appearing at the doorway to the dining room—first the butler, then the chef and the servers, and finally the maids and laundress. I expected the keepers, but they, fortunately, were in the gunroom. Just then, George decided to shuck his pants for a kilt in the form of a bath towel, which he wrapped around himself.

During this change of costume, I observed the piper leave the room. I followed him thinking that he might be going to call the sheriff. You can imagine how relieved I was when I found that he was only phoning his wife to tell her he was going to be late, as he knew the beginning of a riotous party when he saw one. I shall never forget his description to his wife. "Hoot lass! It's the bravest sight since I piped for the queen!"

The costume change completed, George returned to the table, which we all supported with our knees, and gave a proper interpretation of Jack Be Nimble, Jack Be Quick as he tiptoed in and out of glasses, plates, wine bottles, and so on. By some miracle bestowed by the Gods of Intoxication, the table, the chairs, and all the embellishments survived, and his Lordship invited us back in future years. When I want to leave a party early, I sometimes say, "Alice, do you think I should show them how George danced on the table at Milden?"

Lord Dalhousie invited us up for a drink at his Queen Anne castle, which was nearby. A great sweeping staircase divided and went to either side to take you up to the balcony. On the wall facing this staircase were portraits of many of his ancestors prominent in the history of the empire. I let him select which of these to tell us about, as one could inadvertently get off on the wrong foot. All lines seemed to lead to King James I, and we had a very pleasurable history lesson.

Speaking of getting off on the wrong foot, it was fresh in my mind that William Weir had been invited to Balmoral for dinner with Her Majesty and was seated to her right. I could imagine his perplexity when he felt a nudge against his foot under the table. He shifted slightly in his chair, thereby moving his foot while still giving his undivided attention to what the queen was saying. Then he felt it again—an unmistakable pressure on the retrieved foot. Fortunately, he had the presence of mind, before displaying any familiarity with his royal hostess, to drop his napkin and lean over to pick it up while taking a peek under the table. There he saw one of the queen's corgis, thoroughly relaxed, using William's shoe for a pillow.

There were many interesting people I met grouse shooting, not only the owners, the hosts, and the guns, but also among the keepers, the beaters, and the loaders. The keepers had been working, some of them all of their lives, to have enough grouse to provide good shooting. More often than not, they came from a long line of keepers. They could debate one another with a real passion on what was the best way to drive a certain beat when the wind was blowing out of a certain quadrant. They could stare with scarcely concealed scorn as a weak line of guns missed on an abundant drive. They could come along when you were picking up birds after the drive and conjure up a bird you did not think you had killed. They did it with long, usually blind retrieves by their amazing dogs. Then they would smile, touch the brims of their caps, and say, "That'll be a fiver on the dog." I found out the translation of that. It meant he was adding five pounds to the price of the dog.

After the guns would leave the butts, an army of Labradors and spaniels, referred to as the "hoovers," would carefully hunt the heather from butt one to butt eight. These experienced dog handlers said that the grouse most often overlooked by the guns are the ones closest to the butts.

One friend I made was a retired game control agent come home from fifty years in Africa to watch for the birds that, "flying dead," fall a good distance behind the line. I loved to get him to tell me about his adventures as we rode together to and from the moor. He had known Karamojo Bell and some of the other great Scottish big game hunters, and he told me of their exploits in an accent that I had to strain to understand. Bell, he told me, was the best shot he ever saw, being able to kill seven out of ten sand grouse on the wing with a seven millimeter rifle. Now, if my shooting was not already suffering by comparison to the line I was in, that really gave me a point of reference. "Well," I said, changing the subject with him. "What are you proudest of about your fifty years in Africa?" "I never killed a lion," he replied, "I never killed a lion." "But you must have seen many." "Aye, sir, and it's a terrible temptation to kill a lion when he's got his head in the Land Rover with you."

There was a loader named MacDonald who loaded for me as long as I shot with William. MacDonald was good at his job, had good dogs, and tried to help me stay out of trouble. He took my best day's shooting and my worst with the same stoicism. Then one day after knowing us for several years, he asked Alice when he saw her, "Well, Mrs. Hooker, where have you been since I saw you last year?" "Oh, MacDonald," she answered. "We've been to Brazil and Alaska and the Rocky Mountains and some other places." "How is he going to relate to that?" I thought. "His whole life has been spent right here close by." "Well, Mrs. Hooker," he responded immediately, "I wish I had been carrying your bag." "I do, too," she said and shook his hand.

## Franz Seilern

The most interesting friend I made grouse shooting was Franz Seilern. He spoke English sparingly, as if it were far down the line of languages he knew. A terrific shot, he is the only man I ever saw take two in front, get his second gun, take two overhead, get his first gun back again, and take two behind. His quickness, his economy of motion, and his peripheral vision were remarkable. Sure, he had the marks of a lifetime of shooting. He was a little deaf. He had some little scars on his cheek where he had been shot. I asked about that, and he said it was his best friend who accidentally shot him on a walking shoot.

"What did he say?" I asked Franz.

"My friend asked, 'What happened?' and I said to him, 'You shot me.' My friend replied, 'Nein, nein, I am Jägermeister. It is impossible that I shot you.' 'There are two of us here,' I said to him. 'Which one of us do you think did it?'"

"And did you quit shooting with him?" I asked Franz.

"Nein, nein, he is Jägermeister," said Franz with a twinkle.

When Franz heard that my friend George Sloan was going to Pardubice, Czechoslovakia, to ride in the steeplechase there, he told me proudly, "Seven hills overlook Pardubice. On each hill, a castle. Every castle Seilern."

"All of them belong to your family?" I asked.

"Once," he said, "but the Communists took so much."

Then he told me the story that at the end of World War II, he got hold of a map drawn in pencil that showed where the armies of occupation were going to be garrisoned. It showed that the Russians were going to occupy Czechoslovakia and not Austria. Franz immediately went home to his wife and daughter and told his wife to be ready to leave in one hour, never to come back. He had an old farm truck and enough gas to get to the family fortress in Austria. While his wife was preparing to leave, Franz went to her parents to ask them to go with them, but the father refused. Franz could not convince him, so he started to leave. When he got to the front door of the castle, his mother-in-law stepped out of the shadows with something in her hands. It was a heavy box. "These are for my daughter," she said, handing it to him.

"What was in it, Franz?" I asked.

"The crown jewels from the Hundred Years War," Franz replied. "So," he continued, "I went home and got my wife and daughter and we escaped in the old truck. We got to Austria and went to the fort that had belonged to my family since the days of Charlemagne. However, when we got there, we found it occupied by the Russians and they took me to the commandant. I was dirty and ragged, emaciated from the war. But the commandant looked at me and said immediately, 'You are the owner of this castle.' I could do nothing. He had my wife and my daughter. He had the truck full of all the treasures my wife could assemble in an hour. 'Yes, I am,' I told him. The commandant looked at me and at my family. 'You are fortunate,' he said, 'I have been ordered to evacuate at dawn. If you leave and come back after we leave you may be safe, but do not be here if they send me back.' Then he said, 'I am very sorry for all of your servants who died when we came here.'"

Franz put his arms around his family and started back to the truck. Every step seemed to take an eternity. Would the truck start? Would some curious Russian soldier decide to look inside? The truck started and Franz and his family escaped. They later returned to that castle and were still living there when Franz came to Vienna to take me to lunch.

I had just been to the Vienna Museum of Fine Arts, so I could not wait to ask him. "Franz," I said, "there is a whole little room of Rembrandts at that museum and every one of them has on it a little brass plaque that says 'Donat Seilern.'"

"Ja, ja," he said with a twinkle. "It makes you very welcome when you come to a country if you give them a few pictures."

"But did you save any?"

"Ja, ja, for London and New York. Do you know how long it will take the Russians to get here if they come back?"

"A few days?" I ventured.

"By tank, ja. A few seconds by missile."

I looked into his twinkling eyes. He was indeed my friend. How did I know? Because this rich and powerful, urbane European, this carefree international sportsman, had let me see the refugee in his heart.

Not long after this trip, we went to Invermark, another of Lord Dalhousie's moors. Unfortunately, one of our line of guns accidentally shot my good friend Charles Berry in the thumb. It was very painful and frightening, so I was not completely surprised the next morning very early when Derald Ruttenberg, who had invited the accidental shooter, marched into our bedroom and suggested that I ask his friend and guest to stand down. "What if I rigged the draw so as to have him be the meat in the sandwich between guns willing to shoot next to him?" I proposed. "I know you are crazy enough to do that, Hooker, but who else would do such a thing?" Ruttenberg asked. "I have the man," I said and slipped into Sloan's room where he was feigning sleep.

"George," I said, "I have a deal for us."

"They want us to shoot next to that loose gun, don't they?" George said, opening one eye with a smile. "I have been thinking about that. As long as we are going to rig it, can't we rig it so as to get the most birds?"

"You want the most or the least?" I asked him.

"Considering the danger, the most. Might as well die for a lot as for a little," George reasoned in true jockey style.

And so I rigged it, to the relief of the rest of the line. But when we got to the butt and our middleman was swinging his gun to limber up, I could swear I was seeing the firing pins every time he swung toward me. Of course, it was my imagination. I know that now because I can still close my eyes and think of that day and see the dogs, the loaders, the keepers, the beaters, the hillside covered with heather, and those firing pins pointed right at me. We had a good shoot as I remember, but with the percentages improving after the first drive. Now, the gentleman was good company, and he was invited back the next year in spite of the errant pellet of the previous adventure. Better still, he brought his girlfriend, a real beauty, with sun-bright hair, sea-blue eyes, and conformation that made you want to see her walk, trot, and canter under tack. This girl had earlier refused to come down to dinner in Mississippi because she heard there was a Hooker at the table.

I should have suspected something when she arranged to sit by me the first night—and especially when she found my stories and jokes funnier than I did, and when she kept calling for me to tell more. Somehow, among the claret, the Stilton, and the perfume, she laid a line that an old hound like me will honor every time.

I am afraid I did not sleep very well that night and I was slightly bleary the next morning when her boyfriend suggested we make a friendly wager on the number of grouse each of us would take on the first drive. Frankly, I was trying to remember all the jokes I hoped I had not told her the previous evening, and I was delighted that his mind was on shooting and not on my foolish behavior. However, no sooner was the wager sealed by a handshake than she slid in by me on the front passenger seat of the Land Rover. "Gloriously close quarters," I thought. Then she turned to me and said in an intimate voice, "I am taking the first drive with you. They are too far up the hill for me to walk." "Marvelous," I thought. "Now let me see what I should tell her first."

However, we were no sooner in the butt than she picked up the line. "Do you like travel? Do you like sex with music? Then would you like to play off somewhere?" I missed a huge number of birds by so much that they probably didn't even know I had shot at them. There was something in my claret-befuddled brain I was trying to understand. Then she leaned over and said sweetly, "If you don't stop thinking about traveling and playing with me, you are not going to have any birds at all."

Right then I realized I didn't know the difference between come-hither and sic 'em. I suddenly knew that it was all a plan, and my shooting partners were going to come strolling down the hill making inquiries about my bag and that my hopeless preoccupation with itinerant adventures was going to be exposed in all its foolishness. Just then, I began to hit birds and, luckily, there were plenty. As the count began to mount up, the lady began to pout. Then she suddenly became cross, threw down the marker, and ground it into the moor. "If that's all you think of my favors," she said, "you can find your own (blankety-blank) birds." So we finished the drive in silence, with me desperately trying to remember the location of all the fallen birds.

Charlie Grimm, the loader, who had heard the entire conversation but had not said a word, took his dog and began to stack grouse on the front of the butt. My friends came down the hill, laughing and talking.

"Did you have any birds down here?" asked the bettor.

"A few," I replied.

"Did you get any?" he asked. Before I could finish saying "a few" my pretty butt-mate said to him, "Keep walking; you are a poor man."

"What?!" he exclaimed incredulously. "Didn't you ask him about music?"

"Yes."

"And travel?"

"Yes."

"And sex?"

"Yes, I did it all just the way you told me," she replied sullenly, "but he must have figured it out."

"Damn!" he said, eyeing the growing mound of grouse as Charlie continued to pick up and stack them. "We may have to go home early."

The beautiful girl scarcely spoke to me again the rest of the week and never even slightly suggested that she take another drive with me. She probably changed her perfume as well. As for my taciturn loader, Charlie Grimm, he said not a word until we were alone and I, wondering what in the world he must be thinking to hear a lady talking like that, said to him, "You just don't meet them on the moor like that very often, do you Charlie?" He never even smiled as he picked up the gear, signaled his dog, and said, "Nooo," as he started down the hill. From that profound comment, I suppose I gained an understanding of how much a good loader should divulge of incidents of coquettishness on the moor.

## Lord and Lady Rotherwick: The Friendly Game

While we were the guests of William Weir, he took Alice and me to dinner at Lord and Lady Rotherwick's. The other guests were Sonny Marlborough, John Bowes-Lyon (the Queen Mother's nephew), David Dambreunil (the owner of a big maritime insurance company), and a retired lord of the admiralty. I was very flattered when the hostess seated me on her right but I was soon fielding questions that indicated I was barely a step ahead of the savages. She particularly had heard about my carrying a collapsible saw on my saddle and sawing off pine limbs to put on top of barbed-wire fences to stay with hounds. Finally, she leaned over and whispered that perhaps I had noticed that I was the only man at the table without a title.

"Oh, but I do have a title back home," I said. "Really," she said, "what is it?" "That Crazy Son of a Bitch," I replied. She looked at me appraisingly and announced that she would put Alice and me at the gin rummy table after dinner rather than at the bridge table.

The gin rummy game included Sonny, Bowes-Lyon, Dambreunil, and the retired lord of the admiralty. Sonny immediately suggested stakes of one pound a point and I declined, saying that would not be a friendly game. He then asked what would be normal stakes, and I suggested ten pence a point. Assuming this to be settled, we drew for partners. It happened that Alice and I drew Sonny, who seemed somewhat concerned about this turn of events, and immediately suggested that the stakes be lowered, saying that he was only jesting earlier. I declined to lower the stakes, saying that the draw of the partners was part of the luck of the game. So we played the opposite team three across. It happened that we won all three games to naught. In other words, they got not a single score in any game. Of course, this brought on dire penalties making us win quite a lot more.

Winning all of that money was, of course, fun, but hearing the lord of the admiralty curse so colorfully and loudly was the most fun. Moreover, his seaman's language carried to William Weir who looked into my eyes and said, "Well, it's been a wonderful party but we are shooting tomorrow and must go." This certainly did not suit the lord of the admiralty and his hand visibly shook when Alice suggested that all sign one of the stacks of five-pound notes covering the table. Sonny was gleeful, having had a very positive attitude adjustment since the dejection of drawing us as partners. As we were making our manners to leave, Sonny slid over by me and said conspiratorially, "Henry, no one knows you down in Spain do they? We could go down there red-legged partridge shooting and make a lot playing gin rummy until they got the hang of you." Of course, he was jesting again, but I moved on anyway.

## Kate Ireland and Red-legged Partridge

A few years ago, Alice and I did begin going to Spain with Kate Ireland's party. It was an exhilarating experience because of the family and friends with whom Kate surrounded herself, and because it is always memorable to be in the company of a genuinely great lady, recognized by the discerning guides at the Escorial and elsewhere as the focus of an admiring group. Fig Coleman, a longtime resident of Spain during his Central Intelligence Agency career, was the leader. As he has been organizing his shoot for thirty years, it is not surprising that he is an expert on Spanish history and sport. However, the reach of his knowledge extends far beyond the provincial culture on which he is an expert. His scholarship on military history, bullfighting, and the evolution of European society commands his listener's rapt attention. His gift for supplying the explanatory detail makes the shoot into a seminar on life conducted by a brilliant shot who emerges as a courtly gentleman. His elegant toast to the red-legged partridge on the last night of the shoot is a fitting end to the festivities that he so expertly arranges. The Millikens, the father, Gerrish, and son, Peter, were there. Both possess an extraordinary sense of humor, with their contrasting styles keeping the whole party laughing through the shoot. Kate's nephews and nieces, Tom and Nancy Ireland, Bob Ireland, John Dunlap, and Watts and Sally Humphrey, are great shots, as are her Thomasville friends, Richard Mooney and Tom Barron, whose beautiful wives certainly added to the ambiance and the charming dialogue. Will Osborne and George Oliva also added to the bag and the festivities.

El Crespo, the shooting lodge, is on top of a hill. From this romantic setting, it commands a spectacular view of the La Mancha countryside. The fields of grapes and grain and the olive orchards lie around it like a beautiful patchwork quilt. José Manuel Landaluce is the lord of this land. His prowess as a big game hunter and wing shot is everywhere evident in the charming house where he and his family entertain. One of the best parts of shooting at his estancia is his willingness to answer questions and explain the customs and traditions that make such a colorful ritual out of the pursuit of the perdiz roja. When the time comes to thank the staff and leave, it would be very sad except for knowing that another year the lights will be shining to welcome us back to the crest, and the exhilarating drives with plenty of partridges will be waiting below for Kate's march on La Mancha.

# EPILOGUE

If I am ever eloquent, I want it to be in praise and defense of that precious heritage that has allowed me a lifetime of adventure in field sports. Not only the fun of it, but the enduring friendships as well enrich my memory. Those characters who could jest at themselves while jousting with danger taught me much. They are still teaching me whenever I think back over the old times. Sometimes when I read a book, I am about finished with it before I understand it. I do not want hunting, shooting, chasing, and fishing to be the same way. These pastimes, which are so much part of life in our country, are easily taken for granted. However, they must not be. They are endangered species: an ominous storm is gathering over them. The animal rights activists and anti-field sports lobby are already here. They are attacking our way of life at every level with every artifice and weapon at their command. In the media, in the legislatures, even in the county councils, their persistence is unwavering, their passion unstinting. They have seized on ritual and costume to signify class distinctions as symbols to be hated. To finance their stealthy attack, they have raised enormous amounts of money in the name of animal rights. They have spent lavishly to enhance their political power to conduct a war on traditional pastimes of rural society. The political animal lobbies' successes against those they characterize as bloodthirsty have had the ironic effect of causing them to be more bloodthirsty themselves. They refuse to acknowledge or fail to see that hunters and fishermen are the great conservationists, who appreciate the relationship between habitat and game.

How, then, are we going to resist, defy, and defeat them? By uniting that army of hunters, fishermen, and shooters with the pet owners and food growers of our land, and by creating alliances between them and the sympathetically regarded institutions that will identify with the good works of field sports enthusiasts, such as point-to-pointers, steeplechasers, and horse show exhibitors. The Iroquois Steeplechase's alliance with the Vanderbilt Children's Hospital is an excellent example. So are the Grand Prix horse show classes and polo tournaments on behalf of Saddle Up, which treats the physical disabilities of children who are beneficiaries of these activities.

This clash of cultural values will be a long twilight struggle. Patience is required. The opposition has staying power, but so do we. Moreover, we have a long history of frontier experiences. There is in North America still the cultural tradition of respect for the woodsman, the explorer, and the marksman. The sportsman's right to bear arms remains a central tenet of the major American political parties.

An egalitarian self-image goes into the woods with the hunter. These outdoorsmen are an army. We must join with them to defend their sport as they come shoulder to shoulder with us to resist the extinction of ours. When they understand how intertwined our fates must be, they will answer the clarion call and legions will emerge to protect the fields and forests of their homelands. These sportsmen love the land. Their love, like ours, is a passion not a game. This book is not just a reminiscence of amusing and resourceful characters. It is a description of a way of life worth protecting and defending to the last breath and the last rampart. The predicate for an alliance among participants from various walks of life exists in these stories. We must be, each of us, vigilant and determined. Even now, though we may not see them, the foes are at the wall.

For these field sportsmen, the woods are a way of life and they are the descendants of the armies of Andrew Jackson and Sam Houston. Just as the foxhunter never forgets a place where he viewed a fox or a coyote, so the deer hunter, rabbit hunter, or turkey hunter never forgets that hallowed spot where he saw his game.

They have psychological ownership of those places, whatever the property records in the register of deeds office may show. No matter the state of title, their state of mind includes the atmosphere of that moment. They remember the vegetation, the weather, and the light. They remember the excitement. It is for them a memory of how they live and what they live for that remains with them, always.

A sense of place connects them with other parts of the army in defense of the countryside. Conservation easements are making a powerful impact on our country. Landowners who care enough to preserve and protect the land and its inhabitants "in perpetuity" are associating habitat with the lifestyles it encourages. Conservation leads to restoration. The essential element of hunting is that it makes use of the land and the creatures upon it in a sensitive, sustainable way. Every hunter knows that permission is the foundation ingredient of great hunting. From the whistle of wood ducks' wings as they go to roost, to the morning call of doves, the land has its night music and the prowl of its nocturnal predators to excite the imagination. Let us enjoy the fun of our sports but leave as our heritage the opportunity for others to taste the heady wine of danger and discovery as they savor the unequalled exhilaration of the field sportsman. Good hunting. Good racing. Good fishing. Good shooting. Good fun. Home safe.

# CHRONOLOGY

The following historical notes are intended to provide a chronology of the evolution of the Hillsboro Hounds for reference by the reader of the various episodes in the first part of this book.

1932—Mason Houghland, MFH of the Harpeth Hills Hunt Club, left that hunt to establish the Hillsboro Hounds, named by John Sloan Sr., honorary secretary and whipper-in. The country was near Boston, Tennessee, five miles south of Leiper's Fork. Hounds of predominantly Trigg antecedents were from Joe Thomas's famous Grasslands Hunt, which had headquartered in Gallatin, Tennessee, until that same year when it folded. The rest of the superb Grasslands pack was bought by William Dupont Jr. and became the celebrated Foxcatcher Hounds.

1934—The hunt country moved from Williamson County to Robertson County. Felix Peach began a long career as kennelman and then huntsman.

1935—The Hillsboro Hounds relocated to Brentwood at Mason Houghland's Green Pastures on what was once the Harpeth Hills Hunt Club's country. Dr. John Youmans, MFH of the Harpeth Hills, leased its hunt country to the Hillsboro Hounds for one dollar per year. Because of the Hillsboro Hounds' success, Harpeth Hills disbanded.

Mason Houghland was very interested in field trialing and hound breeding. He established great friendships among the noted hound men and night hunters of the day, including Sam Wooldridge, from whom he got Walker hounds for the pack.

1939—A draft of hounds, the so-called refugee pack, was brought over from the North Cotswold in England and split with Vicmead.

1941—The Iroquois Memorial Steeplechase was inaugurated by Mason Houghland and John Sloan Sr. The course was designed by William Dupont. It has been carefully developed through the years by Calvin Houghland and his successor chairman, Henry Hooker, into the leading three-mile, weight-for-age steeplechase in America. One of its keenest competitors, George Sloan, has gone on in separate subsequent seasons to be the only person to be the leading amateur steeplechase rider in both the United States and England, and to become the all-time leading amateur winner in the United States.

1954—Brocklesby Hounds were imported from England and introduced into the pack. The Wartrace country was hunted several times a year until the early sixties.

1958—George Sloan replaced Felix Peach for one year as huntsman.

1959—Upon the death of Mason Houghland, Vernon Sharp and John Sloan Sr. took over as joint MFHs with Robert Harwell Sr. as honorary secretary. Kennels were moved to Sharp's Inglehame, which, along with Sloan's Maple Grove, were favored countries. Calvin Houghland took over the Iroquois Steeplechase. Thus, the stewardship of Mason Houghland's equestrian sport in Middle Tennessee was divided between his successors.

1962—Under the auspices of Robert Harwell Sr. the Cornersville country was developed. At the urging of Henry Hooker, it was made the main country of the Hillsboro Hounds. Many members bought farms there and the country was extensively paneled.

1966—Henry Hooker became honorary secretary and first whipper-in.

1969—Under the initiative of B. R. (Buck) Allison, West Waterford hounds were imported from Ireland. These hounds, the result of

Isaac Bell's selection and breeding, were of English Fell type, white and very tractable.

1971—Buck Allison, as MFH and honorary huntsman, formed the Cedar Knob Hounds in a country near Fayetteville, Tennessee. Hounds were predominantly West Waterford. Bob Gray came from England to assist as kennelman and professional whipper-in of the Hillsboro Hounds.

1973—Walker hounds were infused into the Hillsboro to provide striking power on the poor scenting soil of the Cornersville country.

1974—Felix Peach retired and Bob Gray became huntsman. A group of English Fell hounds from the Milvain were imported. These hounds were very successful, but were not bred soon enough to make a long-term contribution. George Sloan became joint MFH of the Hillsboro, replacing his father, who continued to hunt and to take a very active part in the Iroquois Steeplechase. The Panorama country south of Franklin, Tennessee, was opened.

1975—Bill Carter became joint MFH of the Cedar Knob. Henry Hooker became joint MFH and honorary huntsman of the Cedar Knob. The Trigg hounds bred by Henry Hooker and Bill Brown were added to the Cedar Knob pack. The Hardscuffle Hunt disbanded and sent a draft of hounds with Hardaway breeding to be split between the Hillsboro and the Cedar Knob. These hounds and some subsequent drafts from Hardaway have made very effective additions to the pack.

1977—Henry Hooker became joint MFH of the Hillsboro as well as the Cedar Knob. Virginia Banks became honorary secretary of the Hillsboro. John Gray became huntsman and Karen Gray became professional whipper-in to the Cedar Knob. Coyotes migrated into the countries, providing excellent sport. Hounds accidentally captured a golden eagle in the Cornersville country. The eagle was saved and taken in on horseback by Tom Kenny, who healed the bird and released it in its home country.

1980—The Hillsboro and the Cedar Knob merged, becoming the Hillsboro Cedar Knob Hounds. Vernon Sharp, George Sloan, Bill

Carter Sr., and Henry Hooker became joint MFHs. John Gray became huntsman and Bob Gray retired. Karen Gray became professional whipper-in. The Vanderbilt Children's Hospital became involved in the Iroquois Steeplechase weekend for the upcoming fortieth anniversary of the race. The hunt has since foregone its Calcutta party proceeds, thus making significant annual contributions to the Children's Hospital.

1981—The Pytchley sent a pair of bred bitches to the pack. Sidney McAlister Sr. became honorary secretary. Hunt field numbers increased as interest continued to grow. The Cornersville country became a weekend retreat for foxhunters, trail riders, upland bird shooters, and hill toppers alike. The Foxcatcher, from Maryland, disbanded and sent the bulk of its pack to the Hillsboro Cedar Knob, thus returning to Tennessee the breeding that began both the Foxcatcher and the Hillsboro packs. The Vicmead Hunt, from Delaware, also disbanded and sent their pack to the Hillsboro Cedar Knob. Vernon Sharp retired as joint MFH. During his illustrious career as a foxhunter, he was the only man to be president of the Masters of Foxhounds Association of America, the National Foxhunters Association, and the American Foxhound Club, all three main bodies covering all facets of foxhunting in America.

1982—The breeding was concentrated on the Foxcatcher and Trigg lines, with some Hardaway and Vicmead, to produce a crossbred pack suited to the country.

1984—Sidney McAlister Sr., a subscriber for thirty-seven years, became joint MFH. Dr. Bruce P'Pool became honorary secretary. Robert Harwell Jr. became honorary treasurer.

1986—Hounds were invited to participate in Tennessee Homecoming '86 as part of the Cornersville Froggy Bottom Festival and Parade. In spite of first contacts with steam engines, airplanes, sirens, brass bands, and fancy mule teams, all hounds were eventually recovered.

1987—George Sloan organized and became chairman of the International Steeplechase Group, which held its inaugural Royal Chase in Nashville. The Princess Royal attended and rode in one of the races.

1988—The Hillsboro Cedar Knob became a sponsor and beneficiary of the Royal Chase. The Princess Royal rode a winner to the delight of the crowd. Alex Steele became honorary secretary.

1990—Bill Carter Sr. retired as joint MFH. Dr. Bruce P'Pool succeeded him as joint MFH. Albert Menefee III became honorary secretary.

1991—George Sloan retired as joint MFH. Among his many contributions to the hunt was the stream of visitors from steeplechasing and foxhunting that he attracted to hunt or race. The kennels were named for Vernon Sharp and were moved to Rehwell Farm, where Robert E. Harwell Sr. first took the hunt to the Cornersville country. Henry Hooker became the chairman of the Iroquois Steeplechase Race Committee. Thus, the stewardship of the historically united equestrian sports of hunting and racing in Middle Tennessee was reunited.

1993—Albert Menefee III became joint MFH and Alex Wade became honorary secretary. The hunt became a Tennessee not-for-profit corporation under its original name, the Hillsboro Hounds. The Iroquois Steeplechase went to National fences, which by then were used by most other race meets, and made the transition from amateurs only to any rider licensed by the National Steeplechase Association acceptable to the Race Committee.

1995—L. H. Armistead III became honorary treasurer. Dabney Sloan and Ted Thompson were married at Opening Hunt.

1996—Sidney McAlister Sr. retired as joint MFH. James Reed IV became honorary secretary.

1997—Alex Wade became joint MFH and field master of the second flight. Henry Hooker became a director of the National Steeplechase Association. Mason Houghland was posthumously inducted into the Huntsmen's Room of the Museum of Hounds and Hunting at Morven Park, Leesburg, Virginia.

1998—Stephen K. Heard became honorary secretary. He serves as alternate first flight field master to Albert Menefee III, joint MFH.

1999—Henry Hooker became a director of the Masters of Fox-hounds Association. The Hillsboro Hounds hosted the first Performance Trial run under the Foxhound Club of North America–Masters of Foxhounds Association of America Rules. Hillsboro Swift won the trial.

2001—Calvin Houghland's horse, All Gong, won the Steeplechase Eclipse Award. Calvin was inducted into the Tennessee Sports Hall of Fame in honor of his career and accomplishments in steeple-chasing as a rider, owner, and race meet chairman. Stephen Heard became joint MFH. L. H. Armistead III became honorary secretary. Chip and Sherry Broome became honorary treasurers.

# PROPER NAME INDEX